Teaching EAL

Full details of all our publications can be found on http://www.multilingual-matters.com, or by writing to Multilingual Matters, St Nicholas House, 31–34 High Street, Bristol BS1 2AW, UK.

Teaching EAL

Evidence-based Strategies for the Classroom and School

Robert Sharples

MULTILINGUAL MATTERS
Bristol • Blue Ridge Summit

DOI https://doi.org/10.21832/SHARPL4436
Library of Congress Cataloging in Publication Data
A catalog record for this book is available from the Library of Congress.
Names: Sharples, Robert, 1982- author.
Title: Teaching EAL: Evidence-based Strategies for the Classroom and School/Robert Sharples.
Description: Bristol, UK; Blue Ridge Summit, PA: Multilingual Matters, 2021. | Includes bibliographical references and index. | Summary: "This book offers an evidence-based guide to EAL for everyone who works with multilingual learners. It offers a concise introduction to the latest research underpinning three keys areas of EAL practice: How children acquire additional languages; How language works across the curriculum; How you can establish outstanding EAL practice in your school"—Provided by publisher.
Identifiers: LCCN 2021012480 (print) | LCCN 2021012481 (ebook) | ISBN 9781788924429 (paperback) | ISBN 9781788924436 (hardback) | ISBN 9781788924443 (pdf) | ISBN 9781788924450 (epub)
Subjects: LCSH: English language—Study and teaching—Foreign speakers. | Second language acquisition.
Classification: LCC PE1128.A2 S485 2021 (print) | LCC PE1128.A2 (ebook) | DDC 428.0071—dc23 LC record available at https://lccn.loc.gov/2021012480
LC ebook record available at https://lccn.loc.gov/2021012481

British Library Cataloguing in Publication Data
A catalogue entry for this book is available from the British Library.

ISBN-13: 978-1-78892-443-6 (hbk)
ISBN-13: 978-1-78892-442-9 (pbk)

Multilingual Matters
UK: St Nicholas House, 31–34 High Street, Bristol BS1 2AW, UK.
USA: NBN, Blue Ridge Summit, PA, USA.

Website: www.multilingual-matters.com
Twitter: Multi_Ling_Mat
Facebook: https://www.facebook.com/multilingualmatters
Blog: www.channelviewpublications.wordpress.com

Copyright © 2021 Robert Sharples.

All rights reserved. No part of this work may be reproduced in any form or by any means without permission in writing from the publisher.

The policy of Multilingual Matters/Channel View Publications is to use papers that are natural, renewable and recyclable products, made from wood grown in sustainable forests. In the manufacturing process of our books, and to further support our policy, preference is given to printers that have FSC and PEFC Chain of Custody certification. The FSC and/or PEFC logos will appear on those books where full certification has been granted to the printer concerned.

Typeset by Nova Techset Private Limited, Bengaluru and Chennai, India.

Contents

Figures, Tables and Case Studies — xi
Acknowledgements — xiii
Abbreviations and Acronyms — xv

1 Introduction — 1
    Welcome — 1
    Is This Book for You? — 2
    How Is the Book Organised? — 3

2 EAL in the National and International Context — 5
    A Brief History — 5
    Current EAL Policy — 7
    A Practice-based Approach to EAL — 8
    A Note on EAL Learners — 11
    What We Found in Chapter 2 — 12
    Where Can I Go Next? — 12

Part 1: How Additional Languages Are Learned
    Preface to Part 1 — 15

3 Key Principles and a Theory of Language — 17
    Theory of Language — 18
    Chapter Review — 21
    What We Found in Chapter 3 — 21
    Where Can I Go Next? — 21

4 Learning or Acquiring? — 23
    From First Languages to SLA — 23
    A Starting Point: Krashen's Monitor Model — 24
    Critiques and Current Thinking — 25
    Chapter Review — 27
    What We Found in Chapter 4 — 27
    Where Can I Go Next? — 28

5	Masses of Input	29
	Input, Output and Interaction	29
	Input	30
	Interaction	32
	Output	33
	Chapter Review	34
	What We Found in Chapter 5	35
	Where Can I Go Next?	36
6	Earlier Isn't Necessarily Better	37
	Age of Acquisition, Length of Residence and Ultimate Attainment	39
	Chapter Review	41
	What We Found in Chapter 6	42
	Where Can I Go Next?	42
7	Implicit and Explicit Learning	44
	Three Types of Knowledge	44
	You Gotta Practise	45
	Feedback	46
	Chapter Review	49
	What We Found in Chapter 7	49
	Where Can I Go Next?	50
8	First Languages Are Important for Learning English	51
	The Monolingual Principle	51
	The Role of First Languages in Learning	53
	Bilingualism and the Brain	55
	Chapter Review: Is There Still a Place for 'English-only' Policies?	56
	What We Found in Chapter 8	58
	Where Can I Go Next?	58
9	Pulling It All Together: Learning Trajectories and Second Language Pedagogy	59
	A Practice-based Approach to Additional Language Learning	59
	How Long Does It Take to Develop Proficiency?	62
	What We Found in Chapter 9	65
	Where Can I Go Next?	65
	Part 2: Language Across the Curriculum	
	Preface to Part 2	67
10	Five Principles for Language Across the Curriculum	71
	Five Principles	73
	What We Found in Chapter 10	74
	Where Can I Go Next?	74

Contents vii

11	BICS and CALP	75
	Common Underlying Proficiency	75
	BICS and CALP	76
	CUP, BICS/CALP and Changing Learner Profiles	78
	Chapter Review	78
	What We Found in Chapter 11	79
	Where Can I Go Next?	79
12	Oracy: Talking and Learning	80
	What Is Oracy?	80
	From Talking to Writing	81
	The Quality of Interaction Matters	82
	How Can We Promote Oracy?	83
	Chapter Review	83
	What We Found in Chapter 12	84
	Where Can I Go Next?	84
13	Reading in a New Language	86
	Oracy, Multilingualism and Literacy	86
	Reading as a Skill	87
	What About Phonics?	88
	Vocabulary	89
	Strategies for Developing Confident Readers	91
	Chapter Review	92
	What We Found in Chapter 13	92
	Where Can I Go Next?	92
	Case Study 1: Teaching Poetry in Year 11	93
	Commentary	96
14	Making Meaning in Writing: Field, Tenor and Mode	97
	Introducing SFL	97
	Genre and Audience	98
	Two Contexts: Culture and Situation	99
	Meaning is Multimodal	100
	Chapter Review	101
	What We Found in Chapter 14	101
	Where Can I Go Next?	102
15	Disciplinary Language, Disciplinary Knowledge	103
	From Everyday to Disciplinary Language: The Register Continuum	103
	The Teaching and Learning Cycle (TLC)	105
	Nominalisation and Complex Clauses	106
	Metalanguage and Strategies	107
	Chapter Review	108

	What We Found in Chapter 15	108
	Where Can I Go Next?	109
	Case Study 2: EAL and Maths	109
	Commentary	111
16	Pulling It All Together: What Counts as Proficiency	113
	A Practice-based Approach to EAL, Continued	113
	What Counts as Proficiency?	115
	What We Found in Chapter 16	116
	Where Can I Go Next?	117
	Case Study 3: EAL Is a Mainstream Responsibility	117
	The Welsh Context	117
	EAL: A Mainstream Responsibility	118
	Commentary	120
	Part 3: The EAL Specialist	
	Preface to Part 3	123
	For Newly Appointed EAL Specialists	125
17	Getting to Grips with the Role	127
	Beginning the EAL Audit: Getting to Know your School	127
	Build a Policy Folder and Note the Gaps	128
	What Are your Aspirations for the Role?	129
	Chapter Review	131
	Case Study 4: Working with Families	131
	Commentary	133
18	Establishing Effective Assessments	134
	Basic Features of Language Assessments	134
	What Is an Assessment Framework for?	136
	Choosing the Right Test	137
	Chapter Review	138
19	Welcoming Students	139
	Getting Started	139
	Creating a Welcoming Learning Environment	141
	Chapter Review	143
	Case Study 5: New Arrivals	143
	Commentary	145
20	Getting Connected	147
	Subject Associations	147
	Online Community	148
	For More Established EAL Specialists	150

21 Making Friends and Influencing People	151
Beyond the First Year	151
Models of Provision	153
EAL Specialists as Language Leaders	154
Chapter Review	156
22 From Mono to Multi	158
Monolingual and Multilingual: A Problematic Comparison	158
A Challenge from SLA	160
Chapter Review	161
Case Study 6: Ofsted	162
The Big Picture: EAL Specialists, EAL Data and EAL Practice	163
The Inspection Process	164
Implications for EAL Specialists	167
Questions to Ask	171
Case Study 7: EAL and SEND	174
Communication With Families	174
Linguistic and Cultural Differences	175
Assessment Issues	176
Commentary	177
23 CPD for EAL Specialists	179
Scope and Starting Points	179
Component Parts	180
CPD Across the School	180
We Need to Talk about ITE	181
CPD for EAL: A Practical Guide	181
Chapter Review	183
24 For Everyone	184
Connecting Home and School: Funds of Knowledge	184
Key Messages	185
Where Can I Go Next?	187
Appendix I: Checklist and Activities for the New EAL Specialist	190
Appendix II: Networks and Groups	197
Working with Consultants	199
Courses and Qualifications	200
References	201
Index	211

Figures, Tables and Case Studies

Figures

Figure 2.1	The EAL learner and field of EAL, a conceptual model	10
Figure 6.1	Morphosyntactic and phonological skills of 240 Korean L1 speakers who arrived in the United States between the ages of 1 and 23 years	38
Figure 11.1	Surface features of different languages and common underlying proficiency	76
Figure 11.2	The Cummins quadrants	77
Figure 13.1	A substitution table	90
Figure 13.2	Vocabulary tiers, as portrayed by the Education Endowment Fund (2019) based on the work of Beck et al. (2013)	91
Figure CS1.1	A spaceman	94
Figure 15.1	The register continuum	104
Figure 21.1	The content–language continuum	154
Figure 22.1	Percentage of pupils achieving expected standard in maths at KS1 for EAL pupils at different levels of proficiency in English and monolingual English speakers	159

Tables

Table 17.1	From aspirations to a personal EAL plan	130
Table CS6.1	The six stages of an Ofsted inspection	165
Table CS6.2	Key principles for Ofsted inspections	169

Case Studies

Case Study 1	Teaching Poetry in Year 11, *Manny Vazquez*	93
Case Study 2	EAL and Maths, *Sarah Fowkes*	109
Case Study 3	EAL Is a Mainstream Responsibility, *Pam Cole*	117
Case Study 4	Working with Families, *Erica Field*	131
Case Study 5	New Arrivals, *Christine McCormack*	143
Case Study 6	Ofsted	162
Case Study 7	EAL and SEND, *Anne Margaret Smith*	174

Acknowledgements

Many people contributed to this book and without them it would not have been possible. First and foremost, my thanks go to the young people and teachers whose lives, work and ideas have shaped my understanding of this vibrant and important field. Your generosity and insight are gratefully appreciated. Thanks also to Jean Conteh and James Simpson, incomparable supervisors whose influence resonates through the book.

Many thanks to the anonymous reviewers, case study contributors, friends and colleagues whose comments and suggestions have strengthened the book you hold now.

Finally, thanks to Anna Roderick and the team at Multilingual Matters, who first thought the book was a good idea and whose guidance made it a reality.

Some material in Chapters 2 and 11 was previously published in Sharples *et al.* (2019), and the publisher's permission to reproduce it here is gratefully acknowledged.

Abbreviations and Acronyms

AoA	Age of Acquisition
ASL	American Sign Language
BICS	Basic Interpersonal Communication Skills
CALP	Cognitive Academic Language Proficiency
CEFR	Common European Framework of Reference
CPD	Continuing Professional Development
CUP	Common Underlying Proficiency
DARTs	Directed Activities Related to Texts
DfE	Department for Education (England)
EAL	English as an Additional Language
EF	Executive Function
EIF	Education Inspection Framework
ELF	English as a Lingua Franca
ELL	English Language Learner (predominantly US, equivalent to EAL)
ESL	English as a Second Language
ESOL	English for Speakers of Other Languages (generally used for adult migrants)
EYFS	Early Years Foundation Stage
IP	Input Processing
IRF/IRE	Initiation-Response-Feedback/Evaluation
ITE	Initial Teacher Education
KS1–4	Key Stage (KS1–2 are Primary; KS3–4 are Secondary)
L1, L2	First Language, Second Language
LoR	Length of Residence in the L2 Environment
LTEL	Long-Term English Learners
MFL	Modern Foreign Languages
PiE	Proficiency in English
SAT	Standardised Assessment Test (aka end-of-Key Stage tests and assessments)
SEBD	Social, Emotional and Behavioural Difficulties
SENDs	Special Educational Needs and Disabilities
SFL	Systemic Functional Linguistics
SLA	Second Language Acquisition
TLC	Teaching and Learning Cycle
UG	Universal Grammar
WAL	Welsh as an Additional Language

For Jenny, Isobel and Benjamin

1 Introduction

Welcome

Schools are more richly textured than they used to be. Our collective roots now spread to every corner of the world and draw in young people of widely different experiences and expectations. The sights, sounds and stories of every country are now part of our communities. We haven't really got to grips with this yet. We're still thinking through what it means to teach in a world that is increasingly multilingual and connected, in an education system that was designed for another era and that is under intense pressure.

This is a book about EAL, the specialist discipline of teaching pupils for whom English is an additional language – that richly woven tangle of language, curriculum, meaning, movement, culture and learning that has become part of almost every school in the country. More than one in five pupils in our schools now speaks another language at home, and EAL can fairly be called an 'ordinary' part of every teacher's job (Leung, 2016: 158). Yet newly qualified teachers still report that they feel less well prepared for EAL than for any other aspect of their work (DfE, 2018: 27). There are very few teacher education programmes that allow you to specialise in EAL and similarly few master's programmes dedicated to the discipline. In Scotland, which has perhaps the strongest policy framework for EAL in the UK, changing demographics mean that specialist expertise is greatly in demand. In England, the policy framework is almost entirely absent: there is no real mention of EAL in the Ofsted inspection handbook and no guidance at all from the Department for Education, whose official stance is to maintain only a 'watching brief'. This disparity between the obvious significance of EAL in schools and the glaring absence of any meaningful guidance for EAL specialists is where this book comes in.

Teaching EAL: Evidence-based Strategies for the Classroom and School has a clear goal: to put before you, as simply as possible but with all essential detail, the evidence and principles you need to make informed decisions about your practice. It is written with three principles in mind: first, that EAL is a rich and important discipline, not an add-on or something that happens in the margins of 'real' (meaning subject) teaching. EAL specialists, as we see in Parts 2 and 3, play a vital role in promoting language-rich teaching across the curriculum. Second, that you are a talented and capable educator, able to make good decisions when presented with the evidence ... but that you are also busy and would value clarity. This informs both the structure and the style of the book: references are kept to a minimum but there are extensive notes on further reading at the end of each chapter. We will not shy away from complex ideas, but they will always be expressed clearly and with emphasis on the implications for practice. Finally, that EAL is a specialism but not an exclusive one. Every teacher should know something about how language works in their subject; EAL teachers should know a lot about how language works across the curriculum. This is the basis of the book's contents, of which more below. When read from start to finish, it provides a structured and coherent introduction to the evidence, thinking and principles that underpin EAL provision.

Teaching EAL also makes a series of arguments about what the discipline could (and perhaps should) look like. EAL practice is both diverse and dynamic: the possible combinations of learners, teachers and settings are near infinite, and they change as local communities, school cultures and individuals do. Life never stands still for an EAL teacher and it's easy to feel buffeted by events and the constantly changing needs of your learners. Having a sense of the bigger picture – the historical scope and the international nature of additional language education – allows us to look beyond the day-to-day. EAL teaching has a rich history and relevance beyond a single country, so we can take the transient diktats of government ministers in our stride. We will begin exploring these arguments in the next chapter as we map the national and international context of EAL, and we will develop them throughout the book.

It goes without saying that these arguments are not definitive and the stances adopted are not absolute. Rather, the book offers a series of positions, rooted in evidence that is clearly presented, on which you can base your own work. I have tried to write it as the starting point for a longer conversation, as a curated selection of ideas, findings and thinking from the rich breadth of this interdisciplinary field. I hope it is useful, but most of all I hope it does just what the name implies: that it offers evidence-based strategies that you can use in your classroom and school.

Is This Book for You?

Yes!

The book is written for anyone who works with EAL pupils: teachers, teaching assistants, school leaders, governors and advisors – anyone, in fact, who wants to understand how young bilinguals learn and how they can be supported to achieve highly. If you are interested in EAL but don't see yourself primarily as an EAL specialist (or if you are reading this while you train and haven't decided yet), then Parts 1 and 2 will give you a strong grounding in language acquisition and language in the curriculum. Both of these are essential to the success of bilingual pupils and are well worth knowing about in any role. If you want to develop further, Part 3 focuses on being (or becoming) an 'EAL specialist'. It tackles material that will also be of wide interest (such as how to succeed with Ofsted and how to distinguish between bilingualism and language impairment), but from the perspective of someone who is responsible for EAL provision across the school.

You will notice that the book often uses the term 'EAL specialist' rather than 'teacher', 'coordinator' or similar. Your job title or status in the school isn't particularly important here. What matters is that you want to build up your expertise in EAL. If that's you, welcome.

How Is the Book Organised?

The book is organised in three parts:

Part 1, How Additional Languages Are Learned, gives a concise introduction to second language acquisition. The seven chapters each focus on a key theme, such as whether age makes a difference (Chapter 6) or the importance of first languages (Chapter 8). The discussion is tailored to the needs of EAL specialists, taking into account the diversity of our learners and the specific context of learning English alongside and through the curriculum. Each chapter is written to be short, accessible and grounded in the evidence – just the thing when you need a concise answer or a confident riposte about how bilingual children learn languages.

Part 2, Language Across the Curriculum, examines the shared and subject-specific ways in which language is used in subject learning. It begins by introducing five principles for developing language across the curriculum (Chapter 10). It then distinguishes academic and general English, noting that subject learning is inextricable from subject language, and explores the role of talk and reading in the development of subject knowledge (Chapters 11–13). It introduces the functional approach to language, which allows us to look at how meaning is made in academic text, and discusses some strategies that EAL and subject specialists can use to help learners communicate those meanings (Chapters 14–15). Finally, we look at how what counts as proficiency for EAL learners (Chapter 16).

Part 3, The EAL Specialist, focuses on the ideas and understanding you need to make the role a success. It is organised into two sections, the first for those new in post (or considering the role) and the second for more experienced practitioners who want to reflect on their work so far and how they might develop further. They echo each other: for new EAL specialists we look at how to get to grips with the role, how to establish effective assessments and organise provision and how to connect with other EAL practitioners (Chapters 17–20). We revisit these themes for more experienced specialists – how to influence school policy, how to critique the monolingual ideology of the education system, how to address Ofsted and how to develop a CPD plan for yourself and your colleagues (Chapters 21–23). Part 3 closes with the key messages (Chapter 24).

Each chapter gives suggestions for further reading and at the end of the book you will find two helpful appendices as well as a full list of the references cited.

Case studies

Teaching EAL also includes seven case studies. They are written by experienced practitioners with real, recent experience of EAL. They are drawn from across the UK, from Primary and Secondary contexts, and show how the research evidence can be brought to bear on real-life teaching and learning.

In Part 2, the case studies focus on working across the curriculum. Manny Vazquez follows Chapter 13 on 'Reading in a New Language' by unpacking metaphor in a Year 11 English literature classroom. He shows how EAL knowledge can contribute to subject teaching, enriching reading for all learners. Sarah Fowkes, who follows Chapter 15 on 'Disciplinary Language, Disciplinary Knowledge', writes about her work developing language awareness in Maths. She shows that a 'Word Aware' approach can help Year 4/5 learners with mathematical reasoning. Pam Cole takes a broader focus, linking Parts 2 and 3 of the book by discussing her work embedding EAL across the curriculum. She argues that EAL is a mainstream responsibility, rooted in partnership between EAL and subject teachers, and shows how this ethos can be used to build capacity across schools and regions.

In Part 3, the case studies open out to include other aspects of the EAL specialist's role. Erica Field explains her approach to supporting families in and beyond school, and follows Chapter 17 on 'Getting to Grips with the Role'. She argues that spending time with families, especially over a brew, is a great foundation for EAL practice. Christine McCormack follows Chapter 19 on 'Welcoming Students' and describes how she created a city-wide resource pack and CPD programme about new arrivals. Her work draws in colleagues from across the school, making the EAL specialist a key figure in the support provided for new pupils. The two final case studies are slightly different: Anne Margaret Smith gives a concise guide to distinguishing EAL from SEN, and a double-length chapter (based on extensive interviews with senior inspectors) discusses how to work with Ofsted's new inspection framework.

Taken as a whole, then, *Teaching EAL* offers a thorough review of the research evidence, first-hand case studies by experienced practitioners and a set of arguments about how we might approach education differently. It needs something else, too – a set of shared reference points that create common ground as we discuss how to support bilingual pupils. We need a clear sense of what EAL means now, who our learners are and what our colleagues in other schools are doing. This is the focus of the next chapter.

2 EAL in the National and International Context

This chapter begins by putting EAL in its historical context. It then turns to more contemporary matters, outlining the different ways in which EAL is understood in policy and practice, mapping the changing demographics of our learners and introducing a practice-based approach to EAL.

A Brief History

'EAL' emerged as a distinct discipline in the second half of the 20th century. Its history so far can be understood as three broad phases: the early response to large-scale immigration in the 1950s and 1960s; the focus on race and discrimination in the 1970s–1990s; and the contemporary response to an increasingly mobile, globally connected population.

Although the UK has a long history of inward migration, attention began to focus on multilingual classrooms only with the arrival of young people from the 'New Commonwealth' of newly (re-)independent countries. There was then – as again now – no national approach to majority language education in schools but teachers were encouraged to model Standard English norms through their own speech. The initial policy response was based around the assumption that these young people would settle in the UK for the long term and that the goal was to help them to 'become "invisible", a truly integrated member of the school community [...] as soon as possible' (Derrick, 1977: 16). Specific funding was allocated to support this integration into the mainstream through Section 11 of the Local Government Act 1966. Provision was limited and was often organised through 'language centres' that isolated young migrants from the mainstream and frequently presented English in a 'de-contextualized way [that] did not prepare pupils for curriculum content' (Graf, 2011: 2–3).

The second phase in this short history of EAL – the 1970s, 1980s and 1990s – can be seen as a reflection of a country coming to terms with broader issues of diversity, equality and discrimination. The language centres established in the previous decade came under greater scrutiny as a number of government reports found that isolation from the mainstream did not offer sufficient preparation for academic success (e.g. DES, 1971, 1972). The Bullock Report (1975) was particularly significant because it made a clear argument for multilingualism as part of the mainstream school. A changing political climate also contributed to the increased emphasis on mainstream provision: where previously migrant children had been seen as 'a threat to "standards" and to the quality of education in schools', an increasing awareness of racial discrimination meant that the risk of legal challenges to language centres posed the greater threat (see Leung, 2016: 160–162). The Race Relations Act (1976) allowed for legal challenges on grounds of racism, and the Rampton Report (1981) introduced the notion of institutional racism. The Swann Report (1985) built on Rampton's findings and implied that the use of separate language centres may be discriminatory. The Calderdale Report (Commission for Racial Equality, 1986) found that Calderdale local authority's policy of providing separate English language tuition could not be justified on educational grounds and amounted to indirect racial discrimination. By 1993, when the Local Government (Amendment) Act widened Section 11 funding to all ethnic minority pupils, issues of diversity, equality and discrimination were a robust part of the discourse around multilingual classrooms.

The most recent phase – from the late 1990s to today – can be seen as a period in which global migration flows began to shift, leading to increasing diversity in the classroom. There is still a strong emphasis on monolingualism: early in this period, one policy document referred to children who 'start school without an adequate grasp' of English (DfEE, 1997), but at the same time researchers were beginning to challenge the notion of a 'native speaker' (Leung et al., 1997), to theorise the strategies that young people used to resist classroom power relations (Canagarajah, 1997) and to challenge any sense of language learning as a linear process (Larsen-Freeman, 1997). This literature may have been 'undoubtedly [...] under-used' (Leung, 2001: 1), but it was a period of vibrant debate in which several of today's approaches were first established.

Reforms to the education system since 2010 have led to increasing fragmentation at national level and increasing isolation at school level. Changes to initial teacher education (ITE) have significantly increased the role of schools and multi-academy trusts in training teachers, while the role of universities and local authorities has been reduced. One advantage of the former system was a relatively effective network of EAL support, with expertise shared between schools, local authorities and universities. In a 'school-led' system (see Gilbert et al., 2013), schools are expected to provide that level of expertise themselves. Few can. As a result, very few schools now have access to an experienced EAL specialist. There has been a substantial reduction both in the support available from local authorities and in the number of specialist ITE and postgraduate courses available to EAL teachers. This loss of professional expertise comes at an important time. The pupil population is increasingly multilingual, connected to family and friends around the world and drawing new ideas and influences into the classroom. EAL specialists have an significant contribution to make as we work out how the education system can respond, not least in ensuring that a clear understanding of language and learning informs teaching across the curriculum. Without this insight, it is too easy to default to a deficit model in which pupils' multilingualism and experience is recast as a lack of English proficiency and an inadequate grasp of the curriculum. EAL has never been more important to the work of our schools.

Current EAL Policy

Schools do not operate in isolation, of course. They work within the boundaries set by policy and by teachers' professional standards. These have very little to say about EAL, generally using it to describe bilingual learners without further differentiation. In policy, 'EAL' can perhaps better be seen as an umbrella term for a complex range of characteristics, practices and objectives. This can make it unhelpfully broad, especially when talking to colleagues in other disciplines. It is worth taking a moment to pin down what we mean when we use the term, because its apparent simplicity can quickly lead to practices that marginalise both EAL students and EAL specialists.

Take this simple definition as a starting point:

EAL means that pupils are still learning English.

It is certainly true, as far as it goes, but its simplicity is misleading. The reference to 'learning English', without more detail on the type of English and the reason for learning it, could be taken to mean that EAL is a question of generic language proficiency rather than of subject-specific literacies (see Part 2). The focus on 'learning English' emphasises a linguistic deficit (that they lack full command of their new language), when really our goal is to help learners use their developing English skills to participate fully in the curriculum.

The official definition used by the Department for Education (DfE) is a little more nuanced:

A pupil is recorded as having English as an additional language if she/he is exposed to a language at home that is known or believed to be other than English. *It is not a measure of English language proficiency or a good proxy for recent immigration.* (DfE, 2020: 4, italics added)

This definition has been used for some years. It has the advantage of being inclusive. It encompasses any pupil who has encountered another language in early childhood without requiring schools to evaluate proficiency in English (PiE). This means that British-born bilingual pupils are likely to be counted as EAL, where a less all-encompassing definition might exclude them (especially where, through fear of stigma or devaluation of status, parents play down their other languages to the school). The disadvantage of the DfE definition, however, is that its inclusiveness obscures real and important differences between groups of pupils. The final sentence, in italics, is a relatively recent addition to this definition of EAL. It reflects a growing understanding that exposure to another language is not the most significant factor in bilingual pupils' attainment. The pupil's proficiency in English has a much greater impact on curriculum success.

A measure of proficiency in English was included in the School Census from Autumn 2016 to Spring 2018. While this gave valuable (if short-lived) insight into the English proficiency of bilingual pupils, it also revealed a strongly monolingual view of bilingualism. Take this descriptor, for example, describing pupils at the highest of five stages:

> Fluent [Code 'E']: Can operate across the curriculum to a level of competence equivalent to that of a pupil who uses English as his/her first language. Operates without EAL support across the curriculum. (DfE, 2016: 63)

Fluent bilingual pupils are described in monolingual terms, as having a level of competence equivalent to that of an English first language learner who needs no EAL support. The notion of 'equivalence' with monolingual pupils is a false one. It suggests that bilingual pupils follow a trajectory from inadequate grasp of English towards 'full' or 'native speaker' proficiency in the majority language. This has been extensively criticised for marginalising the linguistic proficiency of bilingual learners – as long ago as 1989, bilingualism researcher François Grosjean warned against seeing bilinguals as 'two monolinguals in one' (Grosjean, 1989). Bilingualism is not simply a question of having monolingual competence in several languages. Instead, languages interact in complex ways that have substantial implications for learning. There is strong evidence that first languages play an important role in the development of additional languages, and even that bilingual pupils outperform monolinguals when both languages are developed to a high level.

An emphasis on monolingualism also creates an artificial separation between subject learning and language development, when the evidence is clear that academic language is best developed in the context of meaningful subject content. EAL provision does not work like the training wheels on a bicycle, something that pupils need for a short while until they are able to 'operate without EAL support'. It is a specialist, 'cross-curriculum' discipline that informs and supports learning in all subjects. Finally, the official definition of EAL reinforces the idea that classrooms are normally monolingual, when the reality is that many classrooms are fundamentally multilingual but operate a monolingual curriculum. This risks reducing EAL specialists to a parallel service whose role is to prepare children to operate without support in the monolingual classroom. This is an impoverished vision for EAL, and one that does not withstand serious scrutiny.

A Practice-based Approach to EAL

A simpler definition is more useful to everyday practice: EAL pupils are learning English as they learn *through* English. They are engaged in the mainstream curriculum and at the same time they are learning the language through which that curriculum is delivered. This has several implications:

(i)   the primary place of learning is the mainstream classroom;
(ii) language is inseparable from content;
(iii) the challenge faced by EAL learners is substantial but not unique – all pupils are developing their command of academic language as they learn.

Each of these implications will be closely examined in the chapters that follow. They are a starting point for a 'practice-based' approach to EAL, one that draws on the rich, interdisciplinary body of evidence available to us but that is rooted in what learners actually have to do to succeed. It draws parallels with the challenge facing all learners – to become experts in their subjects by developing the knowledge, skills and language of that subject – without glossing over the differences that make EAL distinctive. It emphasises their entitlement to the curriculum: except for dual-certified teachers, the subject specialist is usually best placed to teach the subject. It recognises the benefit of peer interaction: rich talk around learning underpins higher level academic language use. It also takes advantage of the fact that mainstream classrooms are not designed primarily for language learners. Subject classrooms tend to include more varied language, less finely tuned to the pupils' level of proficiency and therefore with more opportunities to encounter important but infrequent vocabulary and patterns, exposing pupils to a wider range of speakers and materials. EAL specialists are needed to support language-rich pedagogy across the curriculum and to give higher level support to those that need it, but the overarching aim is for language and subject specialists to 'apprentice' pupils into the discourses of their disciplines – the ways of thinking and doing, as well as speaking and writing, that characterise successful learning.

This practice-based approach has roots in a seminal working paper published by NALDIC, the subject association for EAL, more than 20 years ago. This set the learner's needs in the context of four factors: the process of learning a second or additional language; cognitive development (which is closely related to first language development); the learner's sociocultural background; and the learning context (NALDIC, 1999: 1; see Figure 2.1). As a professional discipline, NALDIC argued, EAL 'is concerned with all four factors. It is [...] primarily about teaching and learning language through the content of the whole curriculum [and] takes place within the mainstream and within all subjects' (NALDIC, 1999: 1–2).

This approach is helpful because it puts the learner at the centre of EAL practice. It does not start by comparing bilingual pupils with an imagined monolingual majority, or judge them solely in terms of proficiency in the majority language. In fact, language is only one aspect of EAL. It is inseparable from the learner's cognitive development and the context of learning. This is particularly significant for EAL pupils because sociocultural development is not limited to what happens in school. Pupils' experience of racism and insecure legal status, of learning in the family and through their faiths, of their sense of their place in a community – all of these and more contribute to the sociocultural context of their learning and help us to see how the full breadth of the learners' lives are connected to our work as teachers. Importantly, this approach shifts the focus from language learning to participation in the curriculum. The obvious implication of this is that EAL cannot be a marginal activity. If language is so intertwined with curriculum learning for bilingual children, it must be so for everyone. EAL pupils have 'distinct and different needs [...] by virtue of the fact that they are learning in and through another language' (NALDIC, 1999: 7), but they equally have much in common with pupils whose first language is English.

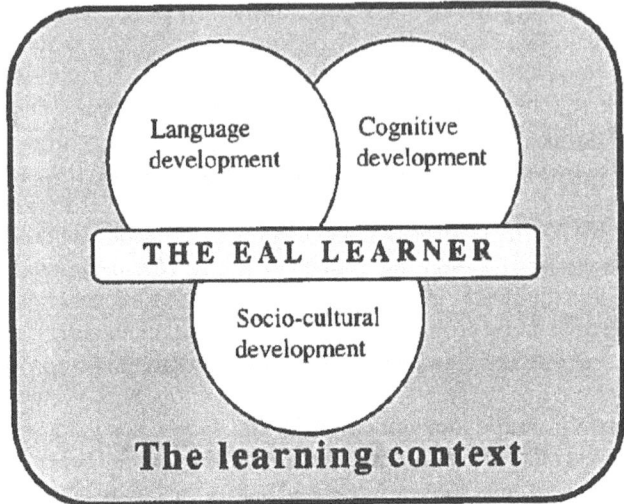

Figure 2.1 The EAL learner and field of EAL, a conceptual model
Source: NALDIC (1999: 3).

Looking at EAL in this way, as a specialist language-education discipline that is deeply rooted in the mainstream curriculum, encourages critical discussion about our field. This might mean asking, for example:

- Is there disciplinary knowledge that is core to all EAL specialists, or is it entirely dependent on the learners and the context?
- Is there a single role for EAL specialists, or is there further specialisation within the field?
- What knowledge and activities should be the domain of the EAL specialist, and what should be taken on by all teachers?
- How should the progress of EAL pupils be assessed and reported, who should receive and act on those reports, and do they provide sufficient insight to support high-quality teaching and learning across the curriculum?
- What do assessments capture about EAL learners, and what do we need to know that is not captured?
- How should provision be organised to support a broad and balanced curriculum at every level of English proficiency?

These questions are important for every discipline. They are especially challenging for EAL because of the heterogeneity of the field. Our critical account of 'EAL' might include the disciplinary knowledge of EAL specialists, the responsibilities of subject teachers, the relationship between different types of assessment and data collection, the role of first language(s), and more. This book does not give definitive answers to these questions – we should be wary of any solution that is meant to fit everyone, everywhere – but it does put forward a body of evidence and argument to help you make your own decisions about your work with EAL learners.

A Note on EAL Learners

It is an understatement to say that EAL pupils are a diverse group. They include learners from all parts of the world, speaking over 360 languages between them and representing every combination of educational, economic and geographical trajectories. It often seems as if the only features that define EAL learners are their diversity and their multilingualism. In fact, there are several trends that we can use to plan robust teaching and learning.

When we talk about EAL learners, we could be talking about any one of several different situations:

- children who were born in the UK and grew up using another language at home but for whom English has become, or is becoming, dominant (advanced bilingual learners);
- pupils who arrive in the school system after the normal year of enrolment, with varying levels of proficiency in English and of literacy in English and other languages (new international arrivals);
- learners with limited or interrupted schooling, insecure legal status and perhaps trauma (such as asylum seekers and refugees);
- learners in schools that have little prior experience of bilingualism, mobility and linguistic diversity (isolated learners and isolated schools); and
- learners whose parents are working or studying in the UK for a short time and who will return to another country either regularly or in due course (sojourners). (Adapted from Conteh, 2012: 12–13)

These are not mutually exclusive. Pupils might have interrupted schooling and be in a school that has little prior experience of EAL, for example. We might also extend the list to add the range of contexts in which such learners study, their existing and emerging literacies, the extent to which they have roots in a local community (here or elsewhere), whether they have secure housing and legal status, their access to learning resources at home and, for new arrivals, whether they are likely to move again or to settle. These characteristics are not unique to EAL pupils – many learners experience insecurity or find the 'fit' with their school difficult – but they demonstrate that EAL responds to much more than language.

A practice-based approach to EAL puts the pupil – the whole person, and everything they bring to the classroom – at the centre. It sometimes feels like the responsibilities can mushroom, from being a language teacher to suddenly having to take every possible aspect of children's complex lives into account. After all, what can you do about only having one pupil from a certain language background, or about a learner's immigration status? Let's set those concerns aside for a moment. Parts 1 and 2 focus on what is more or less universal in EAL: language learning and language across the curriculum. Once we have a good grasp of these essentials we can start tailoring our work to different groups.

Part 3 equips you to do this, setting up the learning context for the learners in *your* school. It includes practical activities for you to make sense of your role and establish provision that fits with your own values and thinking about EAL. In the final section of the book, just before the concluding messages, there is a short discussion of the Funds of Knowledge approach. Originally developed with Spanish-speaking pupils in the United States, this approach is based on the realisation that 'building on what students bring to school and their strengths has been shown to be an incredibly effective teaching strategy' (González *et al.*, 2005: 8). You might want to skip ahead to it now. It's a great way to start thinking about how learners, not language, could be at the centre of EAL provision. If you want to read through the chapters in order, do so. The discussion of Funds of Knowledge can be a point to pause and reflect on your work and the book as a whole, which turns now to the evidence on additional language learning.

What We Found in Chapter 2

In Chapter 2 we reviewed the history of EAL, looked at current policy and outlined a practice-based approach that puts the learner at the centre. We closed with a brief note on the heterogeneity of EAL learners, recognising that there are some common themes that we can use to guide our work. This offers context but is also an important part of current practice: for EAL to be recognised as a discipline we need to know our history, as well as having a well-defined approach to learning and a clear understanding of the learners.

Where Can I Go Next?

For the **history of EAL**, see the excellent journal articles by Tracey Costley (2014) and Constant Leung (2016). The latter includes a particularly helpful 'genealogy' of the discipline for anyone interested in its evolution from 'English as a second language' (ESL). NALDIC's (1999) seminal position paper, 'The distinctiveness of English as an additional language', is also essential reading. It is short, accessible and available free (to members) or cheaply on NALDIC's website. The early policy responses to immigration can still resonate. If you can track down a copy of the 1963 Ministry of Education pamphlet, *English for Immigrants*, you'll find that many of the concerns that policy makers had then are still relevant to us now.

There is a wealth of **EAL data** available online. The key government sources are:

- England: https://www.gov.uk/government/collections/statistics-school-and-pupil-numbers
- Scotland: https://www.gov.scot/collections/school-education-statistics
- Wales: https://statswales.gov.wales/Catalogue/Education-and-Skills
- Northern Ireland: https://www.education-ni.gov.uk/topics/statistics-and-research/statistics

These resources are not always easy to navigate and there are significant gaps in the available data. A helpful (and freely accessible) report by Steve Strand and Annina Hessel (2018) makes important observations about what we can and cannot observe. Further evidence-based criticisms of current EAL data can be found in Jo Hutchinson's (2018) report for the Education Policy Institute.

Part 1
How Additional Languages Are Learned

> *A second language is not just adding rooms to your house by building an extension at the back: it is rebuilding all the internal walls.*
> Vivian Cook, 2008

Preface to Part 1

Language is the heart of our discipline, but it has a dual nature. It is the medium through which we teach: how we bring concepts into being and how we apprentice others into our ways of thinking and doing. It is also a system of rules and procedures. These rules allow us to organise a finite set of units (words and their components) into language of infinite complexity. We acquire this language system in early infancy and each of us carries a mental representation of our languages in our brain. Language is therefore both social and individual. We need to include both approaches in our teaching if we are to give our learners the proficiency and the expertise they need to succeed in the curriculum.

In Part 1 we will focus on *language as a grammatical system*, before turning to more social approaches in Part 2. We will compare formal and functional thinking, asking whether our language system is innate or built up from our interaction with others. In doing so, our discussion will first establish an overarching 'theory of language' so that we have a solid grounding in the concepts and a sense of what end goal we hope our learners will reach (Chapter 3). It will then look at the distinction between learning and acquisition (Chapter 4) and the importance of input, output and interaction (Chapter 5). We draw on early studies that provide an excellent introduction to the field of language acquisition as well as more recent findings. Subsequent chapters extend and apply this thinking, looking at whether age is significant in language acquisition (Chapter 6), what role explicit teaching might play in the EAL classroom (Chapter 7) and why first languages are important for learning English (Chapter 8). Part 1 closes with a brief review of how long it typically takes pupils to reach proficiency in English (Chapter 9), bringing together many of the themes of the preceding chapters as it does so.

In this way the book equips you with a core of knowledge about language acquisition and gives clear links to practice at every stage, so that you can tackle new challenges confidently and effectively.

3 Key Principles and a Theory of Language

This chapter sets out some of the key ideas for the book and introduces a theory of language to underpin our discussion of EAL pedagogy.

Learning a language is a remarkable achievement. Within a few months of birth, babies can recognise their names and begin to distinguish between the sounds of one language and those of another. At around six months they can break down the stream of speech into words and they soon begin to join in by babbling. By two, their vocabulary is growing quickly and they are able to combine words into short phrases and questions. At some point in that second year, grammar emerges in a burst, marking a sudden expansion in their ability to communicate. By the time most children start school, the grammatical system is largely in place and ready for fine-tuning. They have already mastered a large body of words and phrases, a complex grammar and a set of social rules about how these new resources and skills can be used. Even more impressively, they have done this without any formal instruction and based on little more than their interactions with other speakers.

The fact that young children seem to acquire their first language so effortlessly has shaped many of our assumptions about how second languages are learned. These often make intuitive sense: children soak up languages like sponges; language learning gets harder as you get older; parents should speak English at home so their kids get a good model of the language. The problem is that they are neither true nor helpful. Children do soak up language, but without explicit instruction will still struggle with the patterns and registers of academic English. Your ability to pick up a language does change with age, but as you get older you also bring more advanced thinking skills to the task. The quantity and quality of exposure to English is important, but insisting that parents use only English misses the point that first language development also contributes to proficiency in the new language.

What we need is a theoretical framework that can account for all of this. It needs to lie beneath the surface of our practice – not something that we have to puzzle over daily but a coherent set of ideas that tie together the many different aspects of an EAL specialist's job. This chapter sets out one such approach.

Key terms

First, some terminology. In this book and in much of the research literature, the term 'L1' (or first language) is used for all the languages acquired in early childhood. The term 'L2' (second language) is used for all languages acquired later. Another way of putting it would be to distinguish simultaneous bilingualism from sequential bilingualism: 'L1' describes languages acquired together (simultaneously) in early childhood, and 'L2' those learned after the first (in sequence). These L1/L2 labels are useful because the evidence shows that first and subsequent languages are acquired differently, whereas there is less to distinguish between languages learned together in early childhood (L1s) or between the languages learned after the first language was established (L2s). Similarly, the term 'bilingual' is used to mean 'more than one language': current research suggests that there are some differences between the acquisition of second, third, fourth and other languages, but the pedagogical implications are not yet clear. For our purposes, the key distinction is between L1 and L2.

Theory of Language

Any successful approach to language education needs to be underpinned by a theory of language. This is just as it sounds – it is your understanding of the *nature of language* and *how it is learned or acquired*. This has implications for a further aspect – the end goal of language learning (or *target*) and how we help learners to reach it. When we don't take the time to specify these, we tend to rely on everyday assumptions about language that aren't robust enough for high-quality teaching. For example, we often default to a more restrictive view of language and learning than is necessary, or focus on the surface-level features at the expense of those that underpin deeper learning. A coherent theory of language helps us to make sound decisions in our practice.

The nature of language: Two starting points

Is language better seen as a *formal system* of discrete elements (words and their components), organised according to grammatical rules and procedures, or as a *functional system*, organised around the meanings that speakers exchange with each other? Our answer to this question has profound implications for how we think about EAL and how we put our thinking into practice. We will look from both perspectives in this book, recognising that – for teachers concerned with supporting bilingual learners in the curriculum – language is 'partly functional and partly structural' (Hopper, 2012: 302). In Part 1, where we are interested in how the language system is acquired and what factors influence proficiency, we will draw on the work of those who describe the formal system. We then turn to functional approaches in Part 2 to examine how language works across the curriculum.

In the formal tradition, language is understood as an abstract system, separate from the errors, slips and self-corrections of our everyday usage. We need just two elements to describe it: the rules for word formation (*morphology*) and the rules for combining those words into sentences (*syntax*). These two, commonly grouped together as *morphosyntax*, produce a system of startling beauty and complexity. They describe how we can produce an almost infinite variety of language from a finite set of rules, and even give us tools to explore the way in which children acquire language in the first place.

Our first starting point is therefore an observation – that children acquire grammatical patterns which are often missing from the language they are exposed to. This is known as the 'poverty of the stimulus' argument and is most associated with the work of American linguist Noam Chomsky. It is taken as evidence that language must be innate to us: if we are able to produce language in patterns that we haven't heard before, then acquisition cannot be based on imitation alone. Chomsky reasoned that there must be some internal mechanism by which our brains are built for language. He also noted that infants acquire whatever language (or languages) they hear around them in early childhood, so our in-built mechanism must be flexible enough to adapt to whatever language we are exposed to first. He called this innate mechanism 'universal grammar' (or UG), and it has become 'one of the most active and developing theories' in the field (Mitchell *et al.*, 2019: 119).

However, it is very hard (if not impossible) to prove that children are *never* exposed to a particular structure. This has caused some to question whether the poverty of the stimulus is a valid starting point for a theory of language. Far better, they argue, to ask *how much* exposure is needed and *how far* young children can extrapolate from limited input to a rich grammatical system. These are often known as 'usage-based' theories because they focus on how we develop a grammar system from the language we hear and use, rather than from an innate template. In this view, the brain constantly sifts language input for meaningful patterns. When we encounter a given pattern frequently, and when it is meaningful to us, it is reinforced. Over time, these recurring patterns are slowly sedimented into a relatively stable grammatical system. This system is neither innate nor unchanging, but is better understood as a 'structured inventory of meaningful grammatical constructions' (Tomasello, 2012: 84) that is 'always provisional [and] always negotiable' (Hopper, 1987: 142).

These two positions stand in for a much wider range of theories and perspectives in the research literature. The contrast tells us something that is immediately relevant to teaching – that the language children are exposed to is consistently important for language acquisition. This underpins our work in Chapters 4 and 5, and throughout the book. More broadly, it is clear that we need to recognise the important contribution played by Chomsky's UG. It underpinned much of the early research into L2 acquisition that we explore in the coming chapters, but it does not cover everything that we need for an EAL-ready theory of language. First, because UG views the language system in isolation, it has less to say about how language is used in real-life interaction, which is crucial for EAL pupils to master. Second, the emphasis on description means that some of the things we most need to know – such as how learners process the language they are exposed to, or how psychology and emotions affect acquisition – fall outside the scope of UG-based research. Finally, and perhaps most significantly, it is not clear how

UG applies to the acquisition of subsequent languages, and whether those languages can be integrated or form separate grammatical systems. New lines of research (including usage-based approaches) are addressing this, showing both the interconnection between languages and the important benefits that multilingualism brings to learning English. Such findings are beginning to respond to the perceived limitations of UG. They are not restricted to L1 acquisition and can incorporate multiple languages in a coherent theoretical perspective. Finally, usage-based theories in particular fit much more easily with the discussion of language across the curriculum in Part 2. However, work in this tradition is still emerging.

So what can we take from these differing approaches to language acquisition? First, that input is crucial. Whether acquisition is powered by an innate, universal grammar or by the slow connecting and layering of patterns, we cannot give pupils too much exposure to rich language in use. Second, that our theory of language really does affect our practice: a broadly usage-based approach, for example, would encourage us to make our pupils' languages a visible part of our teaching, whereas a UG-based approach might lead us to prioritise the use of English in the classroom.

Target language

So far, we have largely focused on the first language. The ultimate goal of L1 acquisition seems straightforward – full, native-like proficiency – and this has been the default expectation for many years. However, this causes serious problems when we think about its implications for L2 learners.

First, there is the question of whether we can ever reach 'full' proficiency. From a UG perspective, it is not clear that the mechanisms of L1 acquisition are fully available for subsequent languages. From a usage-based perspective, in contrast, there is no such thing as 'full proficiency' because our language system is constantly adapting to new input (although the rate of change may be imperceptible for adults in everyday life). Second, and related, there is the problem of what constitutes a 'native speaker'. A usage-based perspective suggests that the language system emerges as people interact: it is hard to put boundaries around a 'native speaker standard' because we cannot seal off social groups in that way. From a UG perspective, the speaker is an abstract concept, a way of thinking about the language system that lies behind our everyday language use and setting aside all our errors, misspeaking and moments of forgetfulness. In the real world, however, it's not clear that any two people do speak in exactly the same way. Language is a moving target, constantly evolving and varying in small ways between even close groups.

The idea of 'native-speaker competence' has also been criticised for lacking precision: not all native speakers are alike, and often what we really mean is an 'educated native speaker', a privileged sub-set of language users who are elevated to the default standard. It also mixes together more than just our mastery of the grammar and our breadth of vocabulary. It draws in our command of academic (or professional) registers, our social class, the sense of affiliation and inheritance that we feel for a language, and much more. This disadvantages monolingual and bilingual pupils alike, but it especially disadvantages bilingual learners because it omits the many ways in which speaking several languages can be a benefit. Many EAL pupils will go beyond the linguistic and communicative proficiency that the 'monolingual native speaker' standard implies. Acquiring a new language is a complex and dynamic process, one that draws on all your knowledge and experience of other languages, as the next chapter will show.

Chapter Review

This chapter introduced some key principles and a theory of language to underpin our discussion of how additional languages are learned and used. It began by clarifying some key terms, including the distinction between first and subsequent languages (L1 and L2), or simultaneous and sequential bilingualism. It then looked at two broad theories of language (which, for our purposes, stand in for a wide range of theories and positions in the research literature). We found a debate between those who see language acquisition as the activation of an innate capacity (our 'universal grammar') and those who see it as the slow sifting of the language around us, so that the most meaningful patterns are reinforced until they constitute the language system. In either perspective, the child's exposure to language was crucial: we will expand on this insight in the coming chapters.

What We Found in Chapter 3

Chapter 3 examined key terms and a theory of language. The main points were:

- A distinction between the languages learned together in early childhood (L1) and those learned subsequently (L2).
- A broad contrast between a theory of language acquisition based on innate (universal) grammar and one based on usage.
- The central importance of exposure to language (input) for first language acquisition.

Where Can I Go Next?

The **title of Part 1** is a nod to a widely used book by Patsy Lightbown and Nina Spada, *How Languages are Learned* (4th edn, 2013). It covers much of the basics and is written in a clear, accessible style. A more comprehensive volume, presenting the theories behind the practice, is *Second Language Learning Theories* by Rosamund Mitchell, Florence Myles and Emma Marsden (4th edn, 2019). The latter is excellent and is highly recommended for anyone who wants to delve more deeply into the theories and evidence of L2 learning.

There has been a great deal of research into **different theories of language and language acquisition.** Stephen Pinker's (1994) book, *The Language Instinct*, is good primer on UG-based approaches, written for a general audience. An entertaining and polemical challenge to Chomskyan theory is provided by Geoffrey Sampson's (2017) book, *The Linguistics Delusion*. Many scholars have argued that we should use multiple theories to make sense of language learning. Lourdes Ortega's book on *Understanding Second Language Acquisition* (published in 2009) is a rich and accessible place to start.

For those who want to delve more deeply into the research, a special issue of the journal *Language and Cognition* has papers by leading scholars. The first paper, by Andrea Tyler and Lourdes Ortega (2016), sets the scene.

On **whether the processes of acquisition differ between second and subsequent languages**, see Hammarberg (2014) for a clear account of the terms from the perspective of someone interested in *third* language acquisition. There is also a recent systematic review (Puig-Mayenco *et al.*, 2020) and paper (Alonso & Rothman, 2017) that give good overviews of the current research. Pre-publication versions of the latter two are available for free through the University of Reading's repository:

http://centaur.reading.ac.uk/79366/1/18-09-24%20Systematic%20Review%20Accepted.pdf

http://centaur.reading.ac.uk/61776/2/Gonzalez%20Alonso%20and%20Rothman%202016.pdf

4 Learning or Acquiring?

A great deal of acquisition happens when learners are exposed to language in their daily lives. This chapter explores an early model of how this happens and concludes that explicit teaching still plays an important role.

EAL teachers face a conundrum. We know that EAL learners (and probably all learners) benefit from explicit language teaching, but we also know that they need masses of exposure to English and opportunities to use it in a meaningful way. The two seem to pull in opposite directions. The more time is spent teaching *about* English, the less time is spent using it; however, these opportunities for practice are more useful if pupils have a good grasp of how language works. This conundrum is made more urgent by the pressures of time and resources. If you only have short periods of one-to-one or small-group teaching available to you, should you focus on teaching the language or creating opportunities for exposure and meaningful language use? If you co-teach with colleagues, who takes responsibility for what? Does exposure to language in the home and in the playground contribute to the academic English that pupils need to master in school?

These questions are central to the work of EAL specialists, and they are all informed by the theoretical distinction between *learning* a language (for example, in an EAL classroom where the grammar and vocabulary are explicitly taught) and *acquiring* a language (through natural interaction with others). In other words, how much does teaching make a difference, and how much should we just create a language-rich environment and let the learners' brains do the rest? In the early research it was assumed that the two were quite separate – that *learning* happened in classrooms and *acquisition* in the family and community. More recent work has recognised that the reality is more complex: *acquisition* and *learning* may be distinct in theory, but they can both happen in classrooms and the teacher can (to a large extent) create conditions for both. We will look first at an important early position, explore some of the questions it raises and finally clarify the principles that we can take with us into the classroom.

From First Languages to SLA

At this point, we shift our attention from first to second language acquisition (SLA). There are important differences between the two and we will look at these first.

One of the major questions is whether the brain acquires first and subsequent languages in the same way. In other words, should EAL specialists try to recreate the conditions of first language acquisition (masses of exposure to language but no formal teaching) or try something else? Much of the SLA research assumes that they are fundamentally quite similar, and that the mechanisms of L1 acquisition are still available when you come to acquire subsequent languages. There are enough differences, however, for EAL pedagogy to go beyond simply providing input. For one thing, it is not clear that acquisition *does* work in precisely the same way: studies of people who speak three or more languages, for example, show that there is a cumulative effect, so that each language you know contributes to the learning of subsequent languages. It also seems certain that a wide range of cognitive processes are involved, including your working memory, your ability to focus your attention and your ability to use abstract reasoning. All of these change as you move from childhood into adolescence and adulthood. There is, however, a relative lack of research on SLA among school-aged learners and in EAL settings, and so not all findings can be directly applied to additional language learning in schools.

This means that there is no silver bullet for EAL teaching, no single method that will guarantee positive results. The diversity of EAL learners – at different stages of physical, psychological, emotional and social development, with widely varying L1 backgrounds and levels of literacy in different languages – means that we have to proceed cautiously. What we can identify, however, are some broad and well-supported principles to inform the decisions that EAL specialists must make about provision.

A Starting Point: Krashen's Monitor Model

Do EAL pupils acquire English because they receive instruction, or because they are immersed in an English language environment? The answer is probably 'a bit of both'. Learning (the conscious, explicit attention to language rules and procedures) and acquisition (the automatic, unconscious process that happens when we are exposed to language) each play a role in developing proficiency. In the rest of this chapter we unpick the details of that relationship and what it means for EAL practice.

A good place to begin is with the work of Stephen Krashen, whose five-part 'monitor model' represents an early attempt at a coherent theory of learning and acquisition. It remains an important point of reference: even though recent research has offered a sustained critique of his work, it is a widely recognised introduction to an important topic and we can use the critiques to explore our own thinking about learning and acquisition in EAL teaching. Briefly stated, his five hypotheses are:

(a) *The acquisition-learning hypothesis.* Acquisition happens through natural interaction. Given the conditions below, it is unconscious, automatic and very similar to the process of first language acquisition. Learning, in contrast, is the explicit, conscious attention to language rules and procedures.
(b) *The monitor hypothesis.* Learning and acquisition play separate roles. Our acquired language system 'initiates' our utterances and allows for fluency; the learned system acts only as a 'monitor' (or editor), correcting utterances just before or just after production.

(c) *The natural order hypothesis.* Some language features are learned in a specific order, regardless of when they are taught. This has been much qualified by later research.
(d) *The affective filter hypothesis.* Affect (psychological factors such as motivation, anxiety and self-confidence) sits 'outside' the process of language acquisition. Input is the primary driver of acquisition but affect can work as a 'filter', impeding or facilitating acquisition.
(e) *The input hypothesis.* Comprehensible input is the foundation of acquisition. It is defined as input that is slightly above the learner's current level (referred to as '$i + 1$' input). As long as the learner understands the input and there is enough of it, acquisition will automatically follow. (Krashen, 1982, 1985)

What is most valuable about Krashen's monitor model is the way in which he brings together so many of the interlocking concerns that make EAL a rich and challenging discipline. It was very influential in language teacher education in the 1980s and 1990s and is still frequently cited in language education courses today. So what can we make of it?

First, we can consider Krashen's view that acquisition plays a much more significant role than learning. He sees a firm distinction, in which acquisition drives language proficiency forward, and our conscious knowledge about language, the result of our explicit learning, is much less powerful. It allows us to self-correct (by subconsciously 'monitoring' our production, hence the monitor model) but does not contribute to our underlying proficiency. The idea that language acquisition is automatic and innate chimes with the sense that children 'just pick up' a new language. By making a clear distinction between teaching (about) a language and facilitating acquisition, it also offers a rationale for teachers who want to move away from a traditional, grammar-focused syllabus towards more communicative classroom activities. Other aspects make intuitive sense: the idea of a natural order of acquisition would seem to account for learners who are slow to grasp the finer points of morphology, for example. The metaphor of an 'affective filter' that impedes or enables the processing of language input resonates too – especially for teachers who work with new arrivals and children in challenging circumstances.

However, we also need to be cautious about applying any model of SLA directly to practice. On the basis of Krashen's work (and that of others in the same period), many language teachers substantially downgraded grammar teaching and focused on creating language-rich classroom environments. This had the benefit of increasing the range, quality and quantity of language that many learners were exposed to, but at the cost of reducing the explicit teaching that is needed, especially in specialist domains such as EAL (see Chapter 7). We need a more nuanced approach.

Critiques and Current Thinking

The main value of Krashen's model today is as a framework for thinking about acquisition and learning. We need to acknowledge the critiques, but also work with the questions they raise. We can take the hypotheses in turn.

The distinction between **acquisition and learning** has been extensively challenged. McLaughlin (1978: 317), for example, likens it to a 'dubious distinction' between 'rule' and 'feel'. The two are difficult to separate: when you are explaining a grammar point in class, is it the explanation (learning) or the language you are using (acquisition) that makes a difference? (It is for this reason that the two are now often used interchangeably.) The role of the **monitor** is conceptually underdeveloped and is consequently very hard to pin down. Later studies found no advantage for learners who could articulate grammar rules compared with those who could not, for example. The **natural order hypothesis** has only limited relevance to EAL because it can account for only a narrow range of morphological features, and these are only a small part of preparing learners for the curriculum. More recent research in this area (such as processability theory) is very promising but is yet to yield clear guidelines for teaching. The **affective filter** was an early recognition that the learner should be at the centre of learning and that psychological factors strongly influence acquisition. Very little attention was given in Krashen's model to how this might work, but it has become a strong focus in later work (for example, anxiety and motivation).

Two specific areas, however, are useful for us. The first is the nature of **input**, which the previous chapter found to be highly significant for EAL. Krashen's description of '$i + 1$' was quickly challenged for its imprecision (how could we distinguish it from '$i + 2$' or '$i + 3$', for example?) and for the assertion that input alone was sufficient for acquisition (see below and the next chapter), but the general principle is robust. Learners benefit from exposure to rich language, especially when it is slightly above their current level. We can put this into practice in a number of ways. First, we should recognise that it is not possible to pitch classroom talk at the right level for every learner, at every moment. Instead, we need to use a combination of thoughtful classroom talk, broadly differentiated materials and lots of peer interaction to ensure that the classroom is rich in language. It is not necessary (or possible) to measure $i + 1$ for each learner, but language-rich teaching will give plentiful opportunities for EAL pupils to thrive.

Similarly, we can revisit **acquisition and learning** by recognising that a focus on input does not exclude explicit language teaching. A number of scholars have also argued that comprehensible input – while necessary – is not sufficient for proficiency (see next chapter). Patsy Lightbown and Manfred Pienemann (1993), for example, reviewed several studies of grammar interventions and found that they could have a lasting effect on learners' ability to use specific grammatical items accurately (a finding that has been corroborated by more recent research). This may resonate with teachers of advanced bilinguals, who have been shown to benefit from targeted grammar teaching. Many features of academic language are uncommon in everyday usage (and even in academic genres). Pupils will need masses of exposure to such patterns but also careful guidance from the teacher so that they can recognise and consciously use academic language.

Finally, the recurring critique of much SLA research applies here. It is founded on the assumption that learners are monolingual and looking to develop monolingual-like proficiency in different languages. In part this is because Krashen's model was based (explicitly) on L1 acquisition: it left little space for the influence of earlier languages on the one being learned. Such a monolingual perspective is not enough for EAL learners, who continue to use the full range of their languages at home and in school. More recent thinking (such as the multi-competence approach and translanguaging – see Chapter 8) have begun to tackle the interaction between languages more fully and will add a great deal to our understanding of how learners learn.

In summary, Krashen's work gives us three good starting points:

- Exposure to rich language, slightly above the learner's current level, is fundamentally important.
- There is value in explicit language teaching, where it clarifies and supplements a language-rich curriculum.
- Affect (psychological characteristics such as motivation, anxiety and self-confidence) can enable or constrain learning.

We will build on these starting points in the coming chapters.

Chapter Review

In this chapter we moved from first to second language acquisition (or SLA). We noted that this change in focus was significant, both because the learners are older when they start learning a subsequent language and because their first language is already in place. We explored the distinction between *learning* and *acquiring* a language, taking Krashen's monitor model as an example. This yielded three starting points for our principles of EAL practice: the distinction between learning and acquisition, the role played by affect, and the importance of language input. We also considered some of the early criticisms of the monitor model, which are important for two reasons. First, because the model is still widely offered in books for teachers. It has become part of the disciplinary history and a common point of reference for teachers in different traditions. Second, because the criticism has led to a number of valuable findings and brought several linguistic debates into the educational literature. We will continue exploring these in the next chapter.

What We Found in Chapter 4

Chapter 4 examined the distinction between learning and acquiring a language. The main points were:

- Learning (the conscious, explicit attention to language rules and procedures) and acquisition (the automatic, unconscious process that happens when we are exposed to language) each play a role in developing proficiency.
- Current research suggests three important starting points for a theoretically robust approach to EAL provision:
    ○ Exposure to rich language, slightly above the learner's current level, is fundamentally important.

- There is value in explicit language teaching, where it clarifies and supplements a language-rich curriculum.
- Affect (psychological characteristics such as motivation, anxiety and self-confidence) can enable or constrain learning.

Where Can I Go Next?

Two excellent books on **the multilingual turn**, are helpful for the broader issues that this chapter raises. The first, *The Multilingual Turn in Languages Education*, is edited by Jean Conteh and Gabriela Meier (2014) and looks at multilingual learning in settings around the world. The second, *The Multilingual Turn*, edited by Stephen May (2014), connects different academic (sub-)disciplines through a shared focus on multilingualism. It is the more technical of the two, but together they give a very rich picture of how multilingual pupils learn.

There is an excellent special issue on **SLA for children aged 5–18** in the *Annual Review of Applied Linguistics*. The introductory article by Philp *et al.* (2017) gives an excellent overview, as does the review of child SLA by Oliver and Azkarai (2017).

Krashen's work has been extensively discussed in the literature and, despite the criticisms, still serves as an anchor point in the discipline. Several of his books and papers are available free on his website: http://www.sdkrashen.com. An important paper by the Douglas Fir Group (2016, discussed in later chapters) is worth reading for a more contemporary perspective.

5 Masses of Input

Common sense tells us that language input is essential for language learning, but is it enough and what does this mean for EAL provision?

The language that children are exposed to (known as 'input') is crucially important for their developing proficiency. In this chapter, we extend the notion by adding two related concepts: output and interaction. These represent the need for learners to produce language and to do so by exchanging meanings with others. Together, they represent a basic formula for language learning that underpins the language-rich classroom (the role of explicit instruction is covered in Chapter 7).

The basic formula of input, output and interaction is fairly straightforward and is strongly supported by the evidence, and it has far-reaching implications for how we teach EAL. How can we offer masses of input, for example, if we only see pupils for a few hours a week? How can they produce academic language if they are at the early stages of learning English – and what about those at the higher levels who are producing lots of language but not getting it quite right? What counts as a meaningful interaction? What materials, activities and contact time can make this possible? And should I insist on pupils using only English to maximise their opportunities?

We will build up our answers to these questions over the course of the book. The short answer is this: in most EAL settings, the majority of input, output and interaction is going to happen in the mainstream classroom. That is where pupils spend the majority of their time and where they have access to the language, concepts and peers that they need for acquisition to occur. In this chapter, as before, we will start with well-established theories and then look at how the latest research is adding new insights and lines of enquiry. Throughout, we will relate these findings to EAL practice and distil the key points so that we can have evidence-based conversations with our colleagues about language acquisition.

Input, Output and Interaction

We first discussed the importance of input in the previous chapter, in the context of Stephen Krashen's work. We know, because subsequent work has strongly supported it, that exposure to rich language is essential for learners to develop their language proficiency. Krashen's own work imposed a number of conditions on the process. He argued that the interaction must be *successful* (in that both parties make themselves understood) and there must be *enough input* for learners to recognise (subconsciously) the patterns and rules of the language. That means focusing on both the quality and quantity of input. More recent studies have expanded on that starting point.

Input

Recent research has investigated input from a number of different perspectives. We will focus on two that have particular relevance for EAL: the role of attention (because acquisition happens more effectively if learners notice patterns in the input) and the study of input processing (which examines how learners connect language form with meaning).

Input and attention

How do we account for the fact that many learners, immersed in an L2 environment and exposed to masses of input, still appear to miss key features of the target grammar? A strand of research into learner attention suggests that input alone is not enough: we need to *notice* features of the language. This is particularly true in two areas. The first is for features that are less common (including many features of academic language, such as the use of complex noun phrases to convey information – see Chapters 14 and 15) and where they carry less meaning. If features are less common, they appear in the language input less frequently and learners therefore have less opportunity to incorporate them into their developing language system. Similarly, where the meaning of a sentence is expressed in different ways (such as the past meaning in the sentence, 'yesterday I went to the bank'), there is less need to attend to the grammatical form and it is less likely to be acquired. This accounts for the notorious difficulty learners have in remembering the third person '-s' (as in, 'she eats'). In English it is always clear who is involved ('she'), and so the '-s' morpheme does not carry the whole meaning. There is substantial evidence, however, that directing learners' attention to such features helps them to notice and then to acquire them.

So how can we direct learners' attention to key language features? There are several approaches that are relevant to EAL: teaching grammar explicitly, adapting the input, redesigning tasks and giving high-quality feedback. The first can be dealt with fairly briefly. There is some evidence that learners do benefit from grammar preteaching (that is, explaining the grammatical point before they encounter it in the main activity) but with caveats: it has rarely been investigated in an EAL context and it does not seem to be more effective than other techniques. A better approach is to ensure that learners encounter the language feature in a focused way, and that their attention is drawn to it, before the main activity of the class. For example, learners might read a short text that uses the feature several times or the teacher might give some metalinguistic commentary (Did you notice I used a passive there? Why did I do that?). This is likely to have much the same effect as an explicit grammar-teaching stage but fits more easily with the content focus of much EAL support and can potentially be integrated into subject teaching.

The next two techniques are related: adapting the input and redesigning the task. The first suggests that we ensure that learners are exposed to large amounts of a target feature, either by rewriting texts so the feature occurs more frequently, by making the feature more prominent (for example, by putting every instance of the feature in bold text) or by selecting texts in which they are already plentiful. The second suggests that we design classroom tasks so that the learner can only complete them by using the target form. Both are equally effective. Finally, feedback plays a vital role – so important that it gets almost a whole chapter to itself (Chapter 7). It is worth noting here that feedback is already implicit in many of the tasks we set learners – if you don't understand the teacher's instructions in Science, for example, you can't complete the experiment – and so successful participation can be used as a form of feedback. Research on feedback in other subjects also supports this. It is most effective when it is timely, rich in information and targeted at the learner's current stage of development. It is easier to meet these criteria when the feedback is integrated into subject learning.

This research shows that we can use a range of techniques to help learners notice language features, and that this helps them incorporate the feature into their developing language system. We don't need to pre-teach grammar but we can ensure that learners encounter it in the input (for example, in a reading, in a video or in a story told by the teacher). We can draw their attention to language by commenting on how a feature works and on its form (which is easy to incorporate into your classroom talk) and we can ensure that our activities can only be achieved if learners use the language feature correctly. Finally, we can use feedback to draw learners' attention to language. There are some limitations to these findings, however.

Much of the research has examined one language feature at a time, but for EAL this is often unrealistic. Instead, we should look to the subject classroom – rich in the language that our learners need to acquire and with a high degree of context to support learning. EAL specialists are recommended to use subject materials wherever possible to ensure maximum exposure. Where this is not possible, for example at the lower levels of proficiency or with learners whose schooling has been heavily disrupted, we can still select texts that build towards academic language – for example, those featuring increasingly complex noun phrases, or the genres commonly used in academic disciplines (see Chapters 14 and 15) – and that are therefore meaningful to learners.

Input processing and processing instruction

Although Krashen and others have argued that enough input leads to language acquisition, he did not say much about *how* that happens. Research into input processing (IP) is concerned with just that: how we understand the language around us and how we integrate it into our language system. 'Processing', as Bill VanPatten (2004: 6) notes, 'is not the same as *perception* or a form of *noticing*'. It is concerned with how the brain connects language form with meaning. Research in this area has often been highly technical, examining cognitive processes in minute detail, but it has led to important insights for EAL specialists.

The main insight is the important relationship between meaning and form. We often assume that pupils should learn enough grammar and vocabulary to express themselves, but IP studies have shown that the relationship is often reversed. Grammar does not lead to meaning; meaning allows us to acquire grammar. This is connected to the research into learners' attention: learners notice meaning before they notice the grammar in which it is expressed, and they are more interested in what they are trying to say than in accuracy for its own sake. Research also tells us a great deal about how language is processed by learners and what implications this has for teaching (a related field known as processing instruction). Two principles from this research, adapted from VanPatten (2004: Chapter 1), are especially relevant to us:

(1) Learners process input for meaning before they process it for form.

We have limited cognitive resources and understanding a new language is hard. In this situation, research shows that learners prioritise the meaning of what people are saying over the grammatical form in which it is expressed. We also know that learners focus on content words first, and are more likely to get meaning from vocabulary than from grammar.

(2) When it is a sensible option, learners tend to process the first noun in the sentence as the main actor.

Learners pay attention to word order, tending to take the first noun as the subject of the sentence even when they know a grammatical rule to the contrary (in English, the passive is a good example of such a structure). However, this is constrained by the meaning of words: 'the woman was kicked by the horse' is liable to be misinterpreted (both horses and people can kick); 'the fence was kicked by the horse' less so (because fences cannot kick – there is no sensible alternative meaning in that word order). Context plays a similar role – less likely interpretations are less often confused.

As with research into learner attention, we can take some general principles from PI research into the classroom. First, meaning is paramount. Learning is much slower if we only teach the grammar and try to apply it. If we can create situations in which learners are engaged with subject-relevant texts, doing things that require them to find out and exchange meaning, then acquisition is likely to follow. Similarly, a large number of errors may be due to misunderstood meaning rather than a misapplied rule. In general terms, we should clarify understanding and then supply the correct form rather than correcting the grammar directly. Even better, learners can do this by interacting with their peers.

Interaction

Partly in response to Krashen's work, which claimed that input alone was needed for acquisition, a number of researchers began investigating how first and second language speakers interacted with each other. Michael Long (1981, 1983a, 1983b, 1996) looked at the language people used while they were playing games – informal, non-academic settings where participants were motivated to interact. He found that they were rich with examples of negotiation, in which the participants clarified what the other had said, repeated and checked meaning with each other. Second language users, in other words, were far from being passive receivers of L2 input. They were actively engaged in making their input more comprehensible by interacting with the other speaker. These adjustments, made in the course of ordinary, informal interactions, formed the basis of his Interaction Hypothesis.

Interaction has since come to be seen as 'an indispensable component in second language acquisition' (Loewen & Sato, 2018: 285). It has led to a wide range of studies investigating everything from the process of interaction itself to the effect of different types of interlocutors. All are motivated by the broad question: Does interacting with others help learners acquire a new language, and if so, how? We can draw a few conclusions from the evidence of these studies: first, that there is general support for the idea that interaction *does* support acquisition. Many of the details are still under investigation but the evidence is sufficiently settled on the broad point that we can use it to inform pedagogy. Second, interaction does seem to support both vocabulary and grammar learning. Finally, we know that more research is needed on school-age learners in the classroom – both for mainstream subjects and EAL – to show what types of teacher-student and peer interactions most promote language learning.

This has implications for EAL practice. It shows again how important *meaning* is to second language acquisition (SLA). When learners rephrase and repeat something that has been said to them, when they check their understanding and ask for clarification, they are responding to its meaning. In doing so they are also managing the complexity of the input they receive. In other words, if our learners need roughly tuned input, interaction research shows that they at least have a finger on the tuning dial. We can work with that. Activities that require learners to talk together – to exchange meanings and to accomplish a task – are likely to be beneficial. Dialogue with the teacher has a less prominent place: only a small number of pupils will be interacting at any one time, and there tends to be less genuine negotiation of meaning because the teacher knows the answer. This is not to say that teacher-student interaction is unimportant (Chapter 7 shows that it plays an important role), but the evidence does support a re-evaluation of peer interaction for language learning. This research also offers strong empirical evidence for seeing the learner in a social context: we learn language to a great extent through interaction with others. The next section looks at the learner's own role in that process.

Output

Research into output is most associated with Merrill Swain (1985), whose work focused on French immersion schools in Canada. She found that learners could become highly proficient in comprehension (listening and reading) but were often less proficient when asked to produce language (speaking and writing). In particular, she noticed that learners could often understand texts without attending to the full range of grammatical structures they contained. This challenged Krashen's approach. Where the Input Hypothesis held that comprehensible input alone was sufficient for language acquisition, her findings suggested that it was not sufficient – and that something else was therefore needed. Swain (1985) argued that the missing element was output: only when pushed to produce language (that is, to speak or write) would learners fully process the grammar and integrate it into their developing language system.

In subsequent revisions of her Output Hypothesis, Swain (1995, 2005) suggested that output involved three separate functions. Learners have to:

(1) Notice the gap between what they can produce and what they aim to produce.
(2) Make and test hypotheses about what forms are correct and appropriate.
(3) Reflect on the language itself. (Adapted from Swain, 1995: 128)

When learners produce language, then, they have to be aware of what they want to say and what they actually can say, noticing the gap in their abilities. They have to try out new words and phrases to communicate their meaning, and they have to judge whether these worked. These all apply directly to EAL practice. We can easily integrate 'noticing' activities into our work, drawing attention to the language learners use. We can encourage learners to hypothesise (or guess what the correct form should be), giving them time to think and using peer talk so that learners can experiment with different forms in low-stakes activities. We can likewise model thoughtful language use, commenting on our own linguistic choices, praising those of our students and asking students to give feedback on their own writing and that of their peers.

More recent work has extended the Output Hypothesis. It has focused primarily on the first two points – how to get students to notice the gap and to try out new (and better) patterns of language. Different teaching techniques have been investigated, from open-ended prompts to recasts and reformulations (where the teacher re-states or rephrases the learner's words), in order to understand what best encourages learners to adopt new language patterns and incorporate them into their longer term language development. The evidence on such efforts is mixed. Overall, we see consistent evidence that such corrective feedback does play an important role in L2 development, but it is hard to pin down its effects precisely. This is because there are so many variables involved, from the language point being taught to the exact nature of the feedback, the teaching context and the characteristics of the learners themselves. Individual studies can sometimes give suggestions for broader principles. For example, several recent studies have shown that the extent to which learners try to correct their own speech broadly predicts their success in L2 learning, but generally we need to dig into the specifics of how different types of feedback, correction and practice affect learning. This is the focus of Chapter 7.

Chapter Review

This chapter has focused on three central elements of SLA: input, interaction and output. We looked first at the role of input, 'undoubtedly crucial in the process of [L2] learning' (Leow, 2007: 21). We found that it is connected to a wide range of learning and processing systems, and that the process of turning language exposure into language proficiency is a very complex one. We were able to extract several practical principles from the research. First, we recognised that the *quality* and the *quantity* of language are both important. EAL learners need to command patterns that are not frequent in everyday usage and that can only come from extensive exposure to subject materials (including classroom activities, texts and the talk around both). This means that the best place for EAL learners to develop L2 proficiency is in the mainstream classroom. Masses of input, at roughly the right level, is absolutely central to L2 learning.

We looked at how learners process that input. We found that teachers can make processing more effective by directing learners' attention to specific language features and that this can be done in a number of different ways. First, the input itself can be enhanced, either by selecting and arranging texts to maximise exposure to key language patterns or by adapting them. Learners can notice language features more easily when they encounter them often. We can also redesign tasks, asking students to report on progress, share draft work and comment on their language production. This engages their knowledge about language to aid in the task.

We also explored research into language processing, which led to a crucial insight: learners process meaning before form. Effective teaching therefore encourages learners to look at the *meaning* they are trying to express and whether they have got it across successfully. This will be very important when we look at how academic language is structured in Part 2. We are not, primarily, teaching students to use certain vocabulary or grammar patterns. We are immersing them in a subject discipline, with its own ways of organising and communicating knowledge, and ensuring that learners have the right language to participate fully.

Finally, we looked at the Interaction and Output Hypotheses. We found that learners are not passive recipients of input but actively negotiate meaning with the people they are speaking to. They ask for clarification, they rephrase, they check their understanding of what is being said. In other words, they manage the stream of input to make it more comprehensible and therefore more useful for learning. We need to ask ourselves how much scope there is for free negotiation – outside teacher-led question and response sequences – in our classrooms. We also found that output, being pushed to get your meaning across, has a substantial effect on L2 proficiency. Teachers can draw on this by maximising opportunities for learners to use the language with peers as well as with the teacher. All meaningful interaction provides feedback on whether the message was understood, and so contributes to language learning.

What We Found in Chapter 5

Chapter 5 examined input and the related concepts of output and interaction. The main points were:

- The *quality* and the *quantity* of language are both important. This means that the best place for EAL learners to develop L2 proficiency is in the mainstream classroom.

- Teachers can make processing more effective by directing learners' attention to specific language features.
- Learners process meaning before form. Effective teaching therefore encourages learners to look at the *meaning* they are trying to express and whether they got it across successfully.
- Learners are not passive recipients of input but actively negotiate meaning with the people they are speaking to. Teachers can draw on this by maximising opportunities for learners to use the language with peers as well as with the teacher.

Where Can I Go Next?

In a lecture to the 2012 Language Awareness annual conference, Patsy Lightbown discussed how much time a Primary or Secondary language programme could offer and what could be done to 'make the minutes count'. It was published as Lightbown (2014) and is a great place to start exploring the themes of this chapter.

For a short and accessible introduction to **input processing**, see VanPatten (2007). For a fuller discussion see Chapters 1 and 3 of VanPatten (2004). On **interaction**, two recent reviews by Mackey and Goo (2007) and Keck *et al.* (2006) supplement the discussion in Brown (2016). For more on how we can **enhance input in the classroom**, look at Mike Sharwood Smith's original (1993) article, which describes relevant approaches.

Taking these academic publications into your own classroom can be challenging. There is a great deal written online about adapting texts to make certain linguistic features more prominent but there is little in-depth, practical guidance. The best thing to do is to experiment in your own classroom. Start by looking at the range of texts you use. How can we move beyond keywords to focus on the meaning? Which features are important in order to understand the meaning and which do learners struggle with – can they be highlighted or used more frequently? How can you give explicit feedback on language use (Chapter 7) and can you create opportunities for learners to talk about the concepts as they read and before writing (Chapter 12)?

6 Earlier Isn't Necessarily Better

Age has a significant effect on first language learning, but there is less evidence that it is a crucial factor for second language learning.

There is an 'undeniable' relationship between 'age and success in additional language learning', argue Carmen Muñoz and David Singleton (2011). The details of that relationship, however, are not yet fully clear. There are two main proposals for how age affects additional language learning. They are:

(1) that there is a 'window of opportunity (or critical period) – ending at some point during or at the end of childhood – [after which] language acquisition becomes qualitatively different, more arduous and/or less successful'; or
(2) that 'age-related changes' in the capacity to acquire language result from factors other than 'a specifically language-focused critical period'. (Muñoz & Singleton, 2011: 1)

The idea that children 'just pick up' languages is widespread. Here we see a more nuanced view. It may be that childhood and early adolescence are an exceptionally fertile period for the learning of language, and that something happens as the brain matures to make it less so. Or it could be that this is part of a wider set of developmental changes of which language is just one part. We also need to consider what we mean by language, because different systems seem to be affected differently. Morphosyntax (loosely, grammar) is not affected by age in the same way as lexis (vocabulary) and phonology (pronunciation). Finally, we need to reflect on what yardstick we use to measure young bilinguals. Much of the research has focused on the level of monolingual proficiency associated with native speakers but, as we have seen, that term is fraught with complexity.

There is wide agreement on one point: that age correlates with other relevant factors, such as L1 proficiency, frequency of (first and second) language use and the kind of input that learners are exposed to. In an influential paper, Jim Flege and colleagues (1999) examined the morphosyntactic and phonological skills of 240 Korean L1 speakers, who had arrived in the United States between the ages of one and 23 years (see Figure 6.1). At the time of the study they were all experienced users of English and had been in the country for an average of 15 years.

We see the 24 English L1 participants (white dots) clustered in the top left, showing that they 'arrived' in the United States at birth and scored highly on tests of

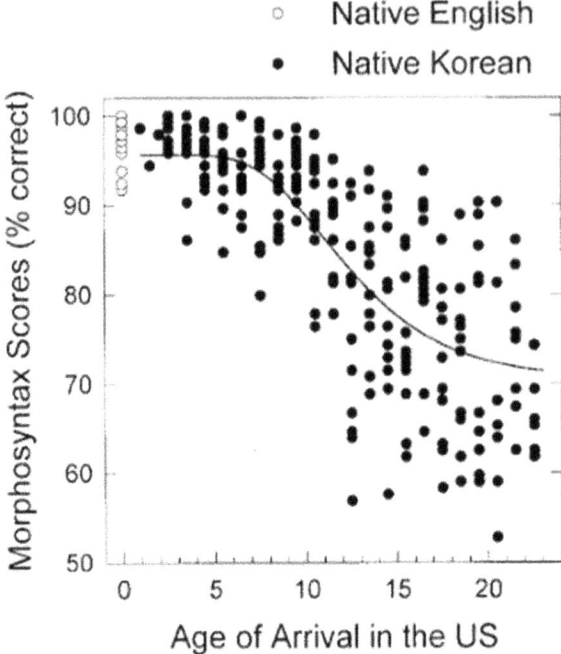

Figure 6.1 Morphosyntactic and phonological skills of 240 Korean L1 speakers who arrived in the United States between the ages of 1 and 23 years
Source: Flege *et al*. (1999: 85).

grammatical judgement. The 240 Korean L1 participants (black dots) are distributed along the line, showing that later arrival in the United States correlated with lower ratings for foreign accent (decided by a panel of US 'native speaking listeners' using anonymised recordings of the participant) and grammaticality (using well-established tests which require participants to decide whether a sample sentence is grammatical or not). However, the study found no sharp cut-off after which performance declined sharply. When researchers controlled for other variables associated with age of arrival, its effect on the grammar test results were not significant. Other studies have supported this: age 'cannot be isolated from other co-occurring factors', as Montrul (2008: 50) puts it.

This is not to say that there is no critical period for language acquisition, but it does suggest that age is one among several influential factors. Some of these are social (such as friendships with people who speak the new language), some are psychological (such as motivation or willingness to take risks) and some are contextual (such as how rich and varied the learner's exposure to the new language is). They also apply differently to different aspects of proficiency. Pronunciation seems to be the most affected by age; numerous studies have found evidence for a 'critical period' for acquiring a native-like accent but not for native-like grammar. However, comparisons with native speakers may be misleading. There is evidence that children who begin learning a second language at a very young age become native-like in many respects but show differences when their language use is subjected to very detailed analysis. This has little immediate application for EAL teachers: pupils who appear in many respects 'native-like' are success stories, not ones to puzzle over.

It may be that experiments will always be able to detect subtle differences between bilingual and monolingual speakers, but for our purposes it is more useful to compare our bilingual learners with a bilingual benchmark. What factors contribute to bilingual proficiency, in which learners maintain their first languages to a high level and also develop the academic English they need to succeed in the curriculum? We explore these questions in the next section.

Age of Acquisition, Length of Residence and Ultimate Attainment

One of the main concerns in this field of research is the relationship between 'age of acquisition' (AoA), length of residence in the L2 environment (LoR) and highest level of language proficiency reached (known as the 'ultimate attainment'). In other words, does your age when you first begin using a new language, or the length of time you have been using it, affect the level of proficiency you will be able to reach in your lifetime? This has some significance for EAL specialists, as it is helpful to understand where our work fits into the learners' broader trajectories of language acquisition.

The main findings in the literature are that both AoA and LoR are significant factors in ultimate attainment, but they are complex and often poorly defined. It makes intuitive sense that the earlier you start learning a language and the longer you have been using it, the higher the level of proficiency you are likely to reach. But consider the EAL context. First, a pupil's use of English may not correspond with their age when they arrive in an English-majority country, nor with how long they have lived there. Many pupils are born in the UK but grow up in bilingual homes in which English plays only a small role. Others may have followed complex migration journeys in which English played a significant role as a means of communication, but not in an English-majority setting. Still others will have studied English regularly as a foreign language, and now find themselves immersed in an Anglophone curriculum. Given this variability, it is more helpful to think of when their first *significant* contact with English started.

There is no single definition of significance. White and Genesee (1996: 242–243) refer to the time when learners are 'called upon to use the L2 for communication', but note that this may not include some language-support programmes if there are low expectations and few opportunities to interact with proficient peers. Muñoz and Singleton (2011: 15) accept 'full immersion in the L2 and interaction with native speakers', but note that a much more detailed appreciation of those interactions is needed. A useful definition for our purposes is given by Andrea Hellman, whose 2008 doctoral thesis defined 'significant' contact as 'daily interaction' with native speakers, which would include the mainstream classroom. The precise definitions vary but the overall message is clear: we need to look closely at the quality and quantity of language that our learners are exposed to, and at their opportunities to use it in meaningful interaction. A lot of this will be with peers, inside and outside the classroom, and we should plan to support this wherever possible.

We also need to consider the range of other languages that the pupils are engaged with in their lives (see Chapter 8). We know that exposure to English is a crucial variable but that sustaining and developing first languages is important for bilingual children to turn that exposure into proficiency. It seems likely that the distance between languages (for example, that English and Dutch are quite close but English and Mandarin are linguistically distant) plays a role, as does the extent to which the different languages are used. This is complicated for EAL, because use is entangled with age and educational experience. Some learners will have had age-appropriate schooling in their first languages. Others will have had limited or interrupted schooling, meaning that their development of cognitively demanding academic language (discussed in Chapter 11) will be more limited. Age is therefore an important factor, but it is only part of the picture.

Some researchers have argued that age-related effects are even 'overshadowed' by family support and other contextual factors. In a longitudinal study, from 2009 to 2016, Pfenninger and Singleton (2019) tracked 636 English learners in and around Zurich, Switzerland. Roughly half had started learning English at the age of eight (and had five years of English tuition at the time of the study) and half at the age of 13 (and had started studying English six months before). The participants were organised into four groups (monolingual, two groups of simultaneous bilinguals with differing levels of literacy, and sequential bilinguals). The study included measures of contextual support, including whether there were few or many books in the home, the level of parental support for activities like homework, and parental attitudes towards learning English. They found that an 'earlier age of learning proved beneficial only for children raised as biliterate simultaneous bilinguals receiving substantial parental support, as opposed to monolinguals and nonbiliterate bilinguals'. In other words, starting a new language early is only an advantage if you have substantial parental support and can sustain literacy development in both languages.

Other studies made similar findings. One, by Johanne Paradis and colleagues (2017), examined language samples from 187 children with English L2 to investigate the development of writing complexity. They found that these children 'used more complex sentences within a few months of English L2 exposure than what is reported for L1 children', suggesting an advantage for an older AoA. One recent study of American Sign Language (ASL) users (Mayberry & Kluender, 2018) offers an interesting insight. It compared signers who became deaf between the ages of eight and 12 (and who learned ASL as a second language) with those who were deaf from birth but who reported minimal exposure to ASL until the same age (and learned ASL as a late first language). This isolated the age-related changes in the brain (such as a critical period) because the AoA of ASL was the same for both groups. The results showed a clear advantage for the group that was exposed to language in infancy: the L2 group performed at near-native levels, whereas the L1 group showed low performance. This demonstrated that infant language acquisition is amodal (spoken language development supports the later development of sign language) and that strong L1 proficiency is crucial to L2 development. Developing EAL learners' first languages will support their growing proficiency in English.

Studies like these point to the shortcomings in the literature, at least as far as EAL specialists are concerned. The relationship between age and acquisition seems robust, but is difficult to distinguish from many other factors. There is debate over whether a 'critical period' for language acquisition exists and studies show conflicting findings over the impact of AoA and LoR, with growing recognition that the quality and quantity of input and use are significant. These findings are relevant for EAL provision. If we knew definitively whether an early start made a difference, we could advise parents and adapt our provision. If there were clear evidence that children learn differently as their brains mature, especially around puberty, it would have a significant effect on curriculum design. But what can we make of the evidence available?

Clearly, age has an effect on language acquisition, but not a determining one. Some pupils will achieve high levels of proficiency very quickly, while others will struggle even after longer periods in an English-medium environment. The evidence for a 'critical period', after which language learning becomes substantially harder, is not clear enough to guide teaching. However, the core principles of maximising exposure to rich, slightly challenging input, with maximum opportunities to use the language for meaningful interaction, *are* supported by the evidence on age and acquisition. The amount of time spent in such an environment, where there is *significant* contact with English, seems to be more important than the overall time: quality beats quantity, which should reassure us.

It can also motivate us to address the literature critically. A great deal of the research accepts monolingual speakers as the benchmark for bilinguals. This is problematic on several counts. From a linguistic perspective, it is not clear that they are alike. Some studies suggest that young L2 learners are like young monolingual speakers in some respects (similarity of age and development), but like older bilingual speakers in others (similarity of language). The skills profiles of bilingual children are often different from those of monolinguals, and measuring them against a monolingual benchmark may miss important abilities that young bilinguals develop but monolinguals generally do not (particularly in communication skills, although studies have suggested effects as varied as phonological awareness and emotional perceptiveness). However, other studies report that socioeconomic status and family support are also significant factors. We should also recognise that, for many bilingual children, their first languages and their use of English are both part of their identity. Some will welcome the challenge of reaching native-like proficiency; others will feel that their speech reflects their heritage and multilingualism, and where their usage differs from that of monolinguals it should not be interpreted as error.

Chapter Review

In this chapter we reviewed the evidence on age and language acquisition. This is important for EAL specialists for two reasons: because the widespread assumption that young children are naturally good at languages is not as straightforward as it sounds, leading to a risk that we have lower expectations of older learners; and because age leads us to an array of other factors that we can take into account in our teaching. First among these is the quality of input: the age at which children first encounter their additional language is less important than the age at which they began rich, sustained exposure. This is useful as we plan progression and calibrate our expectations of bilingual learners. Those who grow up with another language but use English when they come to school will make quick progress, and English will likely become their dominant language before they leave Primary school. Those who come later in their academic careers will make quick progress, too, if they are engaged in a language-rich curriculum. Too often, we feel that we should teach such learners basic or survival English before they join the curriculum. However, the research on AoA and LoR shows that restricted exposure to the language leads to slower acquisition. Balancing these competing demands is a challenge that needs the input of an EAL specialist.

The research on age and language acquisition also pointed to another aspect of that specialism – the need to approach the literature critically. Bilingual learners are frequently – implicitly and explicitly – compared with monolinguals even though their language profiles are often different. This can lead to an artificially negative view of their abilities: bilingual children are like monolinguals in some respects, but not in others. A more holistic view would include their linguistic development in each language and would ensure that they continue to have significant engagement with each. Whether this kind of exposure alone is enough, however, is the focus of the next chapter.

What We Found in Chapter 6

In Chapter 6 we examined the relationship between age and language acquisition. The main points were:

- There is a strong relationship between age and language acquisition. The longer you have been learning a language, the higher the level of proficiency you are likely to reach.
- However, the *quality* and *quantity* of language that children are exposed to is also important – and are key reasons to support the mainstreaming of EAL pupils.
- There is some evidence for a 'critical period' in which children find it much easier to acquire languages, but this is influenced by a range of other factors and should not be a direct consideration in planning EAL support.
- Although exposure to (and meaningful use of) the new language is important, there is great value in supporting the continued development of pupils' first languages.

Where Can I Go Next?

For a general perspective on **raising bilingual children,** see Crisfield (2021) and Festman *et al.* (2017). These practical guides give valuable insight for monolingual practitioners, too. There is a lot written online about the **best age to start learning an additional language,** some of it helpful. From the academic literature, Pfenninger and Singleton's (2019) review provides a robust starting point. Two further book chapters are also very readable: see Cook and Singleton (2014: Chapter 3) and Ellis (2015: Chapter 2).

There has been a great deal of experimental work in this area, and the recommendations are probably more useful for those researching the field (for example, as a dissertation topic) than for everyday practice. If you are researching this, reviews by Unsworth (2016) and Jaekel *et al.* (2017) are good additions to the sources in the chapter.

7 Implicit and Explicit Learning

How can we explain the difference in outcomes among EAL learners, all of whom are fully proficient in their first languages, and what implications does this have for classroom practice?

Children acquire their first languages from just the input they receive. So why do so many L2 learners struggle with a second language? The previous chapter considered the effect of age and found that it does play a role, but not a determining one. The duration and extent of 'significant' contact with English is more relevant. This builds on the findings of earlier chapters that the core principles of L2 learning – masses of input and opportunities to use it for meaningful interaction – are the core of EAL provision. We can now extend the discussion to consider what role practice and feedback play in the classroom. These are underpinned by a distinction between implicit and explicit learning, and lead to clear insights into what subject teachers and EAL specialists can do to promote language proficiency.

Three Types of Knowledge

We should start by recognising that there are different ways of knowing something. Whether we are learning to drive, to cook, to sew or to play video games, we find it easier to describe what we should do than to do it, and it takes practice before we can do anything quickly and consistently. We describe this as a difference between 'declarative knowledge' (knowing the rule) and 'procedural knowledge' (being able to use it). They do not have to go together: plenty of L1 users speak fluently without being able to describe the grammar they use, and plenty of L2 users can describe the rules perfectly without being able to produce those forms reliably or quickly. When we are able to produce language quickly, reliably and accurately, we say that it has become 'automatic knowledge'. These three stages are described by Skill Acquisition Theory, which is most associated with the work of Robert DeKeyser (1997, 2007, 2015). He describes them in the following way:

- *Stage 1: Declarative knowledge.* Learners establish new knowledge, for example through observation or from a teacher's explanation. This might include some explicit description and examples, and it requires a lot of attention to hold in mind.

- *Stage 2: Procedural knowledge.* Knowledge is put into practice, exactly as it was in the example. Some repetition is required, but very little. New practices are stored as 'chunks' or routines, which reduces the demand on attention and working memory but is prone to restructuring. A lot of practice is therefore needed at this stage to make it secure.
- *Stage 3: Automatic knowledge.* Practice allows these chunks to be used reliably and quickly. With practice, the error rate, time taken and amount of attention needed all decrease. New practices become more stable and, because they require little attention, can run in the background. This means that clusters of more complex skills can emerge.

This helps explain why learners often make rapid progress at the beginning but then seem to slow down. When learners encounter new language it is held as 'declarative' knowledge, which requires a lot of attention. As it becomes 'proceduralised' it is organised into chunks and routines. Here, learners are not just storing the language they are exposed to but also organising it. This creates a new type of knowledge that the learner can access with increasing speed and accuracy, given enough practice. It is important to note that this is not a linear process. Very often, the language we encounter is already formed into ready-made 'chunks' (e.g. 'How do you do?'), which make less demand on our attention and are quicker to proceduralise. As other new language patterns are proceduralised (and later automatised), they act as a building block to more complex patterns which themselves become easier to access and produce over time. It is not necessary for us to track our learners' language at this level of detail, however, because the broad pattern is enough to guide our teaching. We need to know that the move from declarative to procedural knowledge happens quite quickly, perhaps even beginning in the first few times it is used. The move from procedural to automatic knowledge is slower and relies on many instances of practice over a longer period. Progress therefore seems slower, but it is an important stage of learning. As Leow (2007: 22) puts it, this 'internalization of the linguistic data' is the 'ultimate goal of receptive practice'.

You Gotta Practise

Practice is essential to language learning. This doesn't require drills, worksheets or grammar practice activities. Everything we do in the classroom should be based around our core principle – masses of input, with lots of opportunities to use it for meaningful interaction. Practice in this sense means 'an attempt to supply the learner with plentiful opportunities for producing targeted structures in controlled and free language use in order to develop fully proceduralised implicit knowledge' (Ellis, 1993: 109). There is still a place for controlled practice, but nothing like to the extent that we often see in English language textbooks. A good rule of thumb for practice activities is to ask whether the language is given in a meaningful context or in decontextualised samples. A worksheet that asks learners to complete sentences with the correct verb form is unlikely to involve more than declarative knowledge. One that asks them to take information prompts and write an email or summary paragraph would require the learners to produce the same grammatical forms but to do so by responding to the meaning of the prompts. This is more likely to help students proceduralise (and then automatise) their knowledge of the rule.

It is clear that practice does more than just help learners to access knowledge more quickly. As Diane Larsen-Freeman (2003: 114) says, 'Doing and learning are synonymous'. The research suggests that there is some transfer between receptive and productive skills and vice versa, meaning that work on speaking and writing will support proficiency in listening and reading, but the nature of this relationship is still under investigation. Similarly, there is more work to be done to understand how far we should break down the complex skills of language learning into smaller components (as was common in earlier, grammar-led teaching approaches) or focus on communication as a whole (as in communicative or task-based approaches, see Ellis *et al.*, 2019). The balance is, again, likely to rest on a number of factors, some related to the language features being taught and some to the learner and the context. What we do know, though, is that practice is important and that it is more effective with the right feedback.

Feedback

We talk about 'feedback' all the time in education: we get feedback on our teaching after an observed lesson; we give feedback to learners when we evaluate their work and give advice on how it can be improved. We even feed back, as a verb, when we respond to requests for information. In language learning, we can add a further, specialised meaning: feedback describes the signals we get from others to indicate how our speech has been received. It is often unconscious, such as our nods and uh hums when we are listening intently to someone. It includes our requests for – sorry, what was that? – clarification and (did you mean) confirmation in ordinary conversation. In accordance with our principle that meaning reigns supreme, these signals tell us if our message has been understood. When we are sufficiently skilled in the relevant language and conversational norms, we do this automatically and it underpins successful communication. When our language skills are not sufficient, or we bring different conversational norms from those of our partner, the lack of effective feedback signals can cause communication to break down.

This is important for EAL because it takes the spotlight – to a certain extent – off the teacher. Peers are equally good at giving this kind of feedback and can do so to a greater extent than the teacher can (there being a lot more learners than teachers in a typical class). That changes the teacher's role somewhat. Rather than being the only or main source of language knowledge, they become the person who can give higher level feedback and organise the extensive practice and meaningful peer interaction that supports deeper learning. Research can tell us quite a lot about what form that feedback should take.

What role does feedback play in learning?

A substantial meta-analysis on feedback in learning generally (Wisniewski et al., 2020) found that it is 'more effective the more information it contains'. High-information feedback, the authors note, 'contains information on task, process and (sometimes) self-regulation level'. That means it goes beyond saying whether the learner's performance was right or wrong and incorporates feedback on how they got there and perhaps on how they managed their work. In a language-learning context, we might be interested in whether the learner made their meaning understood, but also in the effect their chosen words had and how they responded to conversational cues. This is more straightforward than it sounds. When learners are working together in pairs or groups, make notes on the language they use. Have these notes to hand when you bring the class together at the end of the activity and use them to discuss language choices with the class. If you can suggest alternatives – and show why they would be more appropriate – then so much the better.

Feedback does not necessarily have a direct or immediate effect on learners' production. There are several reasons for this. First, language learning is not a linear process. It will take time for new patterns to be incorporated into the learner's language system and to be used regularly and reliably. Second, people aren't all the same. We know that attention and memory play an important role in language learning, and that these vary among individuals. The same feedback techniques might therefore have a different effect on different pupils. Third, different language features and tasks place different demands on us, leading to variation in how quickly we acquire particular patterns. So we should not be too concerned if our feedback techniques do not appear to have an immediate effect. They will, and they will be more effective if we can get colleagues to use them as part of a school-wide approach to language-rich teaching (see Part 3 for useful strategies). However we approach it, though, we need a clear understanding of what types of feedback we can use.

Types of feedback

We encountered one type of feedback earlier in the chapter – the conversational cues that tell us whether our message has been understood or not. These are part of natural interaction in any language and we can use peer activities to maximise opportunities for this kind of feedback. The teacher has other tools, too, which allow for more targeted intervention. We commonly talk about six feedback moves, following the influential work of Lyster and Ranta (1997) and their study of Canadian subject and language Primary lessons. These are:

- explicit correction
- recasts
- clarification requests
- metalinguistic feedback
- elicitation
- repetition

These can further be organised into two broad groups: reformulations (recasts and explicit corrections) and prompts (all feedback moves that elicited modified output). These moves are fairly self-explanatory. Explicit correction is where the teacher 'clearly indicates that what the student said was incorrect' and provides the correct form. Recasts are the 'reformulation of all or part of a student's utterance, minus the error'. Clarification requests 'indicate to students either that their utterance has been misunderstood [or] is ill-formed in some way and that a repetition or a reformulation is required'. Metalinguistic feedback 'contains either comments, information, or questions related to the well-formedness of the student's utterance, without explicitly providing the correct form'. Elicitation is where teachers encourage the student to supply the correct form, either by pausing or asking. Finally, repetition 'refers to the teacher's repetition, in isolation, of the student's erroneous utterance. In most cases, teachers adjust their intonation so as to highlight the error' (Lyster & Ranta, 1997: 48–49). To these categories they also added reinforcement, noting that teachers often added language feedback to their positive comments.

Recasts were by far the most common form of oral corrective feedback in their study, accounting for over half of the total. However, along with explicit correction (which was much less frequently used), recasts were the least likely to lead to the student attempting to produce the correct form. Elicitation was substantially more successful, as was metalinguistic feedback. In both cases, a high proportion of corrections led to the learners trying to correct themselves. (Note that in this study it was less important that the learner produce the *correct* form straight away, because language learning does not work in such a linear way. If they attempted the repair, it showed that they had engaged with the correction in a way that would likely lead to change over time.) The result here should be surprising and reassuring in equal measure: the most common feedback technique was the least effective, but the techniques that engaged learners with meaning and encouraged them to find their own reformulation (elicitation and metalinguistic feedback) were the most effective.

A great deal of research into oral corrective feedback has followed. Ellis *et al.* (2006) reviewed a range of studies before conducting their own research to compare recasts and metalinguistic feedback. They found that the metalinguistic feedback was significantly more effective. Two substantial reviews reported different proportions of feedback types: Brown (2016) found that recasts were the most common form of corrective feedback, accounting for over half the total (as in the earlier study); Lyster *et al.* (2013) found greater variation in the 12 studies they examined, with recasts in the majority in only seven reports. Both reviews found that the range of variables involved (from the language focus to the instructional context and learner characteristics) meant that a single approach was unlikely to be fully successful. Teachers need to vary their feedback techniques and reduce their reliance on recasts. Techniques that engage the learners in repairing their language use, rather than using a correction supplied by the teacher, are broadly more likely to be successful. In closing, it is worth noting that several studies report a strong and consistent preference for correction among students – more so than among their teachers, who often avoid correction in favour of encouraging fluent communication.

Chapter Review

This chapter has focused on implicit and explicit learning. It began with a discussion of three types of knowledge: declarative (being able to say that something is so); procedural (being able to use that knowledge with some accuracy and consistency); and automatic (when speed, consistency and accuracy reach a high level). We found that knowledge changed as it was proceduralised, being organised into chunks and stored in ways that made much less demand on cognitive resources, memory and attention. This takes time but allows more complex clusters of knowledge and skill to emerge and goes a long way to explaining why progress can seem to slow after an initial burst. We examined the crucial role of practice, again recognising the importance of meaning. Decontextualised sentences were out; real-life contexts for language use were in.

We then turned to the role of feedback, noting that it has both a specific and a general meaning in language education. The conversational feedback that tells us if our message has been understood is part of natural interaction and can be effectively provided by peers. The high-information feedback that teachers can provide is different but equally valuable. We examined different types of feedback and found that recasts dominated much teacher-student interaction – but were the least effective. Corrective feedback strategies that engaged learners with meaning and provided explicit language feedback were consistently more effective. As we found in earlier chapters, this helps learners to notice the gap between the language they have produced and the language needed to get their meaning across. Finally, we noted that feedback (perhaps surprisingly) is often expected and desired by students. They see it as having great value for their learning and as part of a teacher's job. We see a clear pattern here: by engaging learners more fully, we can create better conditions for language learning. In the next chapter we will see that this even extends to their first languages.

What We Found in Chapter 7

Chapter 7 examined explicit and implicit learning, types of knowledge and feedback. The main points were:

- We can distinguish three types of knowledge: declarative (being able to say that something is so); procedural (being able to use that knowledge with some accuracy and consistency); and automatic (when speed and accuracy reach a high level).
- Knowledge changes as it is proceduralised, being organised into chunks and stored in ways that make much less demand on cognitive resources, memory and attention.
- Feedback is generally most effective when it encourages the learner to find the correct form, rather than repeating one that the teacher supplies.
- Learning is non-linear, so we should not expect correction to lead directly to the correct form.

Where Can I Go Next?

A special issue of *Studies in Second Language Acquisition* explored **implicit and explicit L2 learning**. The introductory article by Jan H. Hulstijn (2005) gives a clear overview of the arguments. Further discussion of recasts as a form of L2 feedback can be found in Goo and Mackey (2013). It is also worth reading the original studies cited in this chapter, including Lyster and Ranta (1997), for their clear discussion of classroom feedback types.

It is really hard to break habits of feedback. We have years of exposure to how our own teachers corrected us, and those experiences can become so deeply ingrained that they feel completely unremarkable. A good way to use the ideas in this chapter is to record yourself for a lesson, transcribe your interactions with the pupils, and categorise them using Lyster and Ranta's (1997) six types of feedback. There are several options thereafter: rewrite them to elicit more, pick one to focus on for the rest of the week, or just use them as a reminder to be aware of your feedback techniques. At some point, it is exceptionally helpful to have a colleague observe your teaching and make notes on each feedback type so that you can get an objective perspective.

8 First Languages Are Important for Learning English

Multilingual pupils do not suddenly forget their first language(s) when they start studying in English. Those languages continue to play an important role in their lives. Can they also support proficiency in the additional language?

Teachers, researchers and activists have long fought over the right for children to use their first languages in school. In the United States the debate has raged over Spanish-English 'dual-language' schooling, and in Canada over French and English immersion. In the UK, where we do not have a dominant L2 and our schools are linguistically highly diverse, it has focused on the rights of children to bring their home languages into the school and into the curriculum. The arguments have some pedigree. The Bullock Report (1975) made clear that young people should not be 'expected to cast off the language and culture of the home as [they cross] the school threshold' (Bullock, 1975: 286), but in many schools the pupils' first languages are still confined to a few wall displays or an occasional presentation in assembly. Rarely do they get into the curriculum and into classroom activities.

Yet there is a substantial body of evidence showing that learners' first languages have a beneficial effect on learning. This chapter will examine the evidence from a number of angles. It will begin by outlining the 'monolingual principle' – a position that is no longer tenable in most schools, but which needs to be set out clearly before we go further. It then turns to the use of first languages to support L2 learning, and considers the latest evidence on how bilingualism affects the brain and what implications this has for classroom learning. Finally, it returns to the 'monolingual principle' to ask whether there is still a place for 'English-only' policies in schools.

The Monolingual Principle

The 'monolingual principle' – that we best teach a language by using only that language – is so well established that it is taken for granted in many education systems. The reasons for this are varied: many people argue that an 'English-only' policy is the best way to give maximum exposure to the new language, or that the linguistic diversity of the class makes it impossible to use all the languages that students bring. Others are concerned that using multiple languages will lead to transfer (or 'interference') errors, or will overload students trying to switch between them. Some concerns are more closely tied to the curriculum itself: that texts and assessments are in English and so classes should focus on building up proficiency in that language. These positions are all underpinned by an assumption that monolingualism is the norm and that bilingual children should achieve something close to native-speaker competence as soon as possible, so that they can go on to achieve highly in the curriculum.

This line of thinking has been challenged in three main ways. The first is the argument that the monolingual 'native speaker' is a poor goal to aim for and that we should instead focus on supporting students to draw on all their languages. The second recognises that pupils continue to use their other languages alongside English: we can exclude them from our consideration but not, in truth, from our classrooms. The third point is related to the second – that as well as being part of a learner's identity and daily life, languages interact with each other at a cognitive level. Supporting proficiency in L1 is a way to support proficiency in L2. We will take these in turn.

Should 'native-like' proficiency be the standard that our learners aspire to? It depends on what we mean. Certainly, we want our learners to have a full and fluent command of the language so that they can thrive in the curriculum and in life, but the 'native speaker' is generally considered a poor benchmark for such aspirations. For one thing, it is very imprecise. Research has shown that the boundaries between native speakers and highly proficient non-natives overlap, so that at a practical level they can be hard to distinguish. However, 'native' carries overtones that 'highly proficient' does not. Alan Davies (2013: 1), for example, argues that the category of 'native speaker' is really an idealisation of an educated user of standard variety which represents only a minority of actual L1 users. This suggests that education and social capital, as well as language, are bound up in being a native speaker, and that the category may exclude both L1 and proficient L2 users. Others have argued that the single term 'native speaker' should be replaced by a more nuanced assessment of affiliation, inheritance and expertise (Leung *et al.*, 1997), by 'L1 versus LX user' (Dewaele, 2018) or by shifting our focus to 'new speakers' of a language (O'Rourke & Pujolar, 2013). These critiques take aim at the assumption that monolingualism is the norm and that bilingual users should be defined in terms of a monolingual majority. As Mauranen (2012: 4) argues, 'Monolingualism is neither the typical condition nor the gold standard'.

A second consideration is whether EAL learners continue to use their other languages alongside English. Most certainly do. Studies of multilingualism in supplementary schools (Blackledge & Creese, 2010), in faith learning (Lytra *et al.*, 2016) and in extended families (Ruby *et al.*, 2010) show the continuing importance of first languages to children's lives. The full breadth of children's language and learning can be brought into classrooms – spaces 'that can be infused with our students' identities' as they learn to become writers, as Jennifer Rowsell and Kate Pahl (2007: 402) suggest. Doing so involves a critical look at our curricula and pedagogies, finding spaces where students might see their lives reflected in what and how they learn. This is challenging to begin with but there have been several book-length studies that give concrete insights to build on (such as Cummins & Early, 2011; Lytra & Martin, 2010).

One reason why this is so important is because it already happens under the surface. English is rarely alone, even in an English-only classroom. We know from studies that record and analyse classroom talk, for example, that pupils use their L1 as they plan, draft and revise their work in the L2: the first language scaffolds their use of the new language and provides a valuable collaborative resource when working with L1 peers. Similar studies have shown that when L1s are excluded, L2 production is more fragmented and less focused. Without the scaffolding provided by the L1, EAL learners find it harder to achieve highly in English.

So far we have met two major challenges to the monolingual principle: first, that the ideal of the 'native speaker' is neither precise nor useful. There are better goals, revolving around expertise but also recognising the importance of feeling a connection to language, culture and community. Second, pupils continue using their other languages anyway. That is reason enough to create spaces where those languages are represented in the curriculum, but they also provide an essential scaffold to L2 and subject learning. The last of our three considerations extends this focus, examining how languages interact beneficially with each other at the level of the individual learner.

The Role of First Languages in Learning

There are many reasons to include learners' L1s in the classroom, from the positive effect it has on young people's wellbeing to the supportive scaffold it offers to L2 use. This section examines why that scaffolding is effective. In short, it is because our proficiency in different languages is connected beneath the surface.

One explanation, first advanced by Jim Cummins in 1979, is that our different languages share a common underlying proficiency (or CUP). When children learn a new language they are not just learning words and grammar patterns; they acquire concepts and skills too. Those concepts and skills are not stored separately for each language, but at a deeper level that can be accessed (once the learner has reached a certain level of proficiency) through any language. A Polish child who had age-appropriate schooling before moving to the UK in mid-adolescence, for example, will be able to use English to access the concepts laid down earlier in the curriculum, once their English proficiency is sufficiently developed. This gives a very strong rationale for supporting the first language alongside the second: it gives pupils a way of accessing and storing concepts and skills that their current level of English would prohibit. Using both languages allows teachers to maintain a high level of challenge, even before the learner reaches a high level of L2 proficiency. The balance can be shifted as L2 proficiency increases, until L1 provides only a minor support (although it is worth maintaining L1 development so that pupils have access to the full range of concepts and skills in both languages).

Several other approaches have been proposed to account for the relationship between languages. Multi-competence, first proposed by Vivian Cook in 1991, is discussed here. It is based on three premises:

(1) multi-competence concerns the total system for all languages (L1, L2, Ln) in a single mind or community and their inter-relationships;
(2) multi-competence does not depend on the monolingual native speaker; and
(3) multi-competence affects the whole mind, i.e. all language and cognitive systems, rather than language alone. (Cook, 2016: 7–16)

This proposes a view of L2 users that is not based on the ideal of a monolingual native speaker, but rather as 'a legitimate, multi-competent language user in their own right' (Li Wei, 2016: 536). It seems obvious to say that research into bilingual learners involves people who use two languages with some degree of proficiency, but most SLA research has tended to focus on only one of those. The same can be said of EAL: if the learner's languages support each other and are connected by a common underlying proficiency, how do we justify our focus on just the language used in the curriculum? Multi-competence research approaches this by challenging the 'monolingual principle', arguing that it yields 'research questions and methods that are inextricably linked to monolingual native speakers [whereas] the multi-competence perspective relates its questions and methods to L2 users' (Cook, 2016: 3).

This raises a number of practical issues for EAL teachers. It asks us to rethink our teaching from a multilingual perspective. In their extensive study of Greek supplementary schools in Europe and Canada, for example, Julie Panagiotopoulou and Lisa Rosen (2019) found teachers and students trying to make sense of monolingual and multilingual perspectives. They were there to teach and learn a national language, Greek, and felt strongly that it was important to keep the boundaries of that language in place so that learners had sufficient exposure to good quality input; however, at the same time they felt equally strongly that the students' lives were multilingual, and that a rigidly monolingual classroom was artificial. The authors note that second-generation teachers found this dichotomy less problematic: they were 'sensitive to their own multilingual realities as well as those of their pupils in the school context and, on this basis, develop multilingual pedagogies' (Panagiotopoulou & Rosen, 2019: 233). This means rethinking both the role of first languages in the classroom and the notion of deficit. A multi-competence perspective views EAL learners as developing bilinguals rather than English learners.

A similar argument has been advanced by advocates of translanguaging, an approach that has much in common with multi-competence and is associated with the work of Ofelia García (García, 2008; García & Li Wei, 2014). Translanguaging has a more explicitly political focus, emerging from work with Spanish-English bilinguals in the United States (although its intellectual roots go back to bilingual learners in Wales), and is commonly defined as 'the deployment of a speaker's full linguistic repertoire without regard for watchful adherence to the socially and politically defined boundaries of named (and usually national and state) languages' (Otheguy *et al.*, 2015: 281). Advocates of translanguaging argue that the boundary between first and second languages is artificial, reflecting a monolingual view of language use that can and should be challenged by teachers. It should be noted that this is a pedagogic stance: the linguistic basis for translanguaging remains controversial. It does, however, offer a well-developed alternative to the monolingual principle that we can use in school; by using 'all their languages [students] are able to be themselves, help one another, and succeed academically' (García et al., 2016: 15). We will explore these ideas further in Part 2, when we discuss academic language across the curriculum. Before that, we return to the bilingual brain.

Bilingualism and the Brain

Researchers have investigated the connection between bilingualism and the brain for more than a century. The early studies viewed bilingualism as a distinct disadvantage. Researchers repeatedly found that bilingual children scored less well on verbal tests of cognitive ability, leading investigators to describe the use of multiple languages in early childhood as a source of hardship and confusion. It is unsurprising that they did: these studies generally did not account for differences in age, socioeconomic status, language proficiency or a range of other factors (such as whether the participant was a refugee), and often used very imprecise definitions of bilingualism and proficiency. Significantly, they did not adequately consider the impact of the tests (administered in English) on the test-takers (who often had limited proficiency in English). Some of those tested in English had little knowledge of that language and unsurprisingly produced 'evidence' that their bilingualism was a disadvantage.

A seminal paper by Elizabeth Peal and Wallace Lambert in 1962 examined these methodological biases. They noted that, while most studies found a bilingual disadvantage, not all did. Few found a clear advantage but a larger number were inconclusive or found no effect. This led them to conduct their own study of monolingual (French) and bilingual (French-English) pupils in six Montreal public schools. The participants were carefully selected (they tested all 10-year-olds, regardless of school year, to include children being held back), and the researchers controlled for variables such as age, gender and socioeconomic status. By measuring verbal and non-verbal intelligence, attitudes towards each language, school grades and self-reported proficiency in English, they found that the 'bilinguals performed significantly better than monolinguals on both verbal and non-verbal intelligence tests'. Bilinguals, they concluded, 'appear to have a more diversified set of mental abilities than the monolinguals' (Peal & Lambert, 1962: 22), but they could only speculate as to the nature of those abilities.

We now know much more about how bilingualism affects the brain. Using neuroimaging techniques, for example, researchers have established that language learning changes the structure of the brain. This is taken as evidence of *neuroplasticity* – the ability of the brain to adapt physically to the demands placed on it. These changes affected children, adults and older people, and studies show that both age of acquisition and proficiency are important. They also happen quickly. Learning a language was shown to cause structural changes to the white and grey matter of the brain in as little as three months. Such research is perhaps far from classroom practice, but it points to the enormous development in the research literature about the cognitive benefits of language learning across the life course. Two researchers in particular have taken this as a prescription: Thomas Bak and Dina Mehmedbegovic's 'healthy linguistic diet' is a good starting point for an evidence-based discussion in schools, based on the idea that 'exposure to different languages, learnt to different levels of proficiency, can have positive effects across the whole lifespan, benefiting individuals and societies' (Bak & Mehmedbegovic, 2017: 1).

Bilingualism brings many advantages beyond the classroom, but there is a lively debate about whether there is a specific, measurable cognitive 'advantage' to being bilingual. A 'bilingual advantage', if one exists, would likely develop as the young person matures into adolescence and would be maintained until old age if (and possibly only if) more than one language were used regularly. There are as many caveats as concrete proposals in this area, but it is worth setting out the main positions because they illustrate the breadth and depth of the research evidence on bilingualism and show the importance of moving beyond a monolingual perspective.

The 'bilingual advantage' debate has largely focused on executive function (EF), a set of 'top-down mental processes needed when you have to concentrate and pay attention' (Diamond, 2013: 136). Bilinguals use these more because the brain activates both languages when one of them is used; it must constantly manage which resources are drawn on as you speak and write. The proposal is therefore that 'repeated experience in language selection creates expertise in executive function' (Kroll & Bialystok, 2013: 506). The proposal is supported by evidence that people who speak more than one language perform better on tests that require EF, as well as in areas such as metalinguistic awareness, phonetic perception and creative thinking.

However, an alternative proposal is that such effects are either very restricted or non-existent. In a detailed refutation of the bilingual advantage, Paap *et al.* (2015) argued that studies finding no or very little advantage for bilingualism were under-reported. It may be that bilingualism brings advantages only in specific situations: some studies have suggested that sequential bilinguals (whose languages are not learned together from birth) may show greater effects because learning a second language once the first is already established involves reconfiguring mental resources to a greater degree. If so, this would suggest again that sustaining all a pupil's languages while they are at school would be an advantage. The debate continues energetically.

Chapter Review: Is There Still a Place for 'English-only' Policies?

English-only policies may still have a role to play in schools, but only in very limited circumstances. This chapter has examined the use of first languages from three angles: first it established the monolingual principle, that we best teach a language by using only that language. While appealing, and appearing on the surface to fit with our key principles of input, output and interaction, we found that it relied on a narrow view of language that is untenable in an increasingly multilingual world. We looked at critiques of the 'native speaker', which I argued is the implicit assumption behind much EAL provision (and much EAL policy). It is not reflected in the way in which young bilinguals use their languages: they use them to scaffold their use of English, and where L1 is strictly prohibited, L2 production is less successful.

We extended this discussion by looking briefly at different ways of conceptualising the language system. We started with the common underlying proficiency (first advanced by Jim Cummins in 1979 and discussed further in Part 2). This proposed that what we see as separate languages are underpinned by a common proficiency; once pupils have reached a sufficient level of proficiency in the L2, they can access the concepts and skills that were first established in the L1 and vice versa. Both languages can provide a route to deeper learning, and where pupils have unequal proficiency (as is the case with EAL pupils), using the L1 alongside English can support learning while the L2 develops.

We then introduced two other ways of conceptualising the linguistic repertoires of young bilinguals. Multi-competence (Cook, 1991, 2016) reconceptualises these language learners as fully competent language users with different levels of proficiency in each of their languages. This has much in common with translanguaging (García, 2008; García & Li Wei, 2014), which prefers the term 'emergent bilingual' to 'learner' or EAL pupil. Translanguaging goes further than multi-competence in challenging monolingual schooling, arguing not only that it poorly reflects the language norms of bilingual pupils but that it is fundamentally unjust, imposing a monolingual worldview that marginalises the experience of bilingual learners.

Finally, we turned from the classroom back to the bilingual brain, considering the history of research into bilinguals. Early studies found a consistent disadvantage that justified excluding learners from mainstream learning. A seminal study in 1962, by Elizabeth Peal and Wallace Lambert, revisited the literature and found evidence of persistent methodological bias. We followed this line through to the current debates over the so-called 'bilingual advantage', based largely on experimental studies of how the brain processes language and where some researchers have argued that methodological biases have led to overly positive findings. What emerges from the debate, though, is a clear picture that the bilingual brain is not two monolingual brains in one. Languages interact with each other in a complex arrangement of sub-systems that adapt and evolve over time.

So is there still a place for English-only policies? It is difficult to see the strict prohibition of learners' first languages as anything more than the imposition of a monolingual worldview. First languages support learning of and through the second language. A more nuanced approach would encourage L1 use on a sliding scale, supporting L2 development as well as the pupils' proficiency in the norms of academic language. It would also encourage full use of L1 in the curriculum at times: you can't really value pupils' languages if you don't make space for them where it counts the most. It would recognise that learners have expertise in languages, and in the experiences and cultures that come with them, that the teacher does not. It would, given half a chance, radically rethink the way in which languages are used to marginalise young bilinguals in favour of a 'native-speaker' standard that few monolingual pupils even meet.

What We Found in Chapter 8

Chapter 8 examined the role that pupils' first languages play in learning. The main points were:

- The 'monolingual principle' – that we best teach a language by using only that language – is so well established that it is taken for granted in many education systems, but it has been challenged on several grounds.
- First languages play an important role in learning, both at a cognitive level and in their contribution to learners' academic and social development.
- There is a lively debate over the specific cognitive advantages that bilingualism brings, but it is clear that languages interact with each other in a complex arrangement of sub-systems that adapt and evolve over time.

Where Can I Go Next?

On the **use of first languages in the classroom**, a good place to start is Hamish Chalmers' (2019) contribution to the OUP Expert series, *The Role of the First Language in English Medium Instruction*. This free and concise guide covers several major topics in the field.

There has been extensive debate over the **role of the native speaker** – and whether such a label is useful or meaningful. A good place to start is Jean-Marc Dewaele's (2018) paper in *Applied Linguistics*, which includes a very accessible overview of the debate before presenting his own argument to replace 'native versus non-native' with 'L1 versus LX'. The book-length treatment by Alan Davies (2013) is well worth reading too. It is short (around 160 pages) and very accessible. Also of interest is the concept of 'new speakers': see O'Rourke and Pujolar (2013).

This chapter introduced two approaches that go beyond monolingualism. On the first, **translanguaging**, see the CUNY-NYSIEB project in the United States: https://www.cuny-nysieb.org. Although focused on a specific North American context, it contains a lot of thought-provoking ideas (some of which we return to in Part 3). A book by Ofelia García, Susanna Ibarra Johnson and Kate Seltzer (2016) explores the 'translanguaging classroom' further. On the term **'emergent bilingual'**, which is gaining traction among some teachers and researchers in the United States, see the short (61-page) report by Ofelia García, Jo Anne Kleifgen and Lorraine Falchi (available from García's personal website: https://ofeliagarciadotorg.files.wordpress.com/2011/02/ell-to-eb.pdf). On **multi-competence**, in addition to the resources in the recommendations for further reading, see Vivian Cook's website: http://www.viviancook.uk/SLA/Multicompetence/index.htm

9 Pulling It All Together: Learning Trajectories and Second Language Pedagogy

This chapter reviews Part 1, highlights key themes and considers the time taken for learners to achieve proficiency in English.

The introductory chapters proposed a 'practice-based approach to EAL', in response to the shortcomings of current policy. That approach had three tenets:

(i) The primary place of learning is the mainstream classroom.
(ii) Language is inseparable from content.
(iii) The challenge faced by EAL learners is substantial but not unique: all learners are developing their command of academic language as they learn.

Chapters 3–8 reviewed the evidence on how additional languages are learned, beginning with a theory of language and concluding with a critique of monolingualism in EAL. This chapter now revisits the practice-based approach in light of these findings. It will then review one final question: the time it takes for a bilingual learner to develop full proficiency in English (PiE). It will be an opportunity to connect our discussion of language learning (Part 1) to the important role that language plays across the curriculum (Part 2).

A Practice-based Approach to Additional Language Learning

Before we examine the tenets of a practice-based approach to EAL in turn, let us take a moment to review the key points made in each chapter.

Chapter 3, Key Principles and a Theory of Language, opened the discussion with some key terms – L1/L2, bilingual/multilingual, learning/acquisition – and established a theoretical distinction between first and second language learning. It introduced a theory of language based in Chomskyan linguistics and contrasted it with a 'usage-based' approach, a good starting point for our exploration of the language acquisition literature but one that we would scrutinise afresh as the chapters progressed. We introduced the terms morphology and syntax (together, morphosyntax) to add some specificity to our use of the general term 'grammar', and we noted the problems with the notion of 'target language'. EAL learners have to address a moving target and one that is defined in terms of a restricted monolingual worldview.

Chapter 4, Learning or Acquiring?, began with a conundrum: the more time is spent learning about English, the less is spent using it. However, we know that practice is more useful if learners have a good grasp of how English works. We made a distinction between learning and acquiring a language, introducing the work of Stephen Krashen to explore (among other things) the important role of language input. We also looked at contemporary critiques of Krashen's model, concluding that learning and acquisition could be treated together in practical terms. What we took away was a firmer position on the role of grammar teaching – important in moderation – and a clearer understanding that language proficiency develops primarily when learners are exposed to masses of input, with plentiful opportunities to use it in meaningful interactions.

Chapter 5, Masses of Input, took this further. It looked at research into attention and input processing, finding that a syllabus organised around covering grammar points does not seem to be particularly effective. Learners are best able to process input when they encounter language features in context – especially if their attention is drawn to a particular feature. This supports the argument that bilingual learners should be in the subject classroom as much as possible; it's here that they will be exposed to the academic and subject-specific language of their discipline. It also suggests that class and subject teachers are necessary for EAL learners to receive language-rich teaching across the curriculum. From research into input processing, we found that learners process meaning before form: cognitive resources are limited, and so learners make sense of the input on the basis of what seems realistic ('dog bites man' is easier to process than 'banana bites man'). They focus on content words before grammatical words and they also get most of their meaning from vocabulary rather than grammar. This suggests that a pedagogy based on input, output and meaningful interaction – topics that were further discussed in this chapter – is likely to be more effective than one designed around grammar points.

Chapter 6, Earlier Isn't Necessarily Better, reviewed the evidence on age and language acquisition. It challenged the idea that 'children just pick up languages', finding that although age does have an effect it is not determining. It found that the length of time since 'significant' contact with English was the most important predictor of proficiency, but also that age effects were overshadowed by contextual factors such as family support and the differences between individual learners. We can expect EAL pupils to make rapid progress when they join the school, given appropriate support in a language-rich curriculum.

Chapter 7, Implicit and Explicit Learning, sought to understand the differences in outcomes between EAL learners, all of whom are fully proficient speakers of their first languages. It began by outlining three types of knowledge (declarative, procedural and automatic) and described how practice leads to the internalisation of linguistic data. It then looked at practice itself, arguing that 'doing and learning are synonymous'. Practice for EAL learners means using the language for meaningful tasks or interactions, so that they have to draw on the knowledge they have stored. This allows them to access it more quickly and accurately over time. Finally, the chapter looked at the important role played by feedback, finding that it is most effective when it is rich in information and requires the learner to work out how to repair the error. Metalinguistic feedback (commenting on the language used) and elicitation (encouraging a self-correction, either by pausing or asking) are much more effective than simply recasting (giving the correct form) – although recasts are very common in teachers' classroom talk.

Chapter 8, First Languages Are Important for Learning English, looked at first languages from a range of perspectives. It began by outlining the 'monolingual principle', finding that the monolingual native speaker was neither a precise nor useful reference point, and that pupils continue to use their first languages anyway. This led to a longer discussion of the role of first languages, introducing alternative views of bilingual proficiency (common underlying proficiency, multi-competence and translanguaging). We considered whether a monolingual approach might be unsuitable for bilingual learners because it fails to take full account of their knowledge, skills and proficiency in their full range of languages. The chapter then returned to the bilingual brain, examining the arguments for a bilingual deficit and a bilingual advantage. Finally, it drew these lines of enquiry together to discuss what role there might be for English-only policies and monolingual teaching generally.

* * *

We can now reconsider the tenets of a practice-based approach to EAL. There are many reasons to think that language proficiency is best developed in the mainstream classroom. It is where learners will be most exposed to masses of subject-specific input and have opportunities to interact meaningfully with their peers in curriculum tasks. This is very difficult to replicate in a withdrawal lesson unless the subject or class teacher contributes to planning and teaching the session. However, subject content alone does not make the mainstream classroom suitable for bilingual learners. It must be rich in language, with feedback techniques used skilfully to probe and support learners' developing language systems. This shows a clear place for EAL specialists to contribute to mainstream teaching: language-rich pedagogy benefits all pupils. Similarly, language is inseparable from content. We have seen that high achievement in the curriculum depends to a large extent on academic language skills. Practice leads to the internalisation of language data but also of skills and concepts, and once stored they can be accessed through any of a learner's languages. Finally, the challenge faced by EAL learners is substantial but not unique. Family support is a major determinant of success for bilingual pupils as it is for monolinguals; the evidence on feedback and learning is not unique to bilingual learners.

There is much that we do not yet know about EAL provision, and finding out will require us to rethink some fundamental assumptions about language and learning. We will see how as we turn to the final section of Part 1, on how long it takes learners to develop proficiency in English.

How Long Does It Take to Develop Proficiency?

There is a short answer and a long answer. The short answer is this: it takes about two to three years for beginner pupils to develop conversational fluency, and five to seven years to reach a level (in subject assessments) equivalent to monolingual pupils. Pupils whose formal schooling has been interrupted may take more time, up to seven to ten years. The longer answer is that we should not be satisfied with this. Given that we all achieve fluency in our first language, why should some pupils find it so hard to master an additional language when they are immersed in it and supported by teachers with expertise in EAL? What are we measuring when we assess proficiency, and is mastery of academic English related to mastery of academic content? Do our assessments record a holistic view of the young person's language proficiency, or do we bring a monolingual lens that allows us to see only part of what they are capable of?

Time to proficiency, in years

The research gives a range of figures for how long it takes pupils to achieve proficiency, but they all revolve around the same two periods. It takes about two to three years to develop conversational proficiency in English and five to seven years to achieve proficiency in *academic* English equivalent to that of a monolingual peer. Children, especially younger ones, will likely show fluency in familiar settings earlier than this (leading to the familiar report: 'she picked it up in a year!'), but it takes a little longer to extend this fluency to a reasonable range of conversational situations. It is very common for bilingual learners to have a 'silent period' when they are first immersed in an L2 environment but this should not be mistaken for inactivity: their brains are deeply engaged with processing linguistic input and this is a vital stage for many learners. Check with parents that their child's first language use is developing as expected (as the silent period can also mask some developmental delays) but otherwise be reassured that the learner is taking some time to figure out what is going on in the new environment. The best advice is to continue to include them, not to demand they speak in front of others before they are ready but to pair them with a more proficient buddy to encourage peer talk.

Full academic proficiency in academic English takes more time and is discussed in Part 2. The figure of five to seven years is commonly attributed to Jim Cummins (1981), who investigated bilingual learners in Toronto, Canada. He found that language proficiency was not a single construct, and that the aspects needed for academic success correlated well with age and educational experience. Older learners therefore had a slight advantage in developing academic proficiency and (for those arriving after the age of six) it took at least five years to reach that level. He drew two further conclusions from this: that policies offering only a few years' English language support are 'arbitrary and may not reflect the needs of ESL children'; and that any measurements in the first five years are 'likely to seriously underestimate their potential academic abilities' (Cummins, 1981: 148).

Later data have corroborated these findings. In the 1980s, Virginia Collier and Wayne Thomas began studying the time taken for learners to reach proficiency. In a 2017 paper they reviewed 32 years of data (comprising 7.5 million learner records) and reported an average of six years 'for those who start in kindergarten and receive quality dual-language schooling in both L1 and L2 for a minimum of 6 years, with at least half of the instructional time in their L1' (Collier & Thomas, 2017: 207). They emphasise dual-language schooling, which has particular relevance for the United States because a great majority of English learners are Spanish-English bilinguals. A large number of state-level studies have reported very similar figures, although there are some outliers – from two to three years (Conger, 2009; MacSwan & Pray, 2005) to eight years (Umansky & Reardon, 2014).

We might note that much of the research comes from North America. In large part, this is because annual proficiency assessments are mandated by the federal No Child Left Behind Act (2001). States are required to monitor how long it takes learners to be reclassified as 'English proficient' – a benchmark that is not used in the UK and that has no consistent meaning across the 50 states of the USA. It comes with substantial caveats: time-to-proficiency is generally interpreted as the number of years between entering the school system and being reclassified. Students' starting points, their educational histories and their L1 literacies are often treated in broad terms, which means that we cannot always draw detailed comparisons with the UK context.

Research from the UK has added important insights. The Department for Education (DfE, 2020) recently released an analysis of its PiE data, collected in 2018 and then discontinued. While the data collection was too brief to support longitudinal analysis, they did compare pupils' proficiency ratings with the number of years since the learner was first registered at an English school. They found that fluent bilinguals had been in school here for an average of 7.3 years (DfE, 2020: 9), at the higher end of international comparisons. A recent and influential study by Steve Strand and Annina Hessel (2018) found that EAL status is a poor indicator of pupils' academic achievement. The category is just too diverse for meaningful conclusions to be drawn. However, PiE does strongly predict achievement. Bilingual pupils with high PiE outperform monolingual pupils at Key Stage 4 (around 16 years old), a finding that has been corroborated by other studies of local authority data (e.g. Demie, 2018). Because most EAL pupils are British-born bilinguals, these data suggest that EAL support is most needed in Primary. This may under-report the needs of later arrivals.

Time to proficiency, a brief critique

What does it mean to be 'proficient' in English? There are both technical and philosophical issues to consider. At a technical level, there is no standard definition of proficiency and so findings cannot be compared across different settings. This is a particular problem in the United States, where such assessments are federally mandated; a major recent study found 'important methodological and measurement issues that complicate interpretation' and the 'generalizability of the findings' (National Academies, 2017:

221.) A similar approach is used in the UK, where the 'fluent' category (DfE, 2016) means that pupils are able to operate without EAL support, but central government has withdrawn proficiency data from the National Pupil Database.

When we measure time-to-proficiency we are explicitly contrasting two constructs: the academic language proficiency of a monolingual reference group, and the limited proficiency of a bilingual group. Neither of these is well defined: monolingual pupils vary widely in their ability to construct academic text, for example. Help with academic English is important for every pupil (and is discussed at length in Part 2), and bilingual pupils can work more independently much earlier in an inclusive, language-rich classroom. Research has found that age (and therefore cognitive maturity), educational history and socio-economic status are all important predictors of academic success, not just language. The broad 'EAL' category can obscure these important distinctions and encourage us to organise provision around language proficiency rather than other salient characteristics. As several recent studies have noted, it is 'profoundly misleading' (Hutchinson, 2018: 7) to rely on average attainment figures for such a diverse group.

Perhaps the most developed critique has come from the United States, where pupils are classified as 'long-term English learners' (LTELs) if they do not reach the proficiency standard within seven years. Such pupils comprise one-third of all English learners in Chicago and New York; one study in Los Angeles found that fully one-quarter of learners had not reached proficiency within nine years. LTEL students are generally orally bilingual but have very limited (oral and written) academic proficiency in either English or their first language; normal provision for English learners does not meet their needs. That is surely an understatement: after seven years in an English-medium school, it is hard to see that their limited academic language is anything other than evidence of an education system failing young people. Flores et al. (2015: 113) go further, arguing that it represents a 'racial project that serves to perpetuate White supremacy through the marginalization of the language practices' of bilinguals.

The US context is different, from the ways in which schools are more locally funded, which can increase disparity, to the use of annual standardised testing to assess progress in English. Still, these arguments have important implications for EAL in the UK too. Our education system collects too little data on language proficiency for teachers to benchmark how well their learners are progressing. We continue to conceptualise EAL as something that happens before or parallel to subject teaching, instead of looking at how language works for all pupils in the curriculum. And we are too ready to accept the monolingual principle, that we best teach a language by using only that language. If we moved away from that monolingual lens, we might ask whether pupils could use multiple languages in their curriculum learning, and how the discipline of EAL might change as a result.

What We Found in Chapter 9

Chapter 9 reviewed the main themes of each chapter so far and examined the time taken to reach proficiency. The main points were:

- Headline figures are two to three years for conversational fluency and five to seven years for academic proficiency equivalent to monolingual peers.
- These figures are fairly consistent across settings but there are underlying weaknesses in the data. They are based on a monolingual reference group and obscure very wide differences in learner characteristics.
- The strongest response is to challenge the premise that being 'equivalent' to a monolingual peer is a meaningful goal. Instead, we should look at measures of proficiency that reflect learners' abilities to use multiple languages in their curriculum learning.

Where Can I Go Next?

On time to proficiency, the work of Collier and Thomas is extensive. Their website is recommended as a starting point for reading about their approach: https://www.thomasandcollier.com. There is further discussion in Genesee *et al.* (2006: Chapter 5) and in a report by the US National Academies of Sciences, Engineering, and Medicine (2017). The practice of labelling some emerging bilinguals as 'LTELs' has been extensively criticised (see, for example, Flores *et al.*, 2015; Menken *et al.*, 2012).

Part 2

Language Across the Curriculum

> *Academic language is ... no one's mother tongue.*
> Pierre Bourdieu and Jean-Claude Passeron, 1994

Preface to Part 2

In Part 1, we looked at how the bilingual brain processes and acquires language. We established a basic formula for language learning – masses of input, with plentiful opportunities to use it in meaningful interaction – and found that repeated practice allows learners to proceduralise and automatise knowledge, which is essential for the emergence of complex skills and understanding. We saw that feedback is an important part of developing proficiency. We found that age and the time since the first *significant* exposure to English are both important but not determining factors. We also found that classroom feedback is most effective when it is rich in information and asks learners to engage with their language choices, but less so when the teacher just supplies the correct word or phrase. Feedback from peers, as part of natural interaction, is also valuable but is different in kind; peer work could therefore form a large proportion of classroom interaction but cannot replace the teacher's input. Finally, we examined the crucial role played by first languages in learning English, not just at the level of language processing but also at the level of conceptual development. This gave us strong reasons to challenge the 'monolingual assumption' that EAL pupils should be taught English as a precursor to joining the mainstream curriculum.

Part 1 showed, too, that good EAL practice apprentices young people into subject disciplines. Rather than focusing on language proficiency alone (which often leads to a deficit view because their English is still developing), this takes a broader approach and looks for ways in which the pupil can participate in meaning-making activities in the curriculum. In Part 2, we begin looking in detail at how we make and communicate meaning in the curriculum. Unlike in Part 1, where theories of acquisition focused on the individual learner, Part 2 sees meaning-making as a social activity. It happens when we interact with others, either directly (for example, when talking to a classmate) or indirectly (as when viewing a video or reading a text that someone has created). This means that we treat literacy as a social practice as well as a set of skills. I will show what I mean, using a vignette from my own research with newly arrived EAL learners, and two quotations from the literature:

> **Vignette 1 Noham and the Coke bottle**
>
> In a Maths lesson for the new arrivals group, Ms Cartwright (the newly qualified teacher) takes a few minutes to ask why measurements are important. Noham (14) offers two examples: if you're buying a home, you need to know the floor area, plus for immigration where people might ask (for example) your height. Another student suggests measuring the areas of countries and scales for maps (pointing to the map on the classroom wall). Noham comes back with travelling, working out how far you will go, how long it will take and how much petrol you will waste.

Noham's last example, about measuring the volume of petrol, came up several times in the lesson. It seems to relate to his migration journey, which included a dangerous crossing of the Sahara on the back of a pick-up truck. The more fuel the people-smugglers bring, the fewer paying passengers they can pack on board, but running out of petrol in the desert has deadly consequences for all involved. His other examples, from buying a home to answering the questions of immigration officials, show the breadth of ideas and experiences that he brings to the classroom.

Two quotations put that example in a broader context. The first is from the Language In the National Curriculum (LINC) project:

> The essential purpose of the language and English curriculum is, in fact, to provide opportunities for pupils to compose, communicate and comprehend meanings, their own and other people's, in purposeful contexts. (Richmond, 1990: 28)

In this vignette we see the teacher and student working together to make meaning in a purposeful context. Noham's contribution was different enough from the teacher's expectations that it risked pulling the lesson off at a tangent. For Ms Cartwright, however, it was a glimpse into her pupil's life. She worked hard to meet her learners half way, accepting their ideas and using them to explore curriculum concepts. This negotiated meaning-making is a vital part of subject literacy, as the second quotation shows. It is from Jay Lemke, a theoretical physicist turned linguist and science educator:

> Science is not done, is not communicated, through verbal language alone. It cannot be. The 'concepts' of science are not solely verbal concepts [...] To do science, to talk science, to read and write science it is necessary to juggle and combine in various canonical ways verbal discourse, mathematical expression, graphical-visual representation, and motor operations in the world. (Lemke, 1998: 87)

For EAL learners to succeed in school, they need to learn how to think, act, talk and write like members of a subject (or disciplinary) community. Knowledge itself is important but it is inseparable from the language through which it is developed. Noham is at the early stages of developing this disciplinary literacy. His point of entry to mathematical concepts is his migration journey.

Part 2 examines how meaning is created through language, in written and spoken interactions between teachers and learners in the classroom. The first chapter (Chapter 10) introduces a theoretical framework, systemic functional linguistics (SFL), and offers five principles for working with language across the curriculum. The following chapters distinguish academic language and the language of everyday communication, noting the close relationship between academic and linguistic development (Chapter 11) and describing the role of oracy and reading in academic success (Chapters 12 and 13). The book then focuses on the genres of written text from an SFL perspective (Chapter 14) and on how disciplinary language is organised (Chapter 15). Part 2 closes with a discussion of what counts as proficiency and a review of the key themes (Chapter 16).

The case studies are also introduced here. In the first, Manny Vazquez walks us through a lesson he has taught for Year 11 English. This case study immediately follows the chapter on reading and shows us how to approach metaphor (a perennial difficulty for EAL learners, but one that their bilingual and bicultural repertoires should equip them well for). Sarah Fowkes builds on the discussion of disciplinary language by highlighting the importance of vocabulary learning for Primary Maths, describing her use of the 'Word Aware' approach. Pam Cole, who has cross-phase responsibility for EAL in Swansea, closes Part 2 with an account of building capacity across several schools. She uses a partnership approach to bring language and subject specialists together and to foster language-rich teaching across the curriculum – a goal that this book shares.

10 Five Principles for Language Across the Curriculum

This chapter introduces the theory of language we will use for Part 2, systemic functional linguistics, and sets out five principles for effective EAL practice.

Teaching EAL across the curriculum is hard. You have to get to grips with the different ways in which different subjects use language, as well as the general principles of academic language that apply to all subjects. The learners bring widely different experiences and language skills to the classroom and you need to find the right entry points for each one. Then you have to build up their English proficiency, support the development of their first language and work with others to ensure that they can access the full curriculum.

Let's take a moment to think about what the learners bring to this process:

Vignette 2 Alejandra

Alejandra is a Year 5 pupil from Ecuador who moved to Spain when she was four, and then to the UK when she was eight. Her migration was driven by her parents' need to find work; they speak Spanish together at home and she Skypes regularly with her family and friends in Ecuador and Spain. At school, Alejandra has a group of Spanish- and Portuguese-speaking friends. They mostly use Spanish together – although the boundaries between Spanish, Portuguese and English are not strictly adhered to. Alejandra and her friends are funny and fairly popular: this encourages other pupils to learn some Spanish phrases and Alejandra is a ready teacher.

Alejandra's English is developing slowly and she is receiving intensive support through withdrawal lessons and a class teacher who has a good grasp of EAL pedagogy. She gets by in everyday interaction fairly well but struggles with reading and writing. This makes her frustrated: she doesn't want to be taken out for EAL support but her teachers worry that she'll struggle without it.

72 Part 2: Language Across the Curriculum

> **Vignette 3 Farjaad**
>
> Farjaad is a Year 10 pupil from Afghanistan. He arrived in the UK alone last year after an overland journey lasting two and a half years. His accommodation and legal status are insecure.
>
> Farjaad's first language is Dari and he has some literacy in that language. He speaks some Farsi from his time travelling through Iran (the two languages are very closely related). He also speaks some Hindi and Urdu from his love of Bollywood films (these two languages are also closely related in their spoken form) and has picked up phrases in Greek, Arabic and Spanish. At school he has formed friendships with quite a diverse group: they mostly use English between them, but will use other languages in pairs or smaller groups if that is easier. He finds this fluidity unremarkable.
>
> Farjaad is also making slow progress at school. He is a keen but slow reader. He has missed a lot of his education and finds things difficult, but is very grateful for the space and security that the EAL department offers. His teachers wonder what he will do after Year 11 and are looking for college places for him.

> **Vignette 4 Łukasz**
>
> Łukasz was born in the UK and joined the local Primary with other children of his age, although there are very few EAL children in his year group. His parents are from Poland and speak Polish (fluently) and English (very well). They are trying to bring him up with both languages, so they speak mostly Polish at home but made sure he attended nursery (in English) and has a lot of books in both languages. He is now in Year 2 and his English is a little behind that of his monolingual peers but he is catching up quickly. He loves showing off his Polish knowledge to the teacher, who has bought some Polish books for the class library and reads them to the pupils. She hopes to encourage his enthusiasm for reading and to show the other pupils that all languages are valued. Łukasz rarely mixes his languages now except when he is searching for a word that he knows better in one or the other.

These three pupils are very different: Alejandra and Łukasz both speak another language at home and are learning English at school. Farjaad is older, multilingual and a skilled communicator, but has missed big chunks of schooling and is struggling with both the content and the language of the curriculum. Alejandra and Farjaad are frustrated by the slow pace of their progress in English but have mixed feelings about the EAL support they receive, not least because of their different experiences in getting here. Each uses other languages during the school day: Łukasz is proud of speaking Polish but defaults to English at school; Alejandra lives mostly in Spanish but with English from her teachers and (less often) from her peers; Farjaad lives in a very multilingual environment. He tries hard to use English with his teachers and reads as much possible, although far below the expected level for his age. None of these pupils is immersed in an English-only environment, although Łukasz comes close.

If we want to support such pupils effectively, we need to understand the roles that languages play in their lives and in their learning. We also need to understand how language works in the curriculum: as we will see, it is complex and dynamic, inseparable from those who use it.

Five Principles

With that in mind, here are five evidence-based principles for developing language across the curriculum. They are intended as a shared starting point as we explore disciplinary literacy, drawing on both the findings of Part 1 and the key themes of Part 2.

A. Language and concepts are organised in disciplines

Subject disciplines are communities, each with a body of shared knowledge and ways of thinking and doing. We can think of academic language less in terms of 'right' and 'wrong', but as 'more or less accepted by the community'. Learners therefore need exposure to disciplinary language, practice making choices about how they communicate and guidance on what effect those choices will have on their audience.

B. Scaffold language to support learning

Language and knowledge develop together and so should be taught together. The best place for EAL learners is therefore in the mainstream classroom, where they can be included in disciplinary talk and activities. However, this suggests a very close working relationship between EAL specialists and their subject colleagues (in Secondary) or between the EAL specialist and other class teachers (in Primary), where each contributes to planning for the other and the school offers an integrated approach to supporting bilingual pupils.

C. Prioritise vocabulary

Vocabulary, more than anything, underpins proficiency. This goes beyond the pupils' familiarity with keywords to include a deeper understanding of patterns and how words work in texts. Bilingual pupils need a good knowledge of general academic and subject-specific vocabulary, as being able to compare with words in their first languages will help the development of vocabulary in English.

D. Talk before writing

Learners need practice organising their ideas and marshalling their linguistic resources before they can commit to effective academic writing. Oracy – the purposeful use of talk as part of learning – is an essential stage in doing so. Bilingual learners should be encouraged to use their different languages in this way: it helps them to access concepts that were learned in different languages and to draw on the full range of their language knowledge. This supports higher achievement in English than would be possible if they tried to organise their ideas in a new language straight away.

E. Learning is collaborative

Finally, it is worth stressing that learning happens mostly through interaction with others. Vygotsky (1978) reminds us that dialogue with a more-expert other is crucial. For EAL pupils, this could be a peer or a teacher: our goal is to apprentice the learner into the language, knowledge and practices of subject disciplines. This means including them at every opportunity, but also creating opportunities for them to be experts to others.

If you stop reading at these five principles, you will have the essential messages of Part 2. In the following chapters we will extend and deepen them, but they boil down to this: great EAL provision happens when bilingual learners are integral to the life of the school and when their experiences, languages and aspirations are valued accordingly.

What We Found in Chapter 10

Chapter 10 introduced the second part of this book. It used a series of vignettes to show the diversity of experiences that are captured by the term 'EAL', and introduced five key principles for language across the curriculum. These are:

- Language and concepts are organised in disciplines.
- Scaffold language to support learning.
- Prioritise vocabulary.
- Talk before writing.
- Learning is collaborative.

The main message of this chapter was that language is an essential part of learning and should not be taken for granted. If we want to support bilingual learners effectively, we instead need to understand the roles that languages play in their lives, in their learning and across the curriculum.

Where Can I Go Next?

One of the best books about **language in the curriculum** accompanied the LINC (Language In the National Curriculum) project. Edited by Ron Carter (1990), it includes material from the course as well as original papers.

The concept of **scaffolding** is also introduced here. It draws on the work of Wood, Bruner and Ross (1976), but Pauline Gibbons gives a very clear overview in the introduction to her 2002 book. See also the recommendations for Chapter 13 (Reading in a New Language).

11 BICS and CALP

Pupils acquire everyday spoken fluency quite quickly, but higher level academic language takes longer to develop. In this chapter we see that academic language and higher order thinking are connected, and discuss strategies to develop them together.

A stretching curriculum and high standards of academic English should go hand in hand. You need the language to understand the subject, and your engagement with the subject is what drives your acquisition of academic English. This chapter introduces the work of Jim Cummins, a theorist of bilingual education whose work offers a powerful explanation of the relationship between academic language proficiency and higher order thinking skills.

Common Underlying Proficiency

It used to be believed that bilingual learners had two or more language systems at their disposal, and that these had to be kept separate in order to prevent the first language 'interfering' with the language being taught (hence, for example, the strict English-only policies in many classrooms). Cummins (2001) studied how bilingual children used their languages as they worked in the classroom. He recognised that these languages were not kept separate, but that bilingual pupils drew on them both to communicate effectively. He concluded that instead of having a separate proficiency for each language, all human beings have a 'common underlying proficiency' (CUP). This can be imagined as a reservoir of knowledge and skill that informs communication in all languages, and is often represented using the famous 'dual iceberg diagram' (see Figure 11.1). What appear to be separate languages are better understood as different surface presentations of a bilingual person's deeper language proficiency.

The common underlying proficiency suggests that languages are not completely independent of each other: the skills and resources that make us proficient in our first language are also available to use as we develop our proficiency in additional languages (this is often called 'linguistic interdependence'). Separating them artificially will delay the development of both. This has important implications: it is often assumed that the most effective way to support EAL learners is through immersion or by maximising their 'time-on-task' in English lessons, but the interdependence hypothesis suggests that the opposite is true. Development in one language supports proficiency in the other.

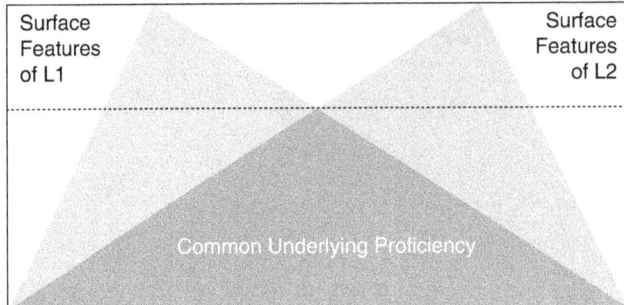

Figure 11.1 Surface features of different languages and common underlying proficiency
Source: Cummins (1984).

EAL learners benefit from using all their languages in challenging, curriculum-based learning to develop the strong English skills they need for academic study.

Learners use the full range of their linguistic and cultural resources to communicate in their wider lives, as we saw in the vignettes, and it is important to make sure that classroom literacy tasks are designed to welcome and reflect those experiences – especially because multilingual learners are likely to have communicative skills in advance of their English language literacy. They may be 'biliterate' (Datta, 2007), and have access to print literacy skills in other languages, or they may have experience of developing and articulating ideas in ways that are unfamiliar to those of us educated in the UK system. One way to look at this is to see how learners' identities become 'sedimented' (Rowsell & Pahl, 2007) in the texts they produce. Noham's discussion of petrol in his Maths lesson, for example, shows clearly how his earlier experiences are part of his learning. These will become fainter over time, as Ms Cartwright works with him to make meanings around the curriculum concepts (as Manny Vazquez does in the first case study, with images to generate talk and ideas around the curriculum concept of metaphor). We might expect that his formative experiences will always be part of his subject literacy, though, and by making these an explicit and valued part of classroom activities, teachers can use them as a base for further literacy development.

BICS and CALP

Cummins (1979, 2001) proposed two terms to describe the types of activities learners might encounter in the classroom. The first describes everyday English, or 'basic interpersonal communication skills' (BICS). The second describes the more challenging, curriculum-based academic skills as cognitive academic language proficiency' (CALP). It is important to note how 'cognitive', 'academic' and 'language' are brought together here: language and thinking are inseparable and are best learned in the context of the subject curriculum. Although they are often presented as distinct categories, everyday and academic language tend to be interwoven and students are exposed to both together in the classroom. It is also worth noting that 'everyday' language is not necessarily simpler or easier to understand: the context and the learner's experience with different ways of using language are both significant. We need to make sure that every lesson – including withdrawal and support sessions – include a rich range of language and cognitive challenge so that the students develop the language, skills and understanding to participate fully in the subject.

The teacher's role in this can be understood in terms of context and cognitive demand. This is illustrated in Figure 11.2. Cummins argued that the level of cognitive challenge was connected to the amount of context given in a task. He conceptualised these as four quadrants (see Figure 11.2), although again we should note that these represent a continuum and not separate activities. The teacher's task, he suggested, is to gradually reduce the amount of contextual support given in the classroom while also increasing the cognitive challenge of the learning activities. In other words, to move learners from high context but low demand (A) towards high demand and low context (D).

High context/low demand activities (A) include, for example, giving instructions for a task, matching exercises or retelling sequences of events. These rely primarily on non-linguistic cues, and the items to be explained, matched or retold give a great deal of context for the task. As the cognitive demand increases, and while the level of context is still relatively high (B), activities might involve generalising from a set of

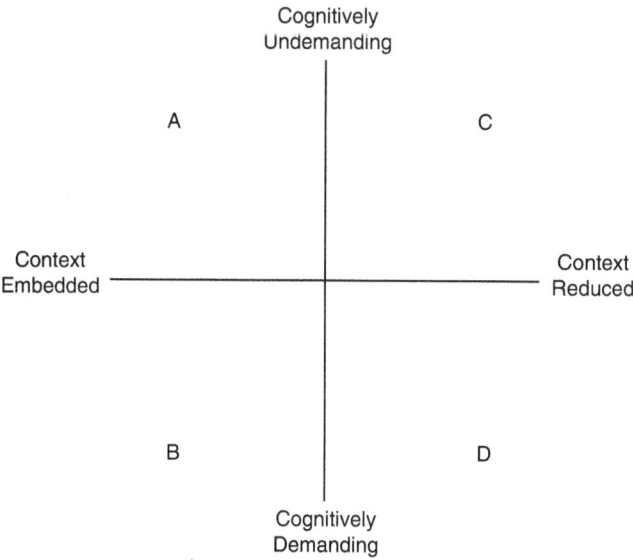

Figure 11.2 The Cummins quadrants
Source: Cummins (1984).

examples, summarising or comparing and contrasting. Activities that are cognitively challenging but less reliant on the context of the task (D) often make greater use of linguistic cues, such as arguing a case from a series of written extracts (common in History), interpreting results (common in Science) or analysing a text (common in English). It is less common that we would want to use activities with low challenge and low contextual support (C), but some valuable activities (such as practising handwriting in a new script) can be placed here.

CUP, BICS/CALP and Changing Learner Profiles

We can make several further observations based on the research in Part 1. The first is that the quadrants are not static: 'cognitively demanding' means different things at different ages. For example, older learners have an advantage in CALP because it is easier to apply analytical thinking as you get older. These do not apply to BICS which, taking into account children's developmental stage and experience of English, are not much affected by age. New arrivals from five to 15 all develop conversational skills in the first year or two, even though their academic language will take much longer to develop and will need targeted support.

The second observation is that the linguistic and cognitive demands of an activity are tied to one another. When work is cognitively demanding, it is harder for learners to extend or consolidate their language. The brain only has so much capacity to process complex tasks at any one moment: recall how much is happening already as we proceduralise and automatise new language (see Chapter 7). This means that part of the teacher's job is to help learners balance these competing demands. We can support challenging subject learning by reducing the linguistic demands (allowing more L1 use, for example, or using visuals to generate language). To maintain the linguistic challenge, in contrast, we can lower the cognitive demands of the task (for example, by allowing more time, more peer support and more context to support understanding). When learners get stuck we don't always need to help them directly with the language or subject material. Instead, we can help with the other part of the language–content equation, reducing the burden and supporting learners to achieve more highly.

Chapter Review

This chapter looked at several related theories from the work of Jim Cummins, an influential researcher of bilingual education. The first is the common underlying proficiency (CUP), which recognises that our different languages are underpinned by a common set of linguistic resources. Development in each language supports proficiency in the other, so using L1 to build understanding of curriculum concepts will also benefit learners' academic English. We also looked at a distinction between basic interpersonal communication skills (BICS) and cognitive academic language proficiency (CALP). Learners develop conversational fluency quite quickly but the ability to use language for cognitively challenging tasks takes much longer to emerge. We can support learners by ensuring that they are engaged with challenging work, varying the amount of context available in classroom tasks as a way of managing the cognitive and linguistic demands of learning. This approach is particularly useful because it helps us to move away from a deficit view of bilingual learners: although their L2 proficiency may be limited, it is not necessarily related to their conceptual development. Using the students' full repertoire – their first languages and their prior experiences – allows us to bring out the full extent of their abilities and to engage them in challenging academic work.

What We Found in Chapter 11

This chapter examined two theories based on the work of Jim Cummins: the common underlying proficiency (CUP), and the balance between basic interpersonal communicative skills (BICS) and cognitive academic language proficiency (CALP). The main points were:

- Our different languages are underpinned by a common underlying proficiency with language. Development in each language supports the other. This is a strong argument for including learners' first languages in the classroom.
- We can make a distinction between everyday and academic language, but we recognise that they do not occur in isolation. In the classroom, students are exposed to and use both.
- The cognitive challenge of an activity is related to the amount of context given.
- We can vary classroom activities to promote higher level language output or higher levels of cognitive challenge.

Taken together, these provide a powerful way to connect subject learning and language development for bilingual pupils.

Where Can I Go Next?

A great deal has been written about **conversational and academic language**. A good place to start is a book by Jim Cummins (2000), called *Language, Power and Pedagogy*. It puts BICS and CALP in a broader context and also addresses several of the criticisms made of this framework. You can also find a short video of Cummins talking about academic language on YouTube: https://youtu.be/qy4vSK4_n6c (a longer video, called 'What do school leaders need to know about students learning the school language?', can be found at https://youtu.be/czOsfsDwfQQ). Jeff MacSwan has been a notable critic and his 2000 paper on the threshold hypothesis is well worth reading.

From a related perspective, **cognitive load theory** has much to offer our discussion of cognitive demands and context. Originally proposed in 1988 by John Sweller, it has seen something of a resurgence of late. There is a free-to-access summary in *Impact*, the journal of the Chartered College of Teaching. A more recent review is provided by Sweller in a 2011 book chapter.

12 Oracy: Talking and Learning

EAL learners need a strong foundation of oral language to support their written language, as well as the development of subject concepts. This chapter discusses what 'oracy' is and what role it plays in learning.

Classrooms are talkative places. Teachers talk to students, students talk to the teacher and to each other; even silent work is recognisable by the muted whisper of even more talk. Used effectively, talk promotes understanding, allowing learners to organise their ideas and find the language to express them. Used badly, it becomes a distraction that contributes little to what learners know and can do. So how do we promote good talk, and what does it do for EAL learners?

What Is Oracy?

What we are looking for is oracy, 'the ability to articulate ideas, develop understanding and engage with others through spoken language' (Voice 21, n.d.). Oracy can be understood as the ability to communicate effectively; in this sense, it is often fostered in debate clubs and classroom discussions. It can also be understood as the skill that underpins speaking, as literacy is to reading and numeracy is to mathematics. In this sense, oracy is the practice of organising your ideas through spoken language. For EAL pupils it has another dimension: oracy is a way to organise your *language*, trying out different phrases and structures, checking what works and what needs changing, before you commit to particular forms. It is a practical realisation of the interaction and output hypotheses, as learners experiment with their language use, get implicit and explicit feedback, and notice the gap between what they can say now and what they need to say to get their meaning across. Oracy is valuable for everyone, but since it supports language acquisition too it is especially important for bilingual pupils.

There is perhaps a danger that oracy comes across as another fad or initiative, something that sounds sensible but gets pushed to the bottom of an already full in-tray. I suggest that it is more than that: for EAL learners who need to reach a high standard of written English in a short space of time, spoken language is the key. It works so well for EAL specialists because it brings together several existing principles of effective practice but is flexible enough to work in the very diverse settings that characterise our field. Talk requires input, output and meaningful interaction – so it already meets our 'basic formula' for language learning. It brings opportunities for both implicit and explicit feedback, as learners try to get their meaning across to others. And – perhaps most usefully of all – it allows us to incorporate first languages seamlessly into the English-medium classroom. Pupils can work towards a piece of writing in English but talk to a partner in any language while they do so, perhaps presenting their rough work *mostly* (but not entirely) in the target language. The final production can be in English, but it will benefit from the scaffolding of the learner's L1 knowledge and existing skills.

From Talking to Writing

Pauline Gibbons (2002: Chapter 3) describes how language changes as it moves from informal group talk to a written report. This example, consisting of four sentences, is taken from a classroom Science experiment:

(1) 'this ... no, it doesn't go ... it doesn't move ... try that ... yes, it does ... a bit ... that won't ... won't work, it's not metal ... these are the best ... going really fast'
(2) 'we tried a pin ... a pencil sharpener ... some iron filings and a piece of plastic ... the magnet didn't attract the pin'
(3) 'Our experiment was to find out what a magnet attracted. We discovered that a magnet attracts some kinds of metal. It attracted the iron filings, but not the pin.'
(4) 'Magnetic attraction occurs only between ferrous metals.'

The first example comes from the talk of a group of 10-year-old students while they were conducting the experiment together. The second was spoken by one of the children about the experiment, reporting to the class. The third was from the same student's written report, and the final example comes from a children's encyclopaedia.

These four examples recognisably refer to the same event, but they are very different from each other. Only the third and fourth would likely be accepted in a student's writing, but it is very difficult for learners to produce that kind of language without going through the earlier stages too. What we see is a 'mode continuum', from the kind of spoken language that is commonly found in face-to-face interactions to written language that conforms to the genre of scientific reports. The first example is impossible to understand without the context: it uses direct references (*this, that, these*) and grammatically incomplete phrases that only make sense alongside the action. In the second example, the speaker gives more detail (naming things and using more precise verbs) because they are recounting the experience to an audience and they do not have the objects in front of them. In the written recount there is even less shared context: processes must be stated clearly (*we discovered that*) and context established (*our experiment was to*). The encyclopaedia entry is less concerned with context: it describes universal properties (*magnetic attraction*) and larger categories (*ferrous metals*).

There are several ways in which we can support effective talk so that learners can develop their ideas and the language needed to express them. First, we can do a lot to improve the quality of interaction between pupils, and between pupils and the teacher, so that classroom talk is maximally effective in developing both language and content. Second, we can design classroom activities so that oral communication is essential – and not just encouraged. Plentiful, meaningful, purposeful and participatory talk is the bedrock of good reading and writing.

The Quality of Interaction Matters

It's not just any talking that makes a difference – the *quality* of classroom talk is important. This happens in different arenas: private, informal talk between pupils, when they are engaged with an activity that requires collaboration and the exchange of meanings, creates the space for ideas to be explored and language practised. As talk becomes less private and more formal – for example, as pupils report to the class and then write up their work – they are pushed to focus on accuracy and the quality of their expression. The teacher plays a vital role in organising talk and in stretching learners to use more challenging language, but too often this has the unintended consequence of closing down opportunities for communication. Take this example:

Teacher:	So, can you read question two, Junya?	(Initiation)
Student:	(*reading from book*) Where was Sabina when this happened?	(Response)
Teacher:	Right, yes, where was Sabina.	(Feedback)
	In Unit 10, where was she?	(Initiation)
Student:	Er, go out …	(Response)
Teacher:	She went out, yes.	(Feedback)

(Walsh, 2015: 17)

Interactions like these are known as 'IRF' or 'IRE' exchanges, because they are built up from an initiation, a response, and feedback or an evaluation. They are very common – studies suggest that the majority of teacher-student interactions may follow this pattern – and they can be effective in developing knowledge through guiding questions. However, they can lead the teacher to dominate classroom talk (because for every one thing a student says, the teacher says two) and they can narrow the range of expressions that students can produce (because they are primarily responding to the teacher's prompts).

EAL pupils learn the communicative rules of the classroom very quickly, especially the unspoken norms that govern who can say what. Walsh argues, though, that we can make a conscious effort to change those norms. The 'prime responsibility for what is said in the classroom', he argues, 'lies with the teacher':

> Learners take their cues from the teacher and [when IRF sequences dominate] rarely initiate a response. Their role, one which they are socialised into from a very early age, is to answer questions, respond to prompts, and so on. (Walsh, 2015: 20)

Oracy needs to be planned into the curriculum and the lesson. Sometimes this will involve the teacher talking more – and a major review of the evidence (Saunders & O'Brien, 2006) suggested that many learners *need* to interact with the teacher to develop oracy – but it will also involve planned peer interaction around meaningful tasks. We saw (in Chapter 7) that peers are very good at giving feedback on spoken language – it's something that happens naturally in interaction – and working with one another means that they have much more practice in using subject language to communicate. However, increased peer interaction does not, by itself, appear to increase proficiency in academic language or academic achievement. Instead, we need to plan for group work that maximises opportunities for practice (input, output, interaction, feedback) and is organised around a task so that talk is meaningful and purposeful.

How Can We Promote Oracy?

Ideally, we would plan for oracy to develop over several activities in a sequence, so that learners can begin working on their ideas informally – with partners and using their full linguistic repertoire – and gradually build up to more complex use of oral language. Good tasks have a number of characteristics. Gibbons (2002: Chapter 2) suggests that they work best when:

- Instructions are clear and explicit.
- Talk is necessary, not just encouraged.
- There is a clear outcome.
- The task is cognitively appropriate to the learners.
- The task is integrated into the curriculum.
- All children are involved.
- Students have time to complete the task.
- Students know how to work in groups.

Take the first of these as an example: How can we set up tasks so that our instructions are clear and explicit? This begins in the planning phase, choosing tasks that engage students with ideas worth expressing (such as realistic curriculum tasks), that are pitched at the right cognitive level (not just their current level of English proficiency) and that have a clear outcome or goal (beyond just encouraging talk, for example, or completing a worksheet based on the activity). The teacher might introduce the task using a number of modes: images, a short video, verbally or through a short reading. Using several modes together means that EAL learners have more opportunity to pick up on the message and greater exposure to the relevant language. Talk can be planned in here, giving learners a few minutes to discuss the task with a partner (in any language, but it is important that the partner can provide a good model of language) and to formulate questions. You might ask a student to confirm back to you what they need to do, or to comment on an example piece of work. Key instructions, including the time limit, can go on the board so that learners don't have to rely on their memory while their brains are engaged with the task itself. Regular reviews throughout the lesson allow the students to engage in purposeful talk with their teacher, which research has shown is an important part of developing oracy and language proficiency.

Chapter Review

Effective talk underpins both academic achievement and academic language proficiency. This chapter began by looking at the different definitions of 'oracy', finding that it meant both the ability to communicate effectively and the practice of organising your ideas through talk. For EAL pupils, it is especially important because talk allows pupils to organise their language as well as their ideas. We then looked at the 'mode continuum', seeing how language changes as it moves from informal, highly contextualised speaking to more formal, decontextualised writing. We linked this to the important role the teacher plays in balancing the linguistic and cognitive demands of tasks. We recognised that the more context we provide, the more support learners have, but also that we should reduce this 'scaffolding' as they progress to more demanding tasks.

We found that the quality, and not just the quantity, of spoken interaction was important. Much classroom talk is actually made up of teacher-led 'initiation, response, feedback/evaluation' patterns, which limit the opportunities for learners to engage in oracy development even if there seems to be a lot of talk happening in the classroom. Finally, we reviewed some key principles for developing effective, talk-rich tasks. These highlighted the importance of subject content to language development: oracy underpins a range of language skills, including the ability to read and write to a high level.

What We Found in Chapter 12

This chapter examined oracy and emphasised the importance of talk for language and subject learning. The main points were:

- Oracy is the skill that underpins speaking, as literacy is to reading and numeracy is to mathematics. For EAL pupils it has another dimension: oracy is a way to organise your *language* before committing to writing.
- We can see classroom talk on a continuum, from the high-context, informal, spoken-like language used in small groups to the low-context, more formal, written-like language used when reporting to the class or writing up work.
- The quality of classroom talk and interaction matters: more isn't necessarily better. Learners take their cues from the teacher; where teacher-led interaction dominates, students quickly learn that their job is to respond rather than to use language to participate in the curriculum.
- There are many ways in which we can promote oracy in the classroom.

Where Can I Go Next?

There is a great **tradition of oracy research and teaching** in the UK. A good place to start is the Oracy Cambridge website (https://oracycambridge.org), which includes a rich library of ideas, reports and resources – including benchmarks and a skills framework to help you introduce oracy in your school. It is led by Neil Mercer, a leading scholar of children's spoken language and literacy. Readers in Wales might be particularly interested in the report on Oracy in the Welsh Curriculum.

Voice 21 (https://voice21.org) is a **national oracy charity** that also produces a lot of useful evidence-based material for schools. They approach it more to develop verbal reasoning, so for L2 development we need to synthesise it with the literature in Part 1.

They also run a programme to become a 'Voice 21 Oracy School' and embed the approach across the curriculum.

Collaborative learning activities can be very beneficial for developing oracy, and Stewart Scott maintains a wealth of resources on the Collaborative Learning website (http://www.collaborativelearning.org). See also a review of collaborative learning generally by the Education Endowment Fund (https://educationendowmentfoundation.org.uk/evidence-summaries/teaching-learning-toolkit/collaborative-learning).

13 Reading in a New Language

The ability to read confidently and effectively is a cornerstone of academic success. This chapter looks at some of the key considerations for helping bilingual learners become successful readers.

Reading is a complex activity. It involves a range of skills that can be taught and practised, but also relies on the readers' experience of similar texts and their familiarity with the content being described. The range of their experiences and linguistic resources means that there are several differences between how bilingual and monolingual pupils learn to read. This chapter explores some of the most important, beginning with the role of oracy and phonics, and then looking at the specific skills involved in reading and the particular importance of vocabulary, before discussing some useful strategies for developing confident bilingual readers.

Oracy, Multilingualism and Literacy

We need to take a more expansive view of how bilinguals learn to read. Compared with their monolingual peers, they have a wider range of linguistic and cultural resources at their disposal, and experience of communicating in different settings. They have often learned to read in at least one other language, whether that was in school, through their faith or at home, and this experience of literacy means that they should make very quick progress in reading. Too often, though, they do not. One of the main reasons for this is that we need to approach literacy differently for EAL pupils, recognising and drawing on their existing resources rather than starting over in English. This is widely recognised in the research literature where, as Riches and Genesee (2006: 64) note, relatively few studies look at EAL pupils' literacy without making reference to their first languages. So what can we do to develop young multilinguals as confident, successful readers?

In the previous chapter we saw that oracy is an important precursor to literacy. Effective EAL teaching draws on them both together, using planned, purposeful talk so that learners have the space to organise their ideas before encountering them in written text. Using the learners' first languages brings a double advantage: it allows them to access concepts that were originally laid down through that language, and it supports the development of the L1 in its own right. This is true at all levels of proficiency and at all different ages, although the way it is done will necessarily vary. For advanced bilingual learners, the first language can scaffold very high achievement: when you read the first case study (which follows this chapter), imagine the students discussing tethers and family obligations in L1, for example, and how that might open the door to deeper comprehension and generate more sophisticated ideas ready for expression in English. At lower levels of proficiency, the use of L1 can bridge gaps in vocabulary so that learners need not stop every time they meet an unfamiliar word. This allows them to participate fully, for example by asking questions of their peers (using L1 and English) that they would struggle to formulate in English alone.

We should also use our knowledge of bilingual literacies to advocate for our learners. We know that vocabulary knowledge is an essential component of successful reading, for example, and that early reading comprehension builds on children's implicit knowledge of grammar, of sound-spelling correspondences and of how texts work in their social context. These all develop in L1, which shares space (at first) with the new language in the child's store of vocabulary. Yet when children are assessed for reading difficulties, their apparent lack of English vocabulary or seeming inability to recognise plausible nonsense words is taken as evidence that they are falling behind. These assumptions need to be challenged, because they are based on a partial understanding of what is happening when young bilinguals learn. 'It now seems clear', argues Grabe (2008: 129), 'that L2 reading is not just someone learning to read in another language; rather, L2 reading is a case of learning to read with languages'.

Reading as a Skill

Reading is both a social practice and a technical skill. That skill can be broken down into five areas:

(1) automatic recognition of letters and words;
(2) knowledge of clause- and sentence-level grammar;
(3) knowledge of information selection, structuring and presentation for different types of text;
(4) relevant content and background knowledge in context; and
(5) knowledge and skills in using different strategies.
   (Adapted from Leung, 2001: 8–13)

Before we can become fluent readers, we need to recognise letters and words at sight (that is, our visual processing skills need to become automatised). Children whose first language uses the Roman alphabet will find this easier, but the approach is the same for all children. They need masses of exposure to letters and words, alongside their spoken forms (primarily so that words are linked to meanings, but also to develop awareness of sound-spelling connections). Ask pupils about the letters and words in their surroundings, and use lots of recognition and matching games, flashcards and targeted practice to help learners make quick progress.

Similar principles apply to the teaching of clause- and sentence-level grammar: learners need to read for pleasure and purpose, with explicit attention drawn to key patterns. This can be through classroom talk or through comprehension activities, such as those that reorganise scrambled sentences or sort chunks of a story into the right sequence. Missing word (cloze) activities, where a certain type of word has been removed (e.g. all verbs, all prepositions) can help learners focus on specific features. These can be made easier if the options are given alongside the task. We might also draw attention to the way that tenses are marked (e.g. '-ed' endings), the normal order of words in a sentence, the parts of speech (e.g. noun, verb) and the words we use to connect ideas (e.g. conjunctions such as *and*, *but* and *because*). The principle here is that these grammatical patterns are learned more quickly where learners want to know the meaning, so building lesson activities around meaning-making is more effective than organising learning around grammar points.

Learners also need to know how texts are commonly structured. The way that information is organised in written text can be opaque to EAL learners, even if they have sufficient grammar and vocabulary for the task, and it is easy to take our implicit knowledge of these genre conventions for granted. Any activities that draw learners' attention to text organisation and the language typical of different genres will be effective. DARTs (directed activities related to texts) and graphic organisers, for example, are especially useful. Similarly, activities that involve reorganising or reconstructing texts (e.g. jumbled paragraphs, texts with connecting language removed, gap-fills with vocabulary in different registers) will also help. It is important to note that genres are not universal, so pupils who have studied in another education system will need explicit teaching of the features to help them transfer their knowledge to a new language.

As well as their knowledge and experience of different text types, learners need good subject knowledge and the skills to manage their reading process. We look at how to develop disciplinary literacy in Chapter 15.

What About Phonics?

Will teaching phonics help EAL pupils to read? The answer is … to an extent. We need to be clear about what we mean by phonics, how it affects bilingual learners specifically and how it fits into the broader process of learning to read.

Phonics is a form of explicit instruction that seeks to develop children's phonological awareness (their understanding of the link between sounds and spellings). It came to particular prominence with the introduction of the Primary phonics screening check in 2012 (DfE, 2012), although teaching sounds and spellings has been part of Primary education (and EAL teaching) for much longer. It is important to separate 'phonics' (the explicit instruction) from phonological awareness (the underlying ability). The latter is an important part of learning to decode text and of learning to read. Bilingual children generally have very good phonological awareness and decoding skills but still perform less well than monolingual pupils on measures of reading comprehension. This suggests that phonics instruction alone will not be sufficient.

Other factors also underlie EAL pupils' reading success. Two of the most significant are oral language and vocabulary development: both are affected by the child's early experience with language and both can be supported in the classroom. Oral language is important because it is used to process written language. Bilingual pupils, as discussed in the previous chapter, will have less exposure to English in early childhood (because part of their exposure will be to other languages) and this may affect their early reading development. Creating opportunities for purposeful talk in the classroom will also support reading.

Vocabulary is similarly important. A broad and deep vocabulary (which would include academic and everyday language, collocations and figurative language) is essential for successful reading. Learners need to know what words mean (semantic knowledge) and how they go together (for example, in collocations): decoding individual words is a necessary but not sufficient component of reading. It is important to remember that bilingual learners are developing vocabularies in two (or more) languages. They tend to have smaller vocabularies *in each language* than their monolingual peers, but this does not mean that we should have lower expectations of their reading overall. Instead, we should look for opportunities to promote vocabulary learning (including by explicitly teaching words and phrases) to support reading. It seems likely that vocabulary is the most significant contributor to reading ability for bilingual children.

There is also a risk that overly focusing on one technique – such as phonics – will mean that we lose focus on everything else we should be doing to support EAL pupils to become successful readers. Bilingual children tend to have very good phonological awareness and decoding skills, so while phonics may play a useful part in EAL provision, it should not overshadow our consistent focus on masses of exposure to language and rich opportunities to use it for meaningful communication.

Vocabulary

Vocabulary is a significant predictor of reading success, so time invested in developing EAL learners' vocabulary knowledge is always time well spent. The principles for doing so are fairly straightforward, but can be adapted to suit the pupils' existing language knowledge.

The first principle is that words have friends. They are connected to each other on different levels, from their usage to their grammar and meaning. Take the short sentence, 'they ran to the station', as an example. It introduces learners to one category of words that take an irregular past ('ran', like 'swam' – a morphosyntactic pattern) and another that uses a common but tricky pronunciation: -tion pronounced /ʃən/ ('station', like 'attention' and 'presentation' – a phonological-orthographic pattern). 'Station' is also an example of a transport word – a semantic field that can be extended by introducing other words with similar meanings. We can use substitution tables such as that in Figure 13.1 to help learners extend their knowledge of these patterns.

Substitution is especially effective when it is left to the student to do. You might give an example sentence and ask intermediate learners to complete the table by finding

They	ran	to	the station
We	swam	from	the airport
The people who love grammar		around	Liverpool docks

Figure 13.1 A substitution table

other irregular past verbs in a text, or by finding all the transport words and the prepositions that go with them. At lower levels of proficiency, the students can be asked to circle words of a certain type and to draw a line from each to the next (a technique known as 'vocabulary chains', which works well because it allows learners to engage with text that they can't yet read confidently). Advanced learners can look at increasingly nuanced patterns (see Chapter 15 on disciplinary language).

Pre-teaching vocabulary is a similarly effective way to support reading. To be effective, it needs to be linked to the subject content in both words and meaning. Lists of key vocabulary are of little use because they don't allow students to connect new words with the ones they already know or the patterns that they are part of. If we present the new words in texts, with all the diagrams and other resources that come with them, then students will have a much better chance of connecting language and subject concepts. Even better, we should teach words in phrases, talking explicitly about how they are constructed and what they mean – especially in Science and Mathematics, where Latin, Greek and Arabic roots mean that many specialist terms have very close equivalents in other languages. Gap-fill, reconstruction, sorting and matching activities are especially helpful in pre-teaching vocabulary, as are questions about meaning and asking students to say why they chose a certain word.

We can break down academic vocabulary in two further ways: by its use in subject disciplines and by its relative frequency. Isabel Beck and colleagues (2013) have categorised academic vocabulary in three tiers, from words in everyday usage (Tier 1) to those found in many disciplines (Tier 2) and those that are specific to a single discipline (Tier 3) (see Figure 13.2). Words may seem to appear in several tiers: for example, 'a <u>mean</u>, unfriendly person' (Tier 1) and the 'arithmetic <u>mean</u>' in Mathematics (Tier 3). These can often cause difficulties for EAL learners, who may be familiar with the everyday meaning but not realise that the word also has a specialist or academic application. Words in Tiers 2 and 3 need to be taught explicitly, as Sarah Fowkes does in the second case study (which follows Chapter 15).

Another way to think about words is their frequency. After taking the meaning of the word into account (especially where a work has an abstract or multiple meanings), the more frequently we encounter words in context the more likely we are to learn them and to be able to use them ourselves. This is the basis of the academic word list, or AWL, created by Avril Coxhead. She examined a corpus of over 3.5 million words of academic text, in a range of disciplines, to produce a set of 570 word families. These exclude the 2000 most frequently used words in English, which students are likely to be familiar with because they encounter them so often, and account for 10% of all academic vocabulary

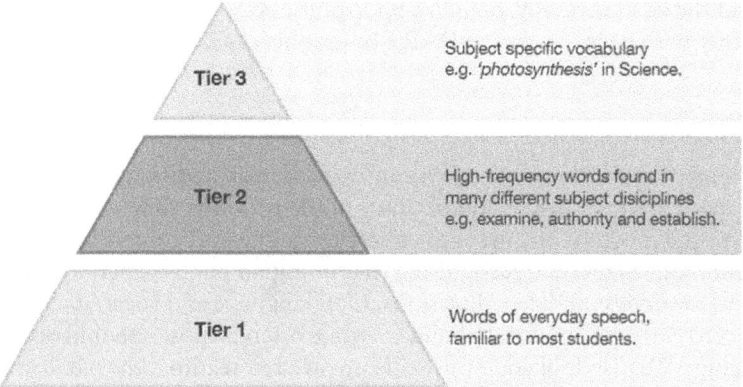

Figure 13.2 Vocabulary tiers, as portrayed by the Education Endowment Fund (2019) based on the work of Beck *et al.* (2013).

(see Coxhead, 2000, for technical details, and https://www.wgtn.ac.nz/lals/resources/academicwordlist/information for more general information and the list itself). These are useful resources in developing strong academic vocabularies and confident readers.

Strategies for Developing Confident Readers

There are two things to prioritise as EAL pupils develop their reading skills. The first is to ensure that learners have rich and sustained exposure to written text, especially in the genres that they will encounter at school. Any reading is good, and there is evidence that reading for pleasure supports literacy development for all pupils, but the specialised registers and vocabulary of academic text mean that much of the vocabulary they need does not occur frequently enough in other genres. The second thing is to teach vocabulary and reading strategies explicitly. Common patterns of word formation (such as the negative prefixes in *unnecessary, irregular and illegal*) and usage (such as the ways in which information is organised in different genres) are not obvious and need to be made transparent for learners. Every lesson, in every subject, should include rich vocabulary teaching. This will benefit all pupils as they become fluent writers in their discipline, but it will especially benefit bilingual pupils.

As learners encounter a text, they draw on their expectations of its content and their knowledge of similar texts they have encountered in the past. Again, we can make this explicit. As well as pre-teaching vocabulary and ensuring that new terms are introduced in rich context, we can activate learners' prior knowledge by asking questions about the content and genre. Any activity that recalls the topic will be beneficial, but especially those that identify the overarching concepts and relevant examples or details, so that learners have a context for the knowledge they are about to encounter. Asking students to predict the content, both after this initial lead-in and at different points during the lesson, keeps students engaged with the text and helps to refine the mental map they activated at the beginning of the lesson. Finally, regular opportunities to clarify, summarise and ask questions, whether with peers or using a DART or graphic organiser, will help too.

Chapter Review

This chapter has examined what it means to read in an additional language. We began by linking reading to the discussion of oracy in the previous chapter, finding that structured talk is an important precursor to effective reading and comprehension. We looked briefly at phonics instruction, recognising that bilingual pupils generally have very good phonological awareness and decoding skills. Oral language and vocabulary are important contributors to early reading, and phonics – while often helpful – should not overshadow EAL pedagogy. We also looked at the skills involved in reading, the particular considerations for EAL learners and the vital role played by vocabulary. Finally, we looked at some strategies for developing confident readers. The idea that we are 'apprenticing' students into our subject disciplines, rather than teaching them the language they need to understand factual content, was again a valuable one. It shifts the focus: rather than emphasising gaps in the learners' understanding, it allows us to look for ways to make the language and practices of our subjects transparent, to share what we do, and how, and why, with our learners. The next chapter explores such disciplinary thinking further.

What We Found in Chapter 13

This chapter examined reading in a new language. The key points were:

- Oracy underpins reading (see previous chapter).
- We need to take a more expansive view of how bilinguals learn to read. They draw on all their language resources and experiences, so they need a different teaching approach.
- Reading is a skill with a series of clear sub-skills. We can teach and promote these to support EAL pupils to achieve highly.

Where Can I Go Next?

There are several useful websites for **practical tools**, including graphic organisers, dictogloss and DARTs (directed activities related to texts). The best for EAL is The Bell Foundation's 'Great Ideas' page: https://www.bell-foundation.org.uk/eal-programme/guidance/effective-teaching-of-eal-learners/great-ideas. The Freyer Model (a long-standing graphic organiser) may also be useful (see https://www.theconfidentteacher.com/2018/04/vocabulary-knowledge-and-the-frayer-model).

On **phonics**, see the research review by Victoria Murphy in the first issue of the *EAL Journal*. It is free to NALDIC members: https://naldic.org.uk/publications/eal-journal.

There is a wealth of research on **vocabulary development and reading**. A good review is Paul Nation and Susan Hunston's (2013) book, *Learning Vocabulary in*

Another Language. Another, with a more practical focus and activities to support the content, is Norbert Schmitt and Diane Schmitt's (2020) *Vocabulary in Language Teaching*. A different perspective is offered by Do Coyle and Oliver Meyer (2021) in their book on pluriliteracies teaching, which argues for a deeper engagement with concepts.

Gibbons (2002) is one of the most accessible introductions to how we can **scaffold reading** in a new language, and her short book is highly recommended as a starting point. On reading, Chapter 7 ('Knowing a Word') of Nation and Hunston's (2013) book is very relevant. On **literacy in secondary schools**, see the recent report by the Education Endowment Fund (2019), which recommends seven principles for improving literacy teaching.

Case Study 1: Teaching Poetry in Year 11

Manny Vazquez is an EAL teacher at St Gregory's Catholic Science College and a consultant at Hounslow Language Service. In this case study, he describes techniques for scaffolding a particularly challenging concept – metaphor – for older EAL learners.

This piece on EAL practice focuses on two key ideas relevant to the EAL classroom context: first, the oft-quoted mantra about the importance of using visuals when working with EAL students; and second, the fact that even in the well-differentiated lesson in a mainstream English class, quite often there is still a pressing need to insert additional steps into the scaffolding, unpacking it a little more, in order to help EAL students with their responses to the text. It is my hope that this piece can also help the EAL specialist have a more meaningful dialogue with their colleagues in the English department in terms of approaches to what can sometimes appear quite challenging texts.

This lesson focuses on the teaching of a poem called 'Mother any distance' by Simon Armitage (reprinted with permission from Faber & Faber Ltd). The opening two lines state the poem's premise. At its most literal, the poem is about the speaker needing help setting up a new house. Specifically, the speaker needs another person there to hold onto the other end of a tape measure while the speaker goes around and measures various parts of the house. However, there is of course a whole world of meaning beyond this literal set-up, as the poem is really about exploring the enduring power of the relationships between mothers and their children:

Mother any distance

1   Mother, any distance greater than a single span
2   requires a second pair of hands.

94　Part 2: Language Across the Curriculum

3　You come to help me measure windows, pelmets, doors,
4　the acres of the walls, the prairies of the floors.

5　You at the zero-end, me with the spool of tape, recording
6　length, reporting metres, centimetres back to base, then leaving
7　up the stairs, the line still feeding out, unreeling
8　years between us. Anchor. Kite.

9　I space-walk through the empty bedrooms, climb
10　the ladder to the loft, to breaking point, where something
11　has to give;
12　two floors below your fingertips still pinch
13　the last one-hundredth of an inch ... I reach
14　towards a hatch that opens on an endless sky
15　to fall or fly

As the poem progresses, we start to see the symbolic significance of the tape, noticing the way that it seems to represent the mother-child bond. Key images and metaphors to explore with students would typically be: the measuring tape as an anchor between mother and son; a kite finally being released as it is untethered; words such as 'acres' and 'prairies' exaggerating the size of the task, words which relate to measurements of land and not walls; the final letting go in the last four lines as the mother can no longer hold on to the tape; and, of course, the final image where we are left to ponder whether the son will successfully thrive (or not), having finally broken free.

One powerful image which serves as an excellent point of discussion and exploration with students relates to Line 9: 'I space-walk through the empty bedrooms ...'. The English department PowerPoint included an image like this one:

Figure CS1.1 A spaceman

The title of this slide was 'Which line matches this image?' In terms of differentiation, the image provides great scope for discussions around tethers, umbilical cords, how far can one reach, 'what if' scenarios, and so on. This image would also be a good example of the need to use visuals to help make meaning with EAL students in mind. Indeed, when teaching this poem to a very able top set Year 11 class, this image allowed an exploration of the words 'empty bedrooms', making the point that poets craft every single word. Similarly, the deliberate use of the adjective 'empty' suggests the son now has to start filling up his own life; both were more than enough to help very able students make meaning.

However, when working in contexts where we know EAL students are going to struggle more with their written outcomes, powerful visuals such as the one above (and related discussions) will not be enough. For such students, the key is to provide them with choices where they have to verbalise ideas around the images. In this case a second image was added, of a new-born baby still attached to its mother by an umbilical cord. The students were presented with both images – baby and spaceman – at the same time. They were then given a number of statements and had to decide whether they applied to one or the other image, or both. Some examples of statements were:

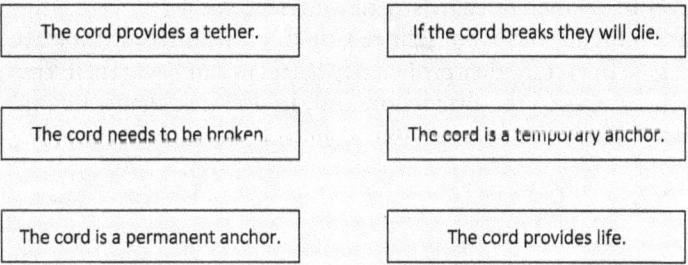

Immediately following this activity, the students were asked to compare the image of the mother holding onto one end of the tape and her son at the other end with the two images of the baby and spaceman. The students were then invited to verbalise the mother and son image using the statements they had just discussed and matched to the baby/spaceman images.

Quite often on training courses we hear the mantra of using visuals with EAL learners. But this is only half the story. The same principle that applies to the use of graphic organisers, or key visuals, should almost always apply to the use of visuals generally: these are not just there for explanatory purposes, but should also be used in a generative way; you need to hook language around them – preferably the kind of language you would be pleased to see in students' written outcomes.

When considering the needs of EAL learners, the lesson may well need that further bit of unpacking, the addition of those extra two steps, in order to help learners make meaning.

Commentary

Manny offers us a powerful example of meaning-making in the classroom. He works very closely with the subject teacher, using the English department's PowerPoint slides and lesson materials but adapting them using principles from his EAL practice. His aim is to generate language – creating 'choices where they have to verbalise ideas around the image' and using images to 'hook language around'.

This fits well with the principles in the previous chapter. Manny gives a lot of time to oracy, getting students to put their ideas into words and generating new ideas through structured talk. The images and the matching activities scaffold learning and create opportunities for learners to compare their own experiences with the curriculum content. The EAL specialist organises and directs the learning, but much of the work is done collaboratively as pupils discuss their responses to the text. This helps them generate more advanced academic language, the kind of language you would be pleased to see in students' written outcomes.

Manny describes this as an opportunity for greater dialogue with subject colleagues and it is clear that these techniques could be adopted into the English teacher's own practice quite easily. By using relatively straightforward techniques that are underpinned by clear principles, he is building up his colleagues' expertise and supporting explicit teaching and language-rich pedagogy across the school (see Part 3). He also supplies a level of challenge that is often missing for advanced bilingual learners. Metaphors are difficult and we might reasonably assume that they are too hard for many EAL pupils. In fact, higher proficiency learners can bring their knowledge of two languages and cultures to the discussion and, in doing so, generate high-quality academic language.

14 Making Meaning in Writing: Field, Tenor and Mode

Our goal is to create confident, purposeful readers and writers. This involves more than skills – it requires an understanding of how meaning is created in its social context. This chapter introduces systemic functional linguistics, an approach to language with meaning-making at its core.

Introducing SFL

Systemic functional linguistics (SFL) is a theory of language that focuses on 'function' – what we can do with language to communicate meaning in the real world. This is a very different approach from the formalism described in Part 1: SFL is not primarily concerned with the rules of syntax and morphology, which describe how grammatically accurate sentences are built up, but instead starts with questions about the choices speakers and writers make as they construct texts. A functional approach recognises the complex reality of teaching EAL. In the words of M.A.K. Halliday, the founding figure in the discipline, there is:

> a real-life contradiction between those two modes of processing language: that of learning it for future use, and that of using it. [Students] can no longer both learn and 'mean it' at the same time. (Halliday, 1990/2003: 141)

EAL pupils, in other words, face a particular challenge because they are learning English as they learn through English. SFL is valuable to us because it gives us tools to manage this contradiction. It focuses on meaning rather than on grammar, on using the language purposefully rather than describing its structure accurately.

SFL begins with the belief that 'language does not passively reflect reality; language actively creates reality' (Halliday, 1990/2003: 145). Our understanding of the world is shaped by the ways in which we use language to describe it. This is especially relevant to curriculum subjects, where knowledge and understanding are created within disciplinary communities that each have well-established patterns of language use. Our understanding of the scientific method, for example, and of concepts such as rigour and objectivity, are intertwined with the way that we write as scientists. Likewise, the skills and aesthetic of literary criticism, our expectations of authorship (and the legal framing of the author's 'moral right' to recognition) and stylistic features such as the authorial voice can all be seen in how we write creatively and as critics. Creating these texts involves making linguistic choices, and these choices both reflect and are sustained by our understanding of our subject. From an SFL perspective, we can analyse those choices both to understand the text and to make those linguistic choices explicit as we apprentice students into our subject disciplines.

Genre and Audience

A key concept in SFL is that texts are produced for a purpose and an audience. Every text carries a message (or multiple messages): it is about *something*, addressed to *someone*, and is designed to have an *effect*. To see what effect this has for EAL learners, we can look at the samples of everyday university-level writing collected by SFL researcher Meg Gebhard. They give a fair sense of what will be expected of learners when they leave school. Here, a student is writing a short email asking to join her class:

> Dear Professor, I am a second year UTS student in the STEP English program. I am very interested in your required EDUC 684 course and I am wondering if I might be able to register despite the fact that SPIRE states that the course is full. I look forward to hearing from you. Sincerely Isabel Johnson (Gebhard, 2019: 76)

The email appears fairly straightforward: the writer introduces herself, gives a little context and then makes her request before signing off in a polite way. These elements, organised in this way, make it recognisably an email request. They also reveal a lot about the writer: she is a confident user of this genre, someone who knows both appropriate phrasing ('Dear Professor', 'I am wondering if I might be able to …', 'Sincerely', and so on) and who knows what is expected of her (the largely informational content, the expression of interest). She positions the tutor as someone who is able to overcome the university bureaucracy ('required' and 'despite the fact that SPIRE states …'), and the closing line ('I look forward to hearing from you') signals that the reader is expected to respond. Different choices could be made about each element: other emails in Gebhard's corpus began with 'Hi Meg' for 'Dear Professor', and included requests such as 'I am wanna register for 684 bc I gotta have it for graduation' rather than 'I am wondering if I might be able to register'. These stylistic choices do not change the genre – it is still an email request – but they have a very different effect on the reader.

Genres, then, are sets of social practices that are expressed in the choices we make about language. In school, we often use genre in a very broad way. We talk about types of text such as 'fiction', 'narrative', 'report', 'argumentative essay' and so on. These categories are a useful way to introduce students to the norms of different text types, but are often too broad to capture the writer's topic, audience and intended effect. To apprentice learners into our subject disciplines, we need to show them *in detail* the choices that writers make and help them to understand the effect their own communicative choices will have on others.

Two Contexts: Culture and Situation

SFL proposes that there are two kinds of learning context that teachers should be aware of. The first is the *context of culture*, our implicit knowledge of 'how things work' that comes from both our experience of texts and from our participation in the communities that produce those texts. EAL learners are likely to have less experience of the types of text we use in an English-medium school, so they will have less implicit knowledge of the kind that Gebhard's email-writing student demonstrated. As EAL specialists, we need to work with colleagues to ensure that students get maximum exposure to relevant texts in a range of genres, that the features of these texts are highlighted and discussed and that learners have support to make informed choices about their own writing. They also need experience of participating in the communities that produce these texts.

Charlotte Bowyer, assistant head at King Ecgbert School in Sheffield, gives a practical example of this. She found that she could get her A Level students to a good standard of writing, especially in the longer paragraph answers needed for the exam, but found it very hard to support them to achieve the highest grades. The problem seemed to stem from the fact that the students needed more exposure to authentic subject writing as well as the technical knowledge to be able to write like historians. 'I never imagined that the solution would come from bringing grammar to the fore of my History teaching', she says, but:

> if we teach students to begin each paragraph with a model sentence-starter [...] then we are setting a limit on their academic writing: they don't sound like historians and will struggle to get the highest level. (Bowyer, 2018: 34)

Bowyer gave her mixed EAL/monolingual class a single lesson on nominalisation (see Chapter 15), using subject-specific examples and vocabulary. She then introduced students to writing on their topic (here, the rise of Stalin) by popular historians such as Simon Sebag Montefiore. The students looked for examples of nominalisation and highlighted how the authors created phrases that acted as 'umbrella terms' for groups of events or concepts – an important part of structuring complex texts in History. After some discussion in class, the students were asked to start writing their own texts, consciously drawing on the examples for inspiration. In this way, the pupils were part of a discourse community with expert writers, drawing on those authors as they found their own voices and using the teacher for support as they developed their own ideas on paper. Bowyer found that the benefit of these strategies lasted – and even found evidence of their new skills in their mock exam papers some months later.

The second learning context is the *context of situation*, the circumstances in which a particular text was produced. This depends not on our implicit knowledge and background experience, but on the topic, on the relationship between author and audience, and on whether the text is spoken or written. In a sense, the difference is between what you bring to the task of writing (context of culture) and how you set about a given writing task (context of situation). In SFL, these situational factors are called *field*, *tenor* and *mode*.

- *Field* is the topic.
- *Tenor* is the relationship between participants (speakers, reader and writer).
- *Mode* is the channel (written or spoken).

Together, these form the *register* of our speaking and writing. All children have experience of different registers; talking with different people about different topics is part of everyday life. This everyday experience is a rich resource for literacy. When children read and talk about books with their parents, or learn to participate in worship, or discuss the football match they watched the night before – all these can be used to develop their understanding of how language changes for different topics, audiences and modes. Our challenge is both to develop this understanding and to apply it to academic text.

This approach – thinking about how students can participate in disciplinary communities and come to understand the communicative choices that members of that community make – has a lot of value for EAL learners. First, because they often have little experience of such disciplinary communities in English – although they may have more in other languages, and this can transfer quickly to L2 if their L1 experiences are welcomed and discussed in the classroom. EAL pupils need to participate in the mainstream class to build up this implicit knowledge (the context of culture) and need lots of opportunities to discuss, comment on and get feedback on the communicative choices made by writers, including themselves (context of situation).

Meaning is Multimodal

We have talked about 'mode' as either written or spoken, but learners rarely encounter just one or the other. We see this in 'history textbooks with pictures, maps, and graphics that explain important events; science reports with diagrams, charts, graphs, and equations that prove findings […] and different forms of multilingual social media' (Gebhard, 2019: 8–13). These do not feature so strongly in language-learning materials, which often focus on the four skills of reading, writing, speaking and listening, rather than the ways we draw on multiple skills to take meaning from rich texts.

Texts are not just multimodal; they are used multimodally. A Geography teacher might introduce the topic of volcanoes by using a short video to capture the students' interest. They might then use a diagram with labels, key information in sentences, and examples of different types of volcano to compare. A reading activity might follow, with a table for the students to complete with positive and negative factors. As the lesson progresses, students might be introduced to more complex ideas to evaluate, compare or prioritise – often moving between prose texts, diagrams or tables, peer and teacher talk, and visuals – developing the cognitive academic language proficiency needed for curriculum success.

Chapter Review

This chapter has introduced systemic functional linguistics (SFL), a major approach to studying and teaching language. We began by looking at the challenge that EAL learners face of *learning about* and *learning to use* the language at the same time. SFL is valuable to us because it offers tools for focusing on meaning, rather than language structure. A key concept is that texts are produced for a purpose and an audience; for learners of academic English, we should see these purposes and audiences in terms of the disciplinary (subject) community that pupils are becoming part of as they study.

Disciplines make use of a wide range of genres. In school we tend to take a fairly straightforward view of genres, often seeing them as prototype texts that students need to learn the conventions of. We can go further than this: genres are better seen as sets of social practices, involving unspoken shared knowledge and assumptions. EAL pupils are unlikely to have enough experience of disciplinary communities to share this unspoken knowledge, so they need as many opportunities to participate as possible – this is one of the major arguments in favour of mainstreaming, even at a relatively low proficiency. It is also important that learners are able to make choices in their writing, and have opportunities to talk about and reflect on their choices. Subject and class teachers play a vital role here, ensuring that students get exposure to relevant texts in a range of genres and that learners have support to make informed choices about their own writing.

SFL recognises two different contexts for language use: the context of culture and the context of situation. The 'culture' relates to the implicit knowledge of how texts work that comes from experience; for this, we need to ensure that our EAL students get maximum exposure to relevant academic texts and have experience of participating in the subject communities that create them. The 'situation' refers to the circumstances in which a particular text was produced. In SFL, the situational factors are called *field* (the topic), *tenor* (the relationship between participants) and *mode* (spoken or written). Finally, we noted that pupils do not encounter only spoken or written language at a time: lesson sequences use multiple modes, including images and physical activity, to make meaning. Much of this multimodality comes from the way teachers use resources and sequence learning in the classroom, so it is vital that EAL and subject specialists collaborate on planning and delivery.

What We Found in Chapter 14

Chapter 14 examined systematic functional linguistics (SFL), which begins from the belief that 'language does not passively reflect reality [but] language actively creates reality'. The main points were:

- Three sets of concepts can be used to understand texts:
  - genres are sets of social practices that are expressed in the choices we make about language;
  - field is the topic, tenor is the relationship between participants, and mode is whether the text is spoken or written (or multimodal);

- - the context of culture is the implicit knowledge of how texts work that comes from experience, and the context of situation is the circumstances in which a particular text was produced.
- Texts are not just multimodal; they are used multimodally.
- Together, these give us a powerful set of tools for thinking about language across the curriculum, emphasising the need for learners to participate in the disciplinary community and make choices about their language use as they communicate meaning.

Where Can I Go Next?

The first place to look should be the work of Pauline Gibbons, especially her 2002 book, *Scaffolding Language, Scaffolding Learning: Teaching Second Language Learners in the Mainstream Classroom*. It is a classic introduction to many of the concepts discussed in this chapter.

There is a rich literature on SFL and many resources written especially for teachers. One of the most accessible is Meg Gebhard's (2019) *Teaching and Researching ELLs' Disciplinary Literacies*. It is written for a US audience (so uses ELL rather than EAL) and she discusses the US policy context in some detail, but the book presents the key issues very clearly. Other good books include María Estella Brisk's (2015) *Engaging Students in Academic Literacies*, which is similar but focuses on the Primary phase.

In the UK, a recent special issue of the *Journal of English for Academic Purposes* (2020, Vol. 4) explored Halliday's influence on the teaching of academic English. The collection focuses mainly on tertiary-level EAP programmes but many of the ideas are easily adapted to Secondary-level subject teaching. The introductory article by Sheena Gardner and Jim Donohue gives a helpful overview, and the paper by Gail Forey ('A whole school approach to SFL metalanguage and the explicit teaching of language for curriculum learning') is particularly good.

15 Disciplinary Language, Disciplinary Knowledge

This chapter introduces the key features of disciplinary language, discusses how far we should go in making it explicit and outlines some teaching techniques that will help learners speak, write, think and act like subject specialists.

The preceding chapters have outlined an approach to subject language based on the idea that we 'apprentice' learners into disciplinary communities. These communities (which extend vertically from Primary, through Secondary and into higher education and professional usage) have their own ways of using language to organise and communicate ideas. There are large overlaps between these disciplines: several features of academic language are common to several subject areas, and even a little knowledge about language will make a difference to your conversations with colleagues. Academic language can often be impenetrably dense because it packs a lot of information into single words or short phrases, which in general English would unfold over a sentence or more. (It can also be dense when academic writers are not held to high standards of clarity and style – something that students will enjoy unpicking as they develop as critical academic readers.) Academic language also uses specialist vocabulary (see Chapter 13) and relies on shared assumptions and implicit knowledge (see Chapter 14), which we can make transparent for EAL pupils.

Disciplinary language, in this sense, is not just something on the page to be deciphered. It is part and parcel of disciplinary practice: we teach our students to write like historians, scientists or artists by teaching them to think and act like historians, scientists and artists. The good news is that we don't have to teach this from scratch. Learners bring a great deal of relevant experience to the classroom.

From Everyday to Disciplinary Language: The Register Continuum

Bilingual learners have a head start in understanding disciplinary literacy. They appreciate that you use language differently for different audiences and occasions, whether that means using one language at home and another for worship, or using different registers with siblings and extended family. Our default monolingualism is quite limiting in comparison with many other languages and cultures. Bengali speakers, for example, have a much richer array of terms for family members than English does, and greater differences in how they should be addressed. If we take the time to make space for this knowledge in the classroom – for example by asking pupils to teach the class a little about their language use every week, by making bilingual books or discussing linguistic differences openly in class – we can use it to create a strong foundation for academic language.

We can see this everyday language as one end of a continuum. At the other end is more formal, academic usage (see Figure 15.1, which is based on the work of M.A.K. Halliday, see e.g. Halliday, 2007 and Martin, 1992). This register continuum is a good way to introduce the concept to students. It is straightforward enough to be displayed on the wall and referred to often, and it is easy to use. Learners can place examples of academic writing along the line and discuss the choices they made, creating opportunities for purposeful talk about language. It also captures a wide range of characteristics that make academic language different from everyday conversation – not only from informal to formal, but also everyday to specialised, spontaneous to planned and spoken-like to written-like. The register continuum is also a good foundation for talking about how meaning is created multimodally: formal, written-like academic text is likely to be found with graphs, charts and diagrams. Pictures and videos can be placed at different points on the continuum as students analyse their content, audience and intended effect. Learners will have an implicit understanding of this but it needs explicit teaching.

A good example of this is given by Gail Forey, who has spent several years exploring the use of SFL and metalanguage in different subjects. In this excerpt from a lesson observation, the teacher is introducing the register continuum in a Science lesson. Three sentences were written on the board and the teacher asked students to decide where they should be placed on the continuum:

> The bigger the voltage, the bigger the current.
> As voltage increases, current increases.
> There is a positive correlation between current and voltage.

Figure 15.1 The register continuum

Teacher: We call it the register continuum. Continuum because it is the line continuing that way and continuing that way. This is everyday language [*pointing at the left of the continuum*]; this is academic language [*pointing at the right of the continuum*]. Think about where you'd put each of those statements. Which one of the uh statements will go to the everyday side?
Student: The first one going to the left …
Teacher: Similar order … from left to right?
Alright. How far is that to the left? Is it all the way to the left?
Students: [Yeah
[No … just a bit to the right
(Adapted from Forey, 2020: 8–9)

As the lesson continues, the teacher asks students to explain their choices. To an extent, they agreed, it depended on the *tenor* – they would make different choices for an exam answer and for a report written under less pressure. It gave them insight into the way scientific writing recycles concepts and language to build meaning, and it introduced them to patterns that they could use elsewhere in their writing (such as 'correlation between [noun] and [noun]'). The teacher, interviewed about the approach later, said that the students:

> not only produce texts independently in the focused genre by the end of this cycle but they're also given the tools to assess what they've done so they can be self-critical, and they can give themselves advice about how to improve which is great! (Forey, 2020: 12)

Understanding the register continuum is a great way to get students thinking about disciplinary writing. To take it further, we can embed it in a teaching and learning cycle.

The Teaching and Learning Cycle (TLC)

The teaching and learning cycle (TLC) is a five-stage approach to developing academic literacy, originally developed as a collaboration between researchers and schools in Australia in the 1980s (Rose & Martin, 2012). The stages are:

(1) building the field
(2) supporting reading
(3) deconstructing model texts
(4) jointly constructing a text
(5) independently constructing a text

In the first stage, you draw on pupils' existing knowledge about a topic, using everyday language. In the second stage, you focus on building up their content knowledge so that students can read about the topic with guidance. The third and fourth stages are collaborative: by deconstructing a text together, students can see how expert writers organise information and how they convey subject knowledge (field choices), position themselves as writers (tenor choices) and build up a coherent and cohesive line of argument (mode choices). As the students' understanding of the text grows, they move to jointly constructing a text of their own with support from the teacher. You are very involved at this stage, making sure that new ideas and patterns are used, asking probing questions and advising on the students' language choices. In the final stage the learners become more independent, working as a class but with less guidance from the teacher as they make their own choices about how to incorporate subject knowledge and subject language.

We see a precursor to this in Forey's example, above. The Science teacher was in the early stages of introducing learners to metalanguage, the register continuum and the TLC. Even then, they created opportunities for students to deconstruct text and understand their own language choices. In Manny's English literature case study, he used images and sorting activities to build the field and support reading (TLC Stages 1–2), developing learners' understanding of the topic and generating language that they could use in their own writing.

Nominalisation and Complex Clauses

As writing becomes more academic or technical, it needs to convey information more concisely. We can do this by turning words (particularly verbs), phrases and whole clauses into single nouns, a process called *nominalisation*. Charlotte Bowyer, whose History teaching we met in Chapter 14, gave her students the following examples:

decide (verb)	to	decision (noun)
introduce (verb)		introduction (noun)
invade (verb)		invasion (noun)
make allies (verb + noun)		alliances (noun)

Learners need practice in order to manipulate parts of speech in this way. A useful activity is to get students to highlight examples of nominalisation in academic texts, noting the verb form in the margin or even rewriting the sentence in its un-nominalised form. They will find that nouns are much more common in informational texts, where the focus is on concepts, than in narratives where the focus is on describing actions. Nominalisation is especially worth attention in subjects that use written reports, such as Science. Here, a process is often described and then nominalised. For example:

The beaker was heated until <u>the liquid evaporated</u>.
<u>Evaporation</u> occurred at precisely 100°C.

Students can also highlight chains of nouns and verbs with the same meaning, to see how nominalisation is used to organise ideas in a text. In the example above, the process described using the verb ('evaporated') became the subject of the next sentence ('evaporation'). By looking closely at texts, students will be able to incorporate this 'zig-zag' pattern into their own writing.

It is easy to take this process for granted, so steeped are we in the norms of language use in our own areas of expertise. Nominalisation is more concise, certainly, but it also changes the nature of the information being communicated. When we move from verbs to nouns, we are moving from the event to the concept, the example to the category. This is an important part of pupils' subject development and underpins the abstract thinking they need to succeed in the curriculum, but that abstraction needs to be made transparent for learners who might otherwise take the new noun as just another word to learn. Charlotte Bowyer did this with her A Level History class, as she explored the way in which nominalisation can combine nouns into complex strings of information. For example, her students revised their writing as follows:

> Stalin <u>made allies on</u> the right and used them to defeat the left.
> *rewritten as*
> Stalin's right-wing <u>alliances</u> facilitated his defeat of the left.

The nominalisation moves us from specific instances ('made allies') to the broader concept ('alliances'), allowing more information to be packed into the sentence. For example, the verb 'facilitated' describes the relationship between two nouns ('alliances' … 'defeat') more precisely than would otherwise be possible. This is true even of academic language that is written to be accessible. The following example is taken from a blog post by an academic author:

> The allies turned into sworn enemies and could now base their mutual hatred on long-standing ideological disagreements. (Weber, 2019)

We would place this writing further to the left on our register continuum. It has spoken-like, informal features (colloquial 'sworn enemies', emotive 'hatred') but is underpinned by the noun 'disagreements'. The adjective 'ideological' is part of a broader pattern in the text, which also features concepts expressed as adjective + noun combinations (such as 'geopolitical interests', 'resettlement operations' and 'ideological motives'). Again, learners could be asked to identify all the adjective and noun units, giving examples of specific events that they could refer to, and to plot them on the register continuum.

Metalanguage and Strategies

So what strategies can we use to develop students' disciplinary language? One valuable tool is to develop their vocabulary for talking *about* language: their metalanguage. At a simple level, words like 'noun' and 'verb' allow us to step back from the text and describe how its elements go together. This is evidently useful, but how far should we go in teaching metalanguage to students of varying levels of proficiency? Is it unnecessary 'complex jargon' (Bourke, 2005: 93) or 'a powerful navigational tool' (Macken-Horarik, 2008: 46)?

Metalanguage is important because it creates a shared vocabulary between teacher and student, allowing discussion of the language patterns and features of texts that would otherwise remain opaque. With that in mind, it should be introduced sparingly and slowly, so that learners have time to get comfortable with using each element before they add the next. The first four parts of speech (noun, verb, adjective, adverb) are a good place to start, followed by pronoun, determiner, preposition, conjunction. It is helpful for learners to identify references within a text, discourse markers and the language used to make a text cohesive and coherent. It is important not to stop here: our goal is not to learn the naming of the parts but to give students the tools to describe their own language choices (especially where they differ from the school's norms) and those of others. This has the added benefit of creating common ground with colleagues as well – a vocabulary introduced by the language specialist that describes how class teachers and subject specialists use language.

Chapter Review

This chapter has discussed the way language is used in subject disciplines. It began by saying that disciplinary language is inseparable from disciplinary knowledge. It can be taught in isolation, but for students to understand deeply how language is used to create and share knowledge, they need to experience the connections between speaking, writing, thinking and acting like a member of that community. In practical terms, this means that they need to participate fully in subject lessons. As a consequence, it also means a closer relationship between EAL and subject expertise: each needs the other and students need both.

We looked at the relationship between everyday language and academic language, introducing the register continuum as a conceptual tool for the classroom. This makes the different dimensions of academic language visible and allows pupils to discuss where they would 'put' words, phrases and passages of text. It gives them opportunities to talk about their language choices, to notice patterns used by expert writers and to become more aware of their own use of register. We then discussed the teaching and learning cycle (TLC), a five-stage process of understanding, deconstructing and reconstructing texts. The TLC is a flexible framework that can be used in any subject, giving EAL specialists a core routine for the wide range of texts they must work with.

We explored nominalisation, a key feature of academic text, and looked at how greater use of nouns allowed us to construct more complex and detailed meanings. Finally, we turned to the question of metalanguage and how much we should teach learners about language itself. Too much is certainly unhelpful, but a working knowledge of how language works gives us common ground to talk about the choices writers make to create meaning. This is as useful to share with students as it is with colleagues, and gives us good grounds for building closer links between subject and language specialists.

What We Found in Chapter 15

Chapter 15 examined disciplinary language. The main points were:

- Everyday and disciplinary language are different. Learners may have little exposure to disciplinary language and so this needs explicit teaching.

- The teaching and learning cycle is a good approach to deconstructing and reconstructing texts with learners, helping them understand the choices that writers (including themselves) make about language.
- Nominalisation is a key feature of academic text. It increases information density but also signals a move from the example to the concept, which is important for learners' conceptual development in their subjects.
- Metalanguage is useful if taught sparingly and with purpose.

Where Can I Go Next?

Two books give a thorough introduction to **disciplinary language**. The first, by Esther Daborn and colleagues (2020), is written specifically for UK Secondary teachers. A subject-specific view comes from John Polias. His 2016 book on *Apprenticing Students into Science* unpacks the ways in which scientific knowledge is organised, communicated and (for pupils) created through language. Primary teachers and Secondary Science teachers will find a lot of useful insight here.

Gail Forey has written extensively about **metalanguage**. Her 2020 paper on whole-school approaches (recommended in the previous chapter) is a good place to start, but a quick search will return several others.

Case Study 2: EAL and Maths

Sarah Fowkes is a Year 4/5 teacher at St Barnabas Primary School, Bristol. She has a particular interest in Maths and here describes her work building up her pupils' mathematical language.

Our inner-city school has an extremely high level of EAL, with the majority of children not speaking English at home and therefore limiting their use of English. More recently, we have also welcomed children totally new to English and often new to the whole school experience. In order for these children and all children in our school to progress and access the curriculum, we have used The Bell Foundation's assessments [see Chapter 18] to correctly analyse the levels of EAL in each class. Using these data, we are now able to plan our lessons and set targets with a huge focus on language. We also reintroduced the Word Aware Programme to create a consistent approach throughout the school.

As the Maths lead at that time, it was evident to me that the children struggled with many of the very 'wordy' questions that arose from the reasoning problems that are now asked in order for them to be proficient mathematicians. Within Maths, the EAL problem was two-fold: a lack of knowledge of mathematical vocabulary and an inability to interpret an actual question, which stemmed from their understanding of everyday language.

When introducing new mathematical vocabulary in my mixed Year 4 and 5 class, I use a number of methods. A small group of children who have arrived in the UK more recently go to a short 'pre-teach' session every morning with a teaching assistant, who introduces new words, pronunciations and meanings to them. This enables these children to feel more confident when the new words are introduced to the rest of the class and it has even encouraged some of them to answer questions in class. One Year 5 girl came to me and said that she was so happy going to pre-teach because she could understand so much more in lessons.

I apply the Word Aware strategy when introducing new language. This enables the children to really explore a word: how it sounds; what letter it starts with; what it rhymes with; how many syllables it has; what it means; and one that I have added, what the word is in some of the children's languages. In this last way, I am able to involve parents and families with their child's learning. The children are so enthusiastic to ask for a translation at home and in doing this, they inadvertently learn the word and often its meaning. The word is then placed on the Maths working wall on colour coordinated paper according to its word type. By highlighting the word type, children who are new to English are able to work out the correct grammatical placement by saying the words in a sentence. To further assist them in this, all nouns are featured with a determiner (e.g. 'a triangle') and all verbs in the infinitive (e.g. 'to simplify'). I have found that this works well for vocabulary in all subjects from English to Science.

For the children to use the new word correctly, I use sentence stems so that they are able to say a sentence that helps with the meaning, e.g. 'a two-dimensional shape with three straight sides is called _____'. This also demonstrates how important it is for the children to be given a determiner with a noun so that they can speak in correct sentences. These sentences are then regularly used to revise vocabulary in later lessons.

Once a word has been introduced, I employ a number of other strategies to embed it in the minds of all of the class. Vanishing cloze exercises can help with more technical definitions: these are activities where parts of a definition are removed so that the children insert relevant parts and build up the meaning. Once the children have spoken the definition a number of times, it is surprising how quickly they learn it. Additionally, we play games like the 'hot seat': writing a noun or noun phrase on the board behind a child and the rest of the children have to give clues or describe it using correct language for the child to guess what the word is. Another game is to give a word to a child who then has to describe it to the rest of the class without saying the word but also using mathematical language.

Analysing words, as I would when teaching spelling, has also assisted with learning new mathematical vocabulary. By investigating the root, word family or origin, children gain a better understanding of language and the ultimate meaning of a word. One child, who arrived in my class in September speaking only Arabic, gained much confidence when she realised that our number system is actually Arabic and many words are also derived from her native language. Similarly, sorting words by deciding whether they are purely Maths words or everyday words has helped with understanding. Many words used in Maths often seem to be more accessible if they have an everyday context, e.g. 'circle' can be used in many other subjects other than Mathematics.

Many of the Maths reasoning problems now require explanations and proof of understanding, so I regularly use sentence stems when asking multiple-choice hinge questions to check their understanding. The children are then able to practise this skill and reinforce their knowledge so that they may answer questions in this particular way. An example of this would be when asking an elicitation question with multiple-choice answers. I would provide a sentence stem such as, 'I know the answer is _____ because first I _____ then I_____.'

Although these examples focus on EAL students, this approach has helped to improve language for all children in the class, including non-EAL students. The children in my class now fully embrace the emphasis on understanding and using vocabulary correctly. They are persistent and enthusiastic in questioning me when they hear a word that they do not understand and often request that a word is made our 'word of the day'.

Commentary

Sarah's case study is packed with activities and ideas. She starts with good information about her pupils, using a well-regarded assessment tool (see Chapter 18). She differentiates her provision, using focused withdrawal sessions to prepare learners for the mainstream class – and she keeps track of how the pupils respond to those sessions by eliciting regular feedback. Her use of short withdrawal sessions for pre-teaching is notable: as we will see in Christine McCormack's case study (on new arrivals), the emphasis is firmly on supporting learners in the mainstream classroom. Withdrawal here is very limited, has a clear goal and uses strategies developed with the class teacher – so the pre-teaching and mainstream classroom are highly integrated.

That classroom is rich with language and she uses a wide range of activities and techniques to make language prominent in everyday learning. It is a good example of the connection between BICS and CALP (see Chapter 11). Sarah notes that one of the challenges her children face is to 'interpret an actual question, which stemmed from their understanding of everyday language'. Her approach focuses on developing their understanding of everyday language: the roots, forms and associations of words they mostly know, new vocabulary that they can use in a range of situations, and patterns that they can use in their talk and writing. Here, everyday language is used to describe academic concepts. In other words, the pupils' BICS is their CALP. Sarah's classroom is an important reminder of how integrated everyday and academic language is in reality, and you can feel that it is a vibrant and engaging place to be.

Sarah has a clear goal in mind: to prepare students for the 'reasoning questions that are now asked of them in order to be proficient mathematicians'. She is helping them to develop the thinking skills and disciplinary language of mathematicians in an age- and curriculum-appropriate way. The Word Aware approach, developed by Stephen Parsons and Anna Branagan (2014), is used as an organising theme, alongside lots of activities that help students to notice the surface-level features of English. She uses sentence stems so that learners can move from words to sentences, and she makes the disciplinary vocabulary of Mathematics transparent by explicitly discussing the everyday and subject-specific use of words. She makes a couple of small tweaks to bring in the pupils' first languages and describes how enthusiastically this is received.

This language-rich teaching has a clear impact: Sarah describes the benefits for both L1 and L2 learners. Even though her learners have low overall English proficiency, they are confident and engaged, 'persistent and enthusiastic in questioning me' and making quick progress.

16 Pulling It All Together: What Counts as Proficiency

This chapter reviews Part 2, highlights key themes and asks what counts as proficiency in academic language.

Part 2 began with five principles, starting points as we explored disciplinary literacy and its implications for EAL learners. They were:

(A) Language and concepts are organised in disciplines.
(B) Scaffold language to support learning.
(C) Prioritise vocabulary.
(D) Talk before writing.
(E) Learning is collaborative.

Chapters 10–15 described an approach to curriculum language based on language function the way that linguistic resources are used to communicate meaning. This chapter now revisits those principles, looking at how each chapter has contributed to a coherent approach to EAL in the mainstream curriculum. It then asks what counts as proficiency, using the themes of the book to reflect on the ostensible goal of EAL provision.

A Practice-based Approach to EAL, Continued

Chapter 10, Five Principles for Language Across the Curriculum, began with pen portraits of three EAL learners: Alejandra, Farjaad and Łukasz. Each represented a different profile: two newly arrived pupils who differed in whether they primarily used their first language (Alejandra) or drew on a range of languages to communicate in a multilingual environment (Farjaad); and one bilingual pupil who came to the UK before he started school and is developing his languages alongside each other (Łukasz). These highlighted the significance of pupils' earlier experiences and the role that their languages play in their everyday lives. This chapter then set out the five principles that underpin the discussion in Part 2.

Chapter 11, BICS and CALP, introduced the work of Jim Cummins. His early research showed that bilingual pupils do not keep their languages in strict separation but draw on each of them as they learn. They have a 'common underlying proficiency' (or CUP) – a reservoir of skills and knowledge that underpins proficiency in any language. This has important implications for our approach to learners' first languages, which can offer valuable scaffolding for second language proficiency. It also suggests that concepts established in one language can be accessed through the other, as long as the learner has developed sufficient proficiency. In the classroom, we can think of this as a sliding scale between L1 and L2 use. Learners who arrive with limited English but a good track record of schooling should be encouraged to keep using L1 while their English develops, allowing them to keep pace with the curriculum. We also looked at the Cummins quadrants, a way of visualising the relationship between the context given for a task and the level of cognitive challenge it offers. This is closely connected to its linguistic demands: more advanced thinking skills require more sophisticated language. The quadrants give us a useful way of checking that we are helping our students to move from high-context, low-demand activities towards more challenging material, with enough support to ensure that they have the language to do so.

Chapter 12, Oracy: Talking and Learning, turned our attention to strategies for supporting academic language development. Oracy has several definitions, but common to them all is the understanding that purposeful talk allows learners to organise their ideas and language. For EAL learners, this can be seen as a practical realisation of the input and output hypotheses: learners experiment with their language use, get implicit and explicit feedback and notice the gap between what they can say now and what they want to say. We looked at the work of Pauline Gibbons to see how talk contributes to written language, using the mode continuum. We noted that the quality of interaction matters a great deal: many teacher-student interactions follow the pattern of 'initiation, response, feedback/evaluation' (IRF/IRE). This can be a useful strategy for checking and organising knowledge, but it significantly restricts the learners' opportunities to engage in extended, purposeful talk. We looked then at the characteristics of activities that promoted talk and found that they were well structured, clearly designed and integrated into the curriculum for all learners. It is relatively straightforward to design activities so that purposeful talk is required, but it needs to be planned for.

Chapter 13, Reading in a New Language, started with the connection between oracy and literacy. It showed that the opportunity to organise ideas verbally allowed learners to engage more effectively with written text, both as producers and as consumers. We also recognised that young people use a range of literacies in their daily lives, which can scaffold the development of academic literacy if they are brought into the classroom. We then looked at reading as a skill, identifying five main sub-skills and discussing the implications of each for EAL learners. These ranged from automatic recognition of letters and words to the ability to interpret how information is organised in texts. We noted some of the activities that will be useful here, from DARTs (directed activities related to texts) to jumbled paragraphs. The chapter then turned to vocabulary, recognising the different networks that words belonged to (such as those with the same meaning or using the same morphological patterns). We introduced substitution tables, briefly discussed pre-teaching and described the three tiers of vocabulary, from the everyday to the academic and the subject-specific. Finally, we discussed strategies for developing confident bilingual readers.

Chapter 14, Making Meaning in Writing: Field, Tenor and Mode, introduced concepts from systemic functional linguistics (SFL). We looked first at genre and audience: that texts are about something, addressed to someone and designed to have an effect. The example of a student's email to her tutor showed that genres are social practices that involve a great deal of implicit knowledge, which informs the choices that people make as they write. EAL learners are unlikely to have sufficient experience of English to have developed this implicit knowledge, so we can usefully make it more explicit for them. We then looked at two types of learning context in SFL: the context of culture (the implicit knowledge that we bring to writing generally) and the context of situation (our understanding of a writing task in particular). These can be taught. We looked at the example of an A Level History lesson to see how authentic subject writing and explicit language teaching were used to address these gaps. We also looked at the three elements that make up the register of a text, to better understand what writers are making decisions about. These are the field (topic), tenor (relationship between participants) and mode (spoken or written – although we also discussed multimodality).

Chapter 15, Disciplinary Language, Disciplinary Knowledge, developed the previous chapter's ideas into a discussion of academic disciplines and how we apprentice learners into disciplinary communities. We began with the register continuum, showing how everyday language can be compared with academic language. We used an example from the classroom to see how it can be used in teaching, encouraging students to analyse the writer's choices and apply this thinking to their own. We then looked at the teaching and learning cycle, a five-stage process to develop contextual knowledge, break down a text, rebuild it collaboratively and then write more independently. This gives a core approach that can be adapted to different lessons, from small-group withdrawal to mainstream lessons. The chapter then turned to sentence-level detail, looking at nominalisation and how complex meanings can be built up from sequences of nouns. We found that this was characteristic of academic text but needs to be taught as something that writers *do*, rather than as vocabulary. Learners need to see the choices writers make when they use nominalisation, rather than learning the nouns as a vocabulary list without the underlying process. Finally, we asked how much we should teach students of the language to describe language – metalanguage. A certain amount is useful, integrated over time into teaching and shared with colleagues as well as students, to give common ground for discussing the role of language in disciplinary learning.

What Counts as Proficiency?

In Part 1, we introduced a theory of language based on sentence-level grammar. It used the native speaker's judgement to evaluate grammatically accurate language and deliberately excluded the context in which it was used. This told us a great deal about the language system, but less about how it is used in real life. In Part 2, we have used a contrasting theory of language that focuses on function and use. We see speakers making choices about how to deploy their linguistic resources and find that their (implicit) knowledge of the context is a major factor in the choices they make. Between the two lies a definition of proficiency that we can use. It's not just when sentences are grammatically well formed, and not just when meaning is communicated effectively, although each clearly plays a part. EAL learners need both: knowing what to say, and how, why, when, where and with whom to say it. Misconceptions around proficiency, particularly when we assume that monolinguals and bilinguals should speak in the same way, contribute significantly to the view that EAL pupils are deficient and destined for academic underachievement.

Any definition of proficiency for EAL needs to recognise the policy context, too. The highest stage of proficiency in English, according to the short-lived proficiency measures introduced in 2016 (see DfE, 2016), described learners who operate without EAL support and perform largely like monolinguals do. This says little about their skills in using different languages to communicate, which have significant value outside school. Other UK jurisdictions have similar policies: few match the ambition of bilingual education, for example, and provide for young people's intellectual and social development in two languages (see Baker & Wright, 2021, for an overview of this field). There is no national policy on EAL and very little mention of bilingual learners in teachers' professional standards. It is right that we push back against this lack of ambition and narrow scope.

There are alternatives. Studies of English as a lingua franca (ELF) – where English is used as a means for people of different first languages to communicate – have shown that proficiency is a complex and dynamic construct. When English-L2 users are speaking with each other in English, without the presence of an English-L1 user (a native speaker), proficiency in English:

> only accounts for part of the success or failure of communication; at least as important is a more general communicative capability, such as sensitivity to the limits of shared systemic and schematic knowledge, as well as accommodation skills. (Seidlhofer, 2004: 222)

This suggests that at least part of what we call proficiency is about meeting the expectations of native speakers. Edmund Hamman (2016) described this as a difference between the 'settled' (the 'teachers, administrators and others who shape schools and school systems') and the globally mobile learners. We have talked so far about using pupils' first languages to support learning in English, but the logical extension of this is to incorporate those languages more fully into the curriculum itself. The professional context for doing so is discussed in Part 3.

What We Found in Chapter 16

Chapter 16 reviewed Part 2. It then turned to the notion of proficiency, arguing that:
- Our understanding of proficiency should include both grammatical accuracy and appropriate usage (see Parts 1 and 2).
- There is very little guidance or ambition for EAL at a national level (in England and Wales; there is more in Scotland). It is right for practitioners to push back against

what limited advice does come from central government if that advice does not meet the needs of our learners.
- A monolingual attitude dominates, manifested in the assumption that successful bilingual learners use language like monolinguals. That is an impoverished view and is not supported by the evidence.

Part 3 will look at the professional context for promoting learners' languages in school.

Where Can I Go Next?

This chapter largely reviews Part 2, but it also introduces a number of interesting connections. On **English as a lingua franca**, see Barbara Seidlhofer's 2004 and 2005 papers. The work of Jennifer Jenkins and the Centre for Global Englishes at the University of Southampton (https://www.southampton.ac.uk/cge) are good places to follow up. See, for example, her recent paper with Constant Leung (Jenkins & Leung, 2019) on alternatives to standardised language tests, and her 2015 book on Global Englishes.

On **'life as a bilingual'**, and how it differs from life as a monolingual, see François Grosjean's (2021) book of that name. It collects many of his popular blog posts, reflecting his many years of academic scholarship, into 15 very readable chapters.

Case Study 3: EAL Is a Mainstream Responsibility

Pam Cole is head of the Ethnic Minority Achievement team at Swansea Council. In this case study she introduces the Welsh context, where pupils might be learning English or Welsh as an additional language, and describes the work her team has done to build capacity in schools across the city.

The Welsh Context

Funding for minority ethnic achievement in Wales, while going through turbulent times and decreasing in real terms, remains in place. The majority of local authorities in Wales have retained some kind of central service, although models of delivery vary significantly. In addition, work in this area benefits from a strong collaborative network of minority ethnic lead officers across Wales and collection of EAL data remains part of the annual school census.

It should be noted that in Wales there are schools that teach through the medium of Welsh. The amount of Welsh-medium provision varies from authority to authority. In some authorities, nearly all schools are Welsh medium. EAL learners who are educated through Welsh are termed WAL learners (Welsh as an additional language). This term only applies to learners who have a first language other than English/Welsh; that is, it does not apply to learners from an English-speaking home who are learning through Welsh as a second language in school. All children in English-medium schools learn Welsh up to the age of 16. The term bilingual, which is often used as another term for EAL learners, in Wales refers to English/Welsh. In essence, any 'EAL' learner in Wales is multilingual.

EAL: A Mainstream Responsibility

Over many years, various different support models for EAL learners have been in place in the local authority. This has been against a backdrop of increasing numbers and widening diversity, with now over 140 languages and dialects being spoken over and above English/Welsh. The vast majority of EAL learners attend English-medium schools. Some communities are established while others are more mobile.

In the early days, individualised and bespoke support for EAL learners was possible. Over time, the centrally employed ESL support teacher became the EAL specialist teacher and there was a shift towards attainment in the curriculum as well as English language development. The erosion of funding and increasing EAL learner numbers have made the need for EAL to be a mainstream responsibility more and more pertinent as time has gone on. To try to offset growing EAL learner numbers and dwindling allocations to schools, any pupil support became very targeted and was balanced with 'capacity building' elements. Capacity building incorporated any activity that built up the skills of school staff. This included delivering training but also formalised capacity-building projects that were undertaken in collaboration with mainstream colleagues.

The formal model of capacity building stemmed from work undertaken in one secondary school. While there were many embedded whole-school practices (e.g. admissions, appropriate setting, GCSE community language exams, policy, senior leader link, access arrangements, shared drive with information, etc.) and collaborations with mainstream teachers had been built up over time, the perception that EAL learners were the responsibility of the EAL team still pervaded. There was a need to dispel the dependency culture on 'EAL' staff to be wholly responsible for the EAL learners – the 'your pupils' scenario, often born out of the perception that EAL is purely about pupil support. As the numbers of beginner learners increased, so did the requests for 'support' from every corner of the school.

Taking a more holistic view of EAL provision, it was recognised that due to limited capacity, EAL learner support timetables often focused on core subjects; some areas of the curriculum and the teachers in those subjects were never included. EAL learners remained unsupported in the majority of lessons. The model of support was reactive and bottom-up, working from the learners and timetable possibilities. It needed to shift to being top-down, proactive and strategic, focusing on long-term sustainability. Inherent in this was the need to shift responsibility for EAL to the mainstream.

After evaluating our existing practice, followed by research and a pilot project, the model implemented involved the EAL specialist teachers working with departments in rotation for a specified block of time. To start with, the model was very prescribed in terms of time frames and paperwork that provided a clear framework in which to plan and evaluate impact, but gave flexibility in terms of what was to be achieved in each partnership. It was recognised that team teaching, a core part of Bourne and McPake's (1991) original partnership model, was not necessarily viable in a number of circumstances. The actual key to success was seeing the partnership as two different sets of equal skills, subject and EAL, with both partners moving on from their own starting point. The collaboration with each department and subject teacher was unique and evolved in its own way. The project was highly successful. One of the unpredicted benefits was the shift in the perception of the EAL specialist teachers by mainstream staff, from one of glorified learning support assistant to that of knowledgeable, professional teachers. The ripple effect of this impacted positively on the entirety of EAL work within the school. This was latterly recognised by Estyn (Wales' equivalent of Ofsted), where provision for EAL was deemed a 'highly effective feature' and contributed to the 'excellent' category awarded to the school.

In time, the successful elements were incorporated into an authority-wide capacity-building model, implemented by central staff across schools. The end-of-project evaluations indicated a positive impact on the majority of class teachers that took part. However, there are still questions as to whether the model had a significant impact at whole-school level in the longer term. Excellent classroom practice for EAL learners, while highly important, is not the whole picture, as EAL provision hinges on good practice in many aspects of school life.

Moving on, the funding for EAL is mainly devolved to schools. Devolving ensures that strings are attached with clear expectations on schools around developing practice. The model essentially shifts EAL from a notion of support to one of whole-school improvement. A key aspect is that all schools complete an annual evaluation with a member of the central team. This identifies good practice for sharing across the authority, authority-wide developmental areas and individual actions for schools.

The evaluation tool focuses on key EAL areas, is cross-referenced with the Estyn inspection framework and uses a language and format similar to that used by school improvement colleagues. The tool has a grading system: embedded and sustained; established; developing; not yet developed. For each key area, there is a set of closed questions and then a statement under each of the four headings.

Schools need to consider their answers to the questions and then decide where they sit on a best-fit basis for each area. The questions ensure a consistent interpretation of what the statements in each area refer to. The key areas in the tool are:

- Whole school approach – vision, policy and strategy
- Roles and responsibilities
- Standards and progress
- Inclusive whole school environment and ethos
- Admissions, settling and induction
- Teaching and learning
- Inclusive curriculum
- Assessment of EAL acquisition
- EAL/Additional Learning Needs
- Engagement with parents

The tool pushes schools away from purely thinking about EAL in terms of 'support', attainment in the curriculum and being the responsibility of one person. It widens thinking to encompass all minority ethnic learners and the broader agendas of inclusion and equity. Despite the years of capacity building, what manifested was the dependency culture that had been built up on the central EAL specialist teacher being wholly responsible for the EAL learners.

What also became clear was that schools might well be able to demonstrate good outcomes for EAL learners on key performance indicators, but that this does not necessarily reflect how well they rate on the evaluation tool when the different areas are unpicked. A generally inclusive school may still not be fully inclusive of its EAL learners and their families without an explicit focus on these learners and their needs. EAL is everyone's responsibility and needs to be considered in every aspect of school life in order for EAL to become intrinsic; only then can practice move into the echelons of embedded and sustained.

Commentary

Pam describes how her team is making something positive out of a challenging situation. Decreasing funding has made one-to-one EAL support from a local authority specialist unsustainable, so by necessity that responsibility has moved to schools. That, perhaps, is where it should be. EAL is a cross-curricular specialism and so it needs to be embedded in all aspects of a school's work – but as Pam shows, that's not easy. She had to push back against a prevailing culture of 'dependency' on EAL specialists, where any pupil who didn't speak the majority language (which could be English or Welsh) was pushed out of the curriculum into EAL support. Pam helps us to face an uncomfortable truth: that specialist EAL provision, where it is not fully integrated with the rest of the school, can narrow the curriculum and lead to EAL pupils being marginalised from much of the mainstream curriculum.

Change took time, beginning with a pilot in one school and eventually being rolled out to many. It also meant changing school cultures, recognising that very strong EAL provision hinges on language-rich teaching across the board. It is heartening to hear of the unpredicted benefit, that it led to a wider appreciation of EAL specialists as expert teachers with a valuable contribution to make to all parts of the curriculum.

Part 3
The EAL Specialist

We are faced with the bizarre scenario of schools successfully transforming fluent speakers of foreign languages into monolingual English speakers, at the same time as they struggle, largely unsuccessfully, to transform monolingual English speakers into foreign language speakers.
Jim Cummins, 2005

Never doubt that a small group of thoughtful, committed citizens can change the world: indeed, it's the only thing that ever has.
Margaret Mead (probably)

Preface to Part 3

So far, this book has presented the evidence on language acquisition and shown how language is used in curriculum subjects. It has also developed an argument about EAL teaching that could be summed up as follows:

- EAL is a distinct specialism, resting on an interdisciplinary knowledge base, that contributes to learning across the curriculum.
- Those involved in supporting EAL learners should therefore be seen as specialists, empowered to make professional decisions according to the evidence and encouraged to contribute across the curriculum.

We have focused until now on the first point. The book has described a specialism that is rooted in language – how it is acquired and how it is used in the curriculum – and that therefore draws on a range of approaches and concepts. We looked at findings from second language acquisition research, from bilingualism and studies of multilingual classrooms, from *functional* linguistics and much more. Where possible, we distilled these findings into a series of clear principles for practice, so that the dazzling breadth of knowledge in our discipline can be put at the service of teaching practice.

Knowing your onions, however, will only get you so far. To create the conditions for multilingual learners to thrive we need EAL practice to be embedded at all levels of the school and across the curriculum. This means developing a whole-school approach to language, involving the community and winning over colleagues to the cause. Part 3 now looks at what that involves. It is organised into two main sections, with two audiences in mind. The first addresses EAL specialists who are new in post or who are working without a strong network of like-minded colleagues. This can be a lonely and vulnerable place: many specialists report significant pressure to treat bilingualism as a remedial need, getting students 'classroom-ready' so that they can join the mainstream rather than ensuring that all teaching in the school is linguistically and culturally rich. Others report that training and development budgets have been cut deeply, leaving little opportunity to develop as a subject specialist, or that EAL lacks representation in the school's management structure.

It is important to remember that this is not the natural order of things: the marginalisation of EAL (and of bilingual learners) results from decisions made by people at all levels of the school, the education system and government. Those decisions are often based on limited evidence but they are not immutable. Evidence can be presented, arguments can be won and policies can be changed. Doing so requires concerted effort and the support of a strong professional community. This first section therefore looks at the simple, concrete steps to take as you get to grips with your role. It looks at what assessments you can put in place to get good data on learning (and how to make such assessments work for your learners), and at the major models of provision that you will need to consider as you organise your own work. It closes with information on how to connect with other specialists and to build your own EAL network.

The second section is written for more established colleagues. Perhaps you feel that your position is more secure and your practice is good but you want to develop your work further. Perhaps you have worked through the stages in the first section and are ready to consolidate those gains. Perhaps, also, you want to look beyond the priorities of the first term or two. The second section sets that wider view. It is organised along similar lines to the first – a deliberate echo as we return to the key themes to add information, introduce new ideas and extend the approaches discussed so far. It begins with a brief discussion of the EAL specialist's role: what it means to be a language leader and what makes the specialist's role distinctive. It extends the 'getting to grips' discussion by looking at strategies for 'making friends and influencing people'. Effective EAL practice demands language-rich teaching across the curriculum, and that means having others keen to apply your expertise in their own classrooms.

It then returns to the discussion of assessment by looking at the limitations of national data. Much of the policy around EAL is based on an assumption that bilingual pupils should achieve the same language proficiency as monolingual pupils. We look briefly at findings that show multilingual pupils *outperforming* their monolingual peers when both languages are fully supported, and we discuss recent thinking that suggests a more expansive view of additional language teaching. We look at how to distinguish between language proficiency and specific language and learning needs, and at how strong EAL provision can be articulated to Ofsted. Finally, we consider what continuing professional development (CPD) looks like for EAL specialists, who are in the unusual position of both guiding subject teachers and continuing their own professional development.

The chapter closes with a shorter section for everyone. It takes a longer look at the 'funds of knowledge' that pupils bring with them and explores what is needed to bring about a 'whole-community' approach to language and learning. Because Part 3 is so focused on your own practice, recommendations for further reading are given together at the end rather than with each chapter. The final section distils the findings of the book as a whole into a series of clear, accessible messages for colleagues and parents – and for ourselves.

For Newly Appointed EAL Specialists

If you are new to your EAL role, welcome! The following chapters set out some of the things you will need to address in your first term or so. They are organised around four themes. 'Getting to grips with your role' takes you through an EAL audit, so that you can establish how things are working now and what you need to do first. 'Establishing effective assessments' considers the key principles of assessing language proficiency across the curriculum. It looks at examples from Europe and the United States to see what language assessments should include and what role EAL assessment plays in schools. The section on 'welcoming students' outlines an approach to gathering information about new arrivals and arranging the admissions process. Finally, 'getting connected' introduces the major subject associations, resource sites and social media accounts that make EAL such a rich field to work in.

Throughout the chapter, you'll find short activities to help keep track of everything. They are all reproduced in Appendix I so that you can mark off progress in setting up your provision while doing the thousand other things that fall to EAL specialists every day. Enjoy!

17 Getting to Grips with the Role

New EAL specialists have to cover a lot of ground in their first year. This chapter sets out the main things to consider.

If you are new in post, your first task will be to get to grips with your role. You might be joining a thriving and well-organised department, in which case the following should be a fairly painless process. You might equally be taking on a set of responsibilities with little formal support and too few hours to accomplish everything that you think is important, in which case some urgent triage is in order. One way of working out where things stand is to begin with an EAL audit, then to think about your own goals and aspirations, and finally to look at the practicalities and decide what to prioritise and what to work towards over time.

Beginning the EAL Audit: Getting to Know your School

In the first term, the main priorities are getting to know your school and understanding where the opportunities are. You might start by reflecting on these questions:

- Who is responsible for EAL (especially among senior leaders and governors)?
- Are the needs of the school's EAL pupils understood by the leadership team – and do they share your high aspirations for those learners?
- Is there a clear and widely agreed policy on languages in the school, that celebrates linguistic diversity as well as proficiency in the medium of instruction?
- Does your school keep accurate records on EAL pupils and is this knowledge widely shared?
- Can your subject/class teacher colleagues speak confidently about the EAL learners in their classes and do they share your high aspirations for those learners?
- What tools (assessments, resources, and so on) do subject/class teachers use to support EAL learners?
- Are there visible signs that multilingualism is celebrated in the school? What about the different dialects that pupils bring to the classroom?

These questions all reflect the place of multilingual learners in the school and help us to bring our critical faculties to bear on our workplace. You might find that multilingualism is visibly celebrated but that some teachers are more confident with their EAL pupils than others; this gives a sense of who might be receptive to trying out new ideas and who might need to see them in action before they take the plunge. Likewise, if the school keeps an accurate register of EAL pupils, including their language proficiency and their curriculum attainment, then these data can be your starting point for discussions with the leadership team to appoint an EAL champion at senior level.

Task 1 Getting to know your school

- ☐ Read through the questions above and make notes on your own school. Feel free to go beyond the questions and include your thoughts and impressions.
- ☐ Note one or two points that you would like to prioritise – then move on to Task 2.

Task 2 Establishing your role

- ☐ Make an appointment with your line manager to discuss your initial priorities. Give yourself enough time before the meeting to work through the rest of this chapter as it will give you plenty of solid points for discussion.

The first two tasks are designed to get things moving. Task 1 is all about capturing your thoughts as you begin your new role. If you are being recruited as an EAL specialist then you might start thinking about these issues as you prepare for the interview and add notes from those crucial first impressions. It will be important to test those assumptions as you become the leading advocate for multilingualism and multilingual learners in your school. If you already work in the school, they can be used to look at your environment with fresh eyes. You might find it quicker to pin down exactly what policies are in place already, which teachers are keen to try new strategies and how data are recorded and shared.

Build a Policy Folder and Note the Gaps

In an excellent (and highly recommended) pamphlet, experienced EAL teachers Amanda Bellsham-Revell and Paul Nancarrow suggest that new EAL coordinators build a folder of relevant school policies and make sure that other teachers can access it easily. They recommend starting with the following documents:

- the school's EAL register, listing the learners with EAL, their languages and levels of English proficiency, including the EAL assessment framework used;
- the school's EAL Policy or Language and Literacy Policy – which should include the modes of EAL support, e.g. in-class or withdrawal groups;
- procedures for the welcome and induction of new arrivals;
- the EAL Coordinator's job description, role and responsibilities and line-management structure;
- class teachers' role and responsibilities in teaching learners with EAL;

- the place of EAL in the school's development plan and equality policy;
- the previous coordinator's action plan/teaching support timetable. (Bellsham-Revell & Nancarrow/NALDIC, 2019: 4)

If these are not available, they should be your first priority. You might also find it useful to include the following:

- a list of local supplementary schools and community groups, with contact details for group leaders;
- details of local networks, professional bodies, websites and blogs on EAL, so that you can refer others to useful material easily;
- contact details for bilingual parents who are willing to help with school activities.

These will be your first steps towards building a whole-community approach to language in the school.

Task 3 Building your policy folder

☐ Use the list above to build your policy folder. Note any documents that are missing to discuss with your line manager.
☐ Make the folder accessible to other teachers (for example on a shared drive).

What Are your Aspirations for the Role?

There are as many ways to be an EAL specialist as there are EAL specialists. One of the great things about the job is that you can tailor the role as you get to know your colleagues, your community and the needs of the pupils in your school. That said, there are some common factors and you can use these to start thinking about what kind of EAL specialist you want to be (or, if you are reading this with more experience under your belt, to think about where you stand now and how that compares with your aspirations for the role).

It can be quite hard to pin down your aspirations at the beginning. If we gave new EAL specialists a blank sheet of paper and 20 minutes to write down what came to mind, we would get ... well, let's give it a try.

Task 4 Developing your own EAL plan

☐ Take a blank sheet of paper (or its digital equivalent) and set a timer for 20 minutes.
☐ Write down your aspirations for the role before the timer runs out. Try to keep writing non-stop to get as much on paper as possible.
☐ Develop this into your personal EAL plan (see below).

What's on your list? Read through it and look for any common themes or categories that come up. For example, are there broad aspirations for the well-being of EAL pupils (that they will feel nurtured, valued, confident)? Are there specific targets connected to attainment or proficiency (that they will achieve a certain level within a certain time)? Are there any measures of how you will change the school itself (raising awareness among the staff, organising a 'language of the week' event) or of how you will work (spend more time working with advanced learners, less time doing x, y or z)? Compare these with your job description and the school's language policy (see Task 3): Do your aspirations align with what is expected of you? If not, this can be raised when you meet your line manager to discuss your initial priorities. Finally, match your own goals against the evidence from Part 1 and Part 2 (and your wider reading) so that you have a solid base of evidence when you raise them with colleagues. You might produce a table like that shown in Table 17.1.

Your personal EAL plan might include a combination of the following:

- *Administrative tasks.* Simple but important: the first tasks on the list should be to fill in any gaps in your policy folder and the EAL register, making sure they are accessible to all staff.
- *Goals for specific groups of learners.* What are the main groups of EAL learners in your school and what support is (or should be) in place for them? Your goals here should be detailed and precise, such as developing an induction programme for new arrivals or helping advanced bilingual pupils handle metaphor. These goals should be reviewed termly and will likely involve others across the school.
- *Promoting a whole-school approach to language.* How can you support colleagues to embed a positive, whole-school approach to language? Some of your goals might relate to making multilingualism more visible, for example through the use of displays, assemblies and activities. Others will focus on supporting specific teachers to develop their understanding of language and their ability to use this knowledge in their teaching. Some might address the relationship between the school and the local community, for example by working with local partners (community and faith groups, parents, supplementary schools). These goals should be quite concrete: break down the larger tasks and move the broader aspirations to the section below to maintain a balance of short- and long-term goals.
- *Continuing professional development.* Include your own CPD needs, those of your team (if applicable) and the wider staff. Identify which goals you can meet through

Table 17.1 From aspirations to a personal EAL plan

Goal	Why is it important to me?	How will I put it into practice?	How will I measure success?	How does it fit with my job description?	What theory and evidence support me?

self-study, which need external advisors and which need formal learning (and perhaps higher-level qualifications such as a master's degree). If you can show how your CPD needs fit into the school's needs, it will bolster your chances of getting support from senior leaders. You can also consult Chapter 23, which reviews the evidence for EAL professional development.
- *Long-term aspirations.* These are the points on the horizon you are aiming for. What drew you to working with EAL learners? What do you hope the school will be like? What do you want to achieve in the next few years – for yourself, for your learners and for your school? The aim of this paragraph is two-fold: it gives context to the more concrete goals in the earlier sections and it help you to keep moving forward in your career.

Your personal EAL plan serves two purposes. It helps you to think critically about your school and the community it serves, identifying the opportunities to raise attainment and well as the challenges. It also gives a structured approach to thinking about your own goals and how to achieve them.

Chapter Review

This chapter set out some of the things you'll need to address in your first term or two in the role. It started with an EAL audit, getting to grips with the school environment and building up a strong foundation for your own work. Through a series of tasks, it developed a personal EAL plan and a set of goals for future development. The following chapters build on this: establishing effective assessments so that you have robust data to work with; looking at how you can organise EAL provision and the implications of different approaches for teaching and learning; and getting connected with colleagues locally and nationally.

Case Study 4: Working with Families

Erica Field is an Ethnic Minority Achievement adviser at Rochdale Borough Council and an experienced EAL teacher. In this case study she describes how she brings parents into the conversation.

Language underpins learning. It allows us to frame our thoughts and ideas, to explore through discussion, discover through reading and refine through writing. Oracy and literacy skills weave their way through our curriculum. Schools work hard to help English as an additional language learners get to grips with curriculum language. With access to curriculum language children and young people can take part in classroom learning in a much richer way. How do we support this?

It doesn't really matter which area or phase of education you focus on, parents can make all the difference. In Rochdale, when we think about meeting the needs of bilingual learners in schools, parents are one of the first resources that we consider. So when it comes to supporting the acquisition of curriculum language it's no surprise that our approach goes beyond the curriculum and into families.

International new arrivals don't arrive at our schools as blank slates. Children come with a history of learning, formal or informal, and an ever-expanding set of language skills. And it's worth remembering that a parent is always a child's first teacher.

Alongside common approaches to supporting the acquisition of curriculum language in the classroom (such as pre-teaching vocabulary, experiential learning, collaborative activities, active listening, substitution tables and much more), we look at ways to strengthen partnerships with parents. In Rochdale we have produced a number of bilingual resources, in conjunction with teachers and families, to support the parents of new arrivals to understand education in our schools. For example, we have a guide for getting your child ready for Reception and an introduction to multiplication tables for parents of children joining a Rochdale school in KS2.

We also run parent workshops, inviting parents along to talk about how we can work together to support their children's education. A workshop in EYFS might include an introduction to synthetic phonics and a discussion about how to help your child learn to read in English, even if you don't. A Year 6 workshop might include an explanation about SATs, how translation can aid learning, word problems in Maths and supporting reading for meaning. All parent workshops acknowledge that the parent is the expert on their own child, stress the importance of continuing to develop the first language and share examples of how the first language can be used to deepen an understanding of curriculum.

Parent workshops are supported by translators. This tends to work by grouping parents of the same language together at one table along with the translator. It might be that we have up to half a dozen interpreters present at a session. While this sounds expensive, I assure you that it is invaluable.

If I'm delivering the workshop, one of the first things I do, after making sure everyone has a brew, is to explain how the session will function. Basically, I talk and then pause. At this point all the translators will translate. I talk in short bursts. The translation tends to take a little longer. Once all the translators have finished, and parents have sought any clarity needed, I talk again.

At the end of each workshop we offer the opportunity for parents to ask questions. I've had everything from queries about the Bus Stop Method to what time is a reasonable time for the child to go to bed. It can be helpful to have a couple of members of staff at the session. This gives the opportunity to build relationships and reduces the length of time people have to wait for an answer to their question.

Parent workshops can also be supplemented with handouts, such as the relevant year group spelling list or topic vocabulary, for families to take away.

Because language underpins learning we have found that it helps when we acknowledge that the language the children already have is essential for their education; that the family's first languages are essential. The parent workshop allows us to share curriculum language found in a child's classroom, link it to language and skills the child already has and provide suggestions of ways we can work together to further develop oracy and literacy.

Commentary

It can be hard to make space for families amid the pressures of the school day, but Erica gives us clear strategies to use. She puts a lot of emphasis on the first language, both as a way for the parents to be involved and because it supports achievement in the curriculum. She also works with translators, supplies handouts and creates bilingual resources to make sure that messages are available in different formats. This means that information is delivered in a rich context and the different elements can reinforce each other. By holding meetings several times a year she is also drawing parents into the curriculum, making the links between academic language and the literacies developing in the home explicit. We can see this as a way to nurture multi-competent pupils, whose languages are valued in school for the roles they play in the child's wider lives.

Erica's case study also makes clear how important it is to connect with parents as people: starting with cups of tea, but also making sure that the school provides translators and that there is time to slow down, pause, and wait while parents articulate the questions that matter to them. EAL specialists often have dual roles like this: acting as bridges between school and the community, making sure resources get to the right places and that parents have the right information, but also acting as bulwarks against the rush and pressure of the school day. Carving out time for parents means that pupils can be supported at home and school.

18 Establishing Effective Assessments

To support learners effectively, we need a clear understanding of what they can do and where they need help next. Good assessment is central to this, but not all language assessments are created equal.

Assessment is part of every teacher's life, but the cross-curricular nature of EAL means that we need a particularly rounded understanding of how to measure language and subject content together. Not all assessment frameworks are up to the task; too often, they emphasise a restricted view of grammatical knowledge rather than the learner's ability to use a range of language appropriately and in context. This chapter helps you to make informed decisions about EAL assessment.

The chapter starts by looking at the basic features of effective language assessments – the construct and the rating scale, and formative or summative modes. The next section delves into some of the thinking behind language assessment, asking what purpose it serves and how to choose a test that works for you. Details of high-quality tests are also given, so that you have somewhere reliable to start. Throughout this chapter, we keep two principles in mind. First, select, don't accept. Assessment frameworks provide us with useful information but they must not determine the curriculum; that leads to narrower learning and less effective teaching, for reasons that we explore. Second, the teacher is the key. Assessment results always need interpreting in context; they give us insights, but they can't replace the knowledge and experience of a skilled EAL specialist.

Basic Features of Language Assessments

Every language assessment is built around two parts: the *construct* (what is being measured) and the *rating scale* (how this is described as a series of levels or stages). The rating scales often look quite similar to each other but can relate to very different constructs, so it's important to compare like with like. Two assessment frameworks might both use the descriptor 'intermediate', for example, but actually describe very different sets of skills and knowledge, or describe similar constructs but put the boundaries between levels at different points. We look at two example rating scales in Task 5.

Establishing Effective Assessments 135

Task 5a Identifying the focus of an assessment (i)

☐ Look at these two sample descriptors and note everything you can think of about the construct. Once you have your notes, move on to the next task.

A2	Can find specific information in practical, concrete, predictable texts (e.g. travel guidebooks, recipes), provided they are written in simple language.
	Can understand the main information in short and simple descriptions of goods in brochures and websites (e.g. portable digital devices, cameras, etc.).
	Can find specific, predictable information in simple everyday material such as advertisements, prospectuses, menus, reference lists and timetables.
	Can locate specific information in lists and isolate the information required (e.g. use the 'Yellow Pages' to find a service or tradesman).
	Can understand everyday signs and notices etc. in public places, such as streets, restaurants, railway stations, in workplaces, such as directions, instructions, hazard warnings.

Source: Common European Framework for Reference (CEFR) (Council of Europe, 2018: 62).

CONNECTION: *Common Core Reading Standards for Informational Texts, Integration of Knowledge & Ideas #7:* Integrate and evaluate multiple sources of information presented in different media or formats (e.g., visually, quantitatively) as well as in words in order to address a question or solve a problem.

EXAMPLE CONTEXT FOR LANGUAGE USE: Students review college or career marketing materials (e.g., print or online) according to personal preferences (e.g., affordability, location, time commitment, requirements, interest) to make informed decisions on post-secondary options.

	COGNITIVE FUNCTION: Students at all levels of English language proficiency EVALUATE post-secondary options.					
	Level 1 Entering	Level 2 Emerging	Level 3 Developing	Level 4 Expanding	Level 5 Bridging	
READING	Sort information on post-secondary options from multiple sources with visual support with a partner	Identify important information (e.g., by highlighting) on post-secondary options from multiple sources with visual support with a partner	Categorize (e.g., best, maybe, unlikely) post-secondary options from multiple sources using illustrated graphic organizers	Make judgments about post-secondary options from multiple sources using illustrated graphic organizers (e.g., checklists of types of evidence)	Draw conclusions on post-secondary options from claims in multiple sources of information	Level 6 - Reaching
TOPIC-RELATED LANGUAGE: Students at all levels of English language proficiency interact with grade-level words and expressions, such as: priorities, vocation/trade, merit scholarship, cost of living, room and board, professional reference, résumé-building						

Source: WIDA English Language Development Standards (WIDA, 2012: 40).

Task 5b Identifying the focus of an assessment (ii)

☐ Add to your notes:
  ○ What types of language does each descriptor mention?
  ○ What types of text, situation or interaction are described?
  ○ What learner characteristics are implied by each descriptor?
  ○ What links do they each make to the curriculum and to academic language?
☐ Finally, decide which is most appropriate for your learners and note why.

Task 5 illustrates the difference between rating scales and their underlying constructs, and it shows that we can get a good sense of the construct just by reading the descriptors carefully. The first example is taken from the 'reading for orientation' descriptor at Level A2 (beginner-low intermediate) of the Common European Framework of Reference (CEFR). There are five characteristics described and they address a range of settings and text types (travel guidebooks, recipes, brochures, websites, advertisements, menus, and so on). It focuses on identifying or finding key information in those text types – the sort of thing that is important if you travel abroad but that is not specific to any particular domain or context.

The second example is taken from the WIDA 'social and instructional language' descriptor for Level 2 (emerging) at Grade 11 – UK year 12. The first thing to notice is that they are not obviously comparable: Level A2 (CEFR) and Level 2 (WIDA) are not equivalents, although both are the second level in a six-stage (CEFR) or five-stage (WIDA) scale. The WIDA descriptor notes skills (identify important information) and relevant text types (multiple sources), using tools and techniques (highlighting, visual support, working with a partner) that are common to subject classes. It is concise, but an example context for language use is given (review college or career marketing materials), as are relevant and age-appropriate cognitive functions (evaluate). Topic-specific language is identified but the descriptor notes that – in the subject classroom – students at all levels of proficiency will encounter much the same vocabulary.

Even the best test needs to be used in the right way. One important distinction is between *formative* and *summative* assessment (also known as assessment *for* learning and assessment *of* learning). Formative assessments look forwards; they give us a sense of what the learner knows now and are useful for planning. Summative assessments look backwards (they sum up learning) and tell us something about what was learned. Almost all the assessment done by the EAL specialist should be formative. Curriculum subjects already have summative assessments, so our focus can be on getting learners into the mainstream and supporting them to achieve highly across the curriculum.

What Is an Assessment Framework for?

Simply put, assessment frameworks tell you what students should be able to do at certain stages. The stages themselves are descriptions of an underlying construct: with each stage or descriptor, the test designers are trying to show how different aspects of a learner's abilities relate to each other. A really good way into this is to look at The Bell Foundation's assessment framework (https://www.bell-foundation.org.uk/eal-programme/teaching-resources/eal-assessment-framework), which comes with an extensive set of descriptors, trackers and guidance notes. It also includes a detailed report on the evidence informing the assessment framework. Other useful reference points include the NASSEA (https://www.nassea.org.uk/eal-assessment-framework) and Solihull (https://www.solgrid.org.uk/education/support-services/english-as-an-additional-language/assessment) assessment frameworks.

> **Task 6** Understanding the purpose of an assessment framework
>
> ☐ Go to The Bell Foundation's website and download a copy of the assessment framework (https://www.bell-foundation.org.uk/eal-programme/teaching-resources/eal-assessment-framework). You need to register an account but it is free.
> ☐ Watch the introductory video (five minutes) and read the introduction (two slides).
> ☐ Make a note on what information the assessment provides. Who might find it useful and why?

Each band of the assessment framework (from A – new to English, to D – competent/diversifying) contains 10 descriptors for each of the four skills (Listening, Speaking, Reading and Viewing, Writing). These descriptors allow us to record what the student is able to do, creating a snapshot of their proficiency. To make an assessment, you simply select all the descriptors that apply to the pupil and match them to the band that fits best. The advantage of this approach is that the remaining descriptors give a good sense of what the pupil might be capable of doing soon. The descriptors do not define that progression and are not usually completed in order, but they do give a broad outline of what we can expect to see.

It is up to the teacher to interpret this in context. Assessment profiles are usually 'spiky', meaning they are stronger in some areas than in others, and there are often good reasons why some descriptors are met earlier or later. The pupil might have arrived fairly recently and not yet be ready to demonstrate the full extent of their abilities. You might have been doing more work on one skill area, for example, or one subject teacher might make a particular effort to support EAL learners to work in groups with others, or the school librarian might run a reading club with lots of bilingual books ... many things can affect the pupils' language profiles. The assessment is your snapshot tool; it doesn't tell you how you got there or determine your curriculum and approach.

Choosing the Right Test

The main consideration when choosing an assessment framework is this: Does it give you information you can use, in a format you can use, to support learners to develop proficiency in academic English? This immediately rules out most general English assessments; they don't tell us enough about the distinctive syntax, vocabulary and skills of academic English. Your test should be primarily formative, so that you can assess regularly but unobtrusively, without getting learners to spend precious time sitting tests or doing work that is only for you to assess. Finally, your test should reflect your high aspirations for your learners. Descriptors should put learning in context (as with the examples above) and show flexibility where profiles are stronger in some areas than others. They should be focused on what the learner can do, and not on a sequence of language points to cover.

Good EAL assessments are also embedded in a curriculum context: the skills and texts they refer to should be those that the students will encounter in the subject classroom. This means a stronger emphasis on assessing vocabulary and how it is used than on assessing grammar. Building a deep and wide vocabulary is essential, as is knowledge of the genre conventions of different types of academic text. Testing grammar is less important: if we assess how well students get their meaning across, we will quickly see what grammatical points need explicit teaching.

Chapter Review

This chapter has reviewed several principles in establishing effective assessments. It began with the basic features of language assessment: the construct and rating scale, plus formative and summative modes. We found that different assessment frameworks are not directly comparable because they often assess different things or use different boundaries. We found that EAL assessment should be almost entirely formative, as we want regular snapshots of what pupils can do with their growing language skills. We looked at sample rating scales to see that the EAL specialist plays an important role in contextualising and interpreting assessment results. Pupils' language profiles are often spiky and strongly influenced by the context, so the assessment alone should not define the next steps. The right framework for your school will be one that meets your needs – easy and unobtrusive to use, with a strong focus on vocabulary and content, and reflecting your high aspirations for the learners.

19 Welcoming Students

The more we know about our learners, the better we can support them. This chapter looks at what information we need to collect and how we can use it in the admissions process.

So far we have looked at what you hope to achieve in the first few terms and considered your approach to assessing language. Now it's time to start pulling it together into formally organised provision. This chapter starts from the beginning, both for you in your new role and for your learners as they arrive in the school for the first time. We look at the initial fact-finding you'll need to conduct (which, together with the EAL audit in Chapter 17, should give detailed insight into your school) and at the kind of induction you might offer. We then focus on two key aspects of EAL provision: how to create an environment where the welcome is more than skin deep, and what models you can base your provision on.

Getting Started

Initial fact-finding

Your EAL audit focused on the school and on your role, leading to a personal EAL plan. The initial fact-finding now focuses on the learners. What do you know about their languages, their experiences of school, their learning at home and in the community? A good way to learn about these is through the students' own stories, and Task 7 offers us a thought-provoking starting point.

Task 7 A different perspective on language and community

☐ Visit the Multilingual Digital Storytelling website (https://goldsmithsmdst.com) and watch some of the student-made videos. Make notes on:
- What these videos tell us about the language and literacy skills that children bring into the classroom.[1]
- How we can help colleagues to understand the relevance of these multilingual literacy skills for curriculum learning.

Note: [1] A detailed handbook for teachers accompanies the MDST project and is available from http://goldsmithsmdst.wordpress.com/handbook. See Chapter 8 of that publication for ideas on integrating multilingual literacies into the curriculum.

The Multilingual Digital Storytelling Project was 'a form of life writing about personal and shared experiences'. It took learners from different language backgrounds and gave them the tools to tell stories about their lives and communities. Because it took place outside school, it allows us to see the young people's languages and literacies in a new light. We are particularly interested in:

- What languages can the pupils speak, read and write?
- Who do they use their languages with?
- Have they been to school before? If so, what did they study and for how long?
- What would the children say are their talents and skills?
- What languages do they use on regular basis and for what/with whom?

We hope to get a sense of who our learners are and how they would like to be known. To do that we need to ask them directly, and try to set aside the monolingual assumptions that many of us have grown up with. If you are monolingual, you use one language for everything and develop all your literacy skills in that language. For multilingual children, though, the picture might be quite different. They may not be literate in their main language (because many regional varieties lack a common written form), and have learned to read and write in a more prestigious variety. The majority of people in the world use more than one language as a matter of course, switching between them without thinking. If we only assess multilingual pupils in English, their poor test results would lead us to be concerned about their level of proficiency. But think how strange it must be from the other side, working with teachers who can only speak one language!

There are several good techniques for eliciting this kind of rich insight into the pupils' languages and literacies. Observation is one, but language portraits are also useful for getting pupils to share their ideas. Any kind of multilingual storytelling is also good. This approach can supplement your assessments or – for new arrivals – replace them in the first few months. When pupils are immersed in a new language it is very common for them to be silent for a period, and in any case it is very unlikely that they will show their language skills to their fullest extent. Any formal assessments in the first six months should be reviewed later in the school year to account for this.

Robust admissions, assessment and induction

The richness of our initial fact-finding needs to be reflected in the rigour of our admission, assessment and induction process. As Christine McCormack shows in her case study (which follows this chapter), a very clear process gives confidence to colleagues who might be less certain of what to do when multilingual pupils arrive in class, as well as furnishing us with useful information to plan provision.

The admissions meeting is an important starting point. In addition to the information from the fact-finding, we would need to know about any faith observance and dietary requirements (if your school does not routinely accommodate them), whether they attend a supplementary school, and any special needs or health issues. Joining a new school can be overwhelming and pupils don't always feel able to ask when they need the school to adjust to them – even though the teachers would happily do so if they had known. In a similar vein, it is also worth taking this opportunity to find out from them how the student's name is pronounced and including it in the information that goes out to the teaching staff.

Good admissions meetings include a tour, time to talk to key members of staff (with an interpreter if needed) and a chance for the new child to meet peers. It is often helpful to have a set day for admissions meetings, and a set starting date a short while later so that new arrivals join together and colleagues can be well briefed to welcome them (although this is not always possible in schools with very high or very low numbers of new arrivals). A baseline assessment should be conducted as soon as possible after arrival but need not be very formal: observation will give more insight in the early weeks, and if possible a member of staff who speaks the same language should be involved. Where setting is used, always place the student based on your best estimate of their curriculum learning and not their English proficiency (which will change rapidly). It is better to have high aspirations and support the pupil in a higher set than to place them in a lower set straight away. It is very hard to overcome a first impression that teachers have low expectations of you.

Task 8 From 'new arrival' to 'one of us'

☐ Gather your school's admissions procedures and welcome pack (if there is one). Ask around to find out what information is sent to staff – and whether it is actually used or gets lost in the email blizzard.
☐ On a fresh sheet of paper, draw a timeline from when you first get news of a new arrival, through the induction period, to when you might be confident that they are settling in. Add:
  ○ Your key actions and where you need information or help from others.
  ○ When others might need to act (for example, in their own classrooms) or need more information from you.
  ○ What points the new pupil might find most disconcerting or need your help with.
  ○ When you are going to check in with the pupil's buddies, teachers and family.
☐ Run this past a few colleagues. Does everyone know what's expected and is anything missing?

Creating a Welcoming Learning Environment

It's important to look at our schools through the eyes of new arrivals. Pupils are quick to recognise when their languages and experiences are truly welcome in the school and when they are only paid lip service to. It is very common, for example, to see the word 'welcome' in a couple of dozen languages in the reception area, but then find that the teaching staff don't have information on the languages and literacies that pupils bring into the classroom, or that (in Secondary, particularly) EAL is relegated to a separate corridor with little connection to the mainstream. The physical environment matters, but so do the opportunities for learners to bring their lives and languages into the curriculum.

> **Task 9 Surveying the linguistic landscape**
>
> ☐ Find some time to walk through the school slowly. Start in the reception area and work your way up to your classroom; then go around each department (in Secondary), the common areas and gathering places such as the hall, the dining hall and the playground. Take photos as you go, aiming to capture every instance of language that is visible.
> ☐ On a separate occasion, take a notebook and record what languages you hear. It's often worth pausing at places where students congregate and where they move from one space to another: coming out of lessons, into assembly, in the playground.
> ☐ Compare your notes and the images. Do you see the same languages that you heard? Were there times when you couldn't be sure what language was being used or where languages were mixed? The difference between the (teacher-controlled) visual environment and the (student-controlled) aural environment is a good indicator of how well the school reflects the languages of the pupils.
> ☐ Optionally, you might repeat this, but looking at/listening for cultural references rather than languages.

Some displays do make a difference. When they make students' languages, experiences and cultures visible, they demonstrate that bilingual pupils have a rightful place in the school. Sometimes the difference seems quite small: name trees, for example, take a regular multilingual display and enrich it with information provided by students and their families. Jean Conteh (2012: 76–77) explains:

> [The teacher] began by making a large cut-out tree shape (without leaves) for the classroom wall. Then she showed the children a photo of her own daughter and told them what her name meant and why she had given it to her. After this, she gave each child a letter [...] translated into some of the home languages of the children and a leaf cut out of green paper to take to their parents.

The parents helped their children write their names on one side, with a bilingual explanation of its meaning on the other. Each child presented their leaf and the teacher added her own. Parents were invited in to see the completed tree and it was presented to the school in a special assembly.

There are many other ways to create space for pupils' languages and experiences. Dual-language resources are a great way to develop literacy and connect subject content with both English and first languages. There are a range of resources that explore their use and some excellent ones are listed in the suggestions for further reading. Using the pupils' first languages to discuss subject content is more valuable still, recognising each learner as 'a legitimate, multi-competent language user in their own right' (Li Wei, 2016: 536). The final task of this chapter is designed to give an insight into that person.

Task 10 Shadow a pupil

- ☐ Shadow a pupil for at least a lesson, a short break and a long break (so most of a morning). In Secondary, shadowing pupils in a range of lessons will give a richer insight into their experiences, allowing you to compare how teachers approach different subject areas and how the pupils respond.
- ☐ Note how others speak to the pupil. Is their name used accurately? Does their hand go up and is it noticed? Do teachers and others show patience if they need time to formulate their ideas? Do they have a supportive group of friends? How do they manage differences in language, experience and English proficiency?
- ☐ What specific techniques does the teacher use to ensure the pupil is included, supported and challenged? Do pupils do anything to the same end?
- ☐ What would you change for this pupil if you could?
- ☐ Share your insights with the colleagues concerned and ask if it matches their observations of the pupil. What next steps would they take as a result?

Chapter Review

This chapter has looked at the welcome that the school offers to new pupils. It began by proposing an initial fact-finding about the pupils themselves, their languages, cultures and experiences. This acts as a complement to the EAL audit of Chapter 17, which focused on the school and on your role. It discussed good practice in admissions and looked at how the school environment could be made more welcoming. It is not enough to have different languages on the walls if the pupils do not see themselves reflected in the curriculum – and young people spot the difference very quickly. EAL specialists are in a powerful position to make bilingual and migrant pupils more visible, to advocate and to amplify their voices. We will return to this when we discuss how to make friends and influence provision in Chapter 21.

Case Study 5: New Arrivals

Christine McCormack is an EAL teacher and Area Lead for EAL in Glasgow. She produced a guide and resource pack for working with new arrivals and chairs a working group for local schools to coordinate their support for pupils arriving in the area.

As an EAL teacher, I use a number of strategies when preparing to welcome a new arrival bilingual pupil in school. If we have notice of the learner's arrival, we prepare the class teacher with some basic starter resources and gather some background information which will enable me to ensure that the resources and strategies provided are at the correct age, stage and academic and language level for the learner. More often than not, however, the arrival of a new pupil is unexpected or allows little preparation time. In both cases there are a number of things I would do to ensure that the learner (and their family) feels welcome and has an opportunity to settle relatively quickly.

Prior to arrival (if possible), and assuming we have some knowledge of the learner, I would prepare some resources in the home language and English ('All About Me' activities, dual-language books, websites with dual-language stories and games); this will help with the settling in period of the first few days in class. It is important to give some settling time in class as the learner may be shy, in a silent period or just a little reluctant to communicate at first. An English language level assessment taken too early could be inaccurate.

If possible, it is extremely useful to attend the enrolment meeting with the parents and an interpreter. This is when we can gather important information such as previous schooling, home language skills and academic abilities. It also allows time for the parents to ask questions, perhaps have a short tour of the school and be given some key information about timetabling, curriculum and the school day in general. I would ensure that the importance of maintaining the home language is discussed here also. Whatever information is gathered here would be shared with the relevant staff who would be working directly with the learner.

There can often be a sense of panic when a new arrival bilingual learner appears in school quite unexpectedly. In Glasgow, we have a booklet called *Supporting New Arrivals in Glasgow Schools*. I give this to the class teacher to ensure that they have some background information and strategies to support bilingual learners in the mainstream classroom and to minimise any extra planning and preparation they may need to do.

When the learner arrives, if possible, I buddy them up with a same-language peer who they can speak to about any concerns or misunderstandings they may have. I would also recommend that they are sat with a good role model of English. I use resources such as a communication fan [a pocket-sized set of cards with useful language and often pictures, joined at one end so that they fan out] and a visual timetable to ensure that they can communicate and understand the basics of what is happening.

After a few weeks, I carry out an assessment to determine the English language level of the learner. The assessment would focus on reading, writing, talking and listening activities both in English and the home language. I use a translation app to aid me with this and I aim to provide a text in the home language to demonstrate reading skills. I use the Glasgow City Council English language level descriptors when determining their level of English.

If we assess that the pupil is new to English, I recommend a focus on survival language for the first few weeks in school. In order to communicate basic needs, I believe the learner should concentrate on:

- All About Me
- social language/feelings
- school
- colours
- the body
- clothes
- food
- weather/seasons etc.

As well as providing support for the learner either on a one-to-one basis or within a small group of pupils who are at a similar language level, I would give the class teacher some resources to cover each of these areas and to ensure that survival language can remain a focus in class. I would recommend against initially focusing on a phonics or reading programme, and concentrate on using picture books and creating a bilingual dictionary which can be completed at home with parents.

With regard to homework, it is essential that the parents are informed that it is not important to be able to speak English to support their child. Taking time to meet with parents (and an interpreter) early on to ease any homework worries and discuss ways in which the home language can support learning is important. At this point, I would encourage parents to ask questions and discuss the homework with their children, and stress the importance of supporting their home language. Picture books are useful for this, as no assumptions have to be made or questions asked about the literacy levels at home.

After some weeks, more structured support should be in place to ensure progression and access to the curriculum. Working in class is best, using team teaching and modelling to support the pupil alongside peers, but it is not always possible. Withdrawing the learner for extra support is also an option. Whatever we do, we want to ensure the class teacher has access to resources (both physical and digital) to support continuous progress and help the learner on their journey through the school.

Commentary

It's easy to see why Christine's approach was so well received in Glasgow. She's at the heart of things, making sure she is well informed about each new arrival, working with subject teachers, setting up buddies and getting resources to the right people. She makes life easy for colleagues by supplying them with a pre-prepared guide and information about the pupil, which will go some way to easing the 'panic' that many people feel about new arrivals. Despite all this activity, she makes time for stillness and patience: it can be overwhelming to arrive in a new school, new city and new language, so she holds off assessing the pupil until things have settled down. As with Erica Field (Case Study 4), parents are an integral part of her work and she finds time for a school tour and some one-to-one time with them.

Christine advocates survival English and withdrawal for pupils who are completely new to English. This is one of the few occasions when we might relax our commitment to supporting learners in the mainstream classroom. The withdrawal programme she describes is time-limited (just a few weeks), has clear goals (equip students to get by in everyday school life) and has a clear exit (structured support using team-teaching and modelling in class). It shows a flexible, responsive approach to supporting new arrivals that still adheres to the principles of developing successful bilingual learners.

20 Getting Connected

A strong network will support you as you develop as a specialist. This chapter outlines the main organisations to investigate.

The EAL community is brilliant! You'll find a lot of supportive, experienced people online and in local networks around the UK (and internationally). Connecting with them is especially important as you develop your own role and seek to establish good practices in your school: a strong network will bring people to share ideas and celebrate successes with, bring perspective to challenges and save you from reinventing the wheel. (If your work is more established, then these networks are a great place to support others and meet likeminded peers.) You will find a full list of networks and groups in Appendix II.

Subject Associations

The first place to turn is **NALDIC**, the subject association for EAL (http://naldic.org.uk). It operates a network of regional groups around the UK as well as online groups for international and independent schools. NALDIC's annual conference is a great place to meet other EAL specialists (and EAL-interested colleagues) and to get up to date with developments in the field. Their flagship publication is the *EAL Journal*, published three times a year. It contains accessible research summaries, reports on excellent practice and commentary on issues as varied as policy and professional development. The **EAL-Bilingual Group** (https://groups.google.com/forum/#!forum/eal-bilingual), also managed by NALDIC, is an online peer discussion forum where EAL specialists can ask questions and share resources. It is free to join and messages can be grouped into handy daily or weekly digests so they won't overwhelm your inbox.

The **EAL Research Network** is an academic group that is open to all (see www.ealresearchnetwork.com). They produce and share evidence-based resources and research summaries about EAL, language in the curriculum and more. They particularly welcome practitioners with an interest in research.

NASSEA (the Northern Association of Support Services for Equality and Achievement) has a wealth of resources, including an EAL assessment framework, and runs training events and an annual conference (http://www.nassea.org.uk). For teachers in Scotland, **SATEAL** (the Scottish Association for Teachers of EAL) also organises an annual conference (https://www.sateal.org.uk). The Welsh subject association

(EALAW) is not currently operational, but NALDIC runs a number of regional groups that Welsh members can join.

For international schools, the **Multilingual Learning in International Education** special interest group (part of ECIS, see https://www.ecis.org/mlie) organises a fantastic biannual conference. The event is hosted in a different European country each time and attracts large numbers of teachers from around the world as well as leading researchers. Teachers in state sector schools will find much to value here; MLIE are passionate advocates for multilingualism and multilingual learners, and their work encompasses languages other than English too.

Task 11 Getting to know your subject association

- ☐ Find your subject association. Make a note of how much membership costs and what it offers you.
- ☐ Note three things you can do to build your network within this community. For example, is there a regional group in your area? If so, you could email the convenor to say hi and get details of the next meeting. Do they publish resources (like a blog or magazine)? If so, is there anyone you can buddy with to talk about what you read? Is there a conference that could go in your diary now? If so, add the details to your professional development plan (see Chapter 23).

Subject associations play a vital role in the professional recognition of EAL. They advocate with policy makers and make the sector's voice heard in consultations. They offer a network of colleagues to share ideas with and produce resources to inspire and refresh. They also convene the conferences where you can meet and be inspired by others. Having joined your subject association, the next steps are to build up your online community and identify good resources to draw on.

Online Community

Twitter has become an invaluable source of ideas and connections for many EAL teachers. All the subject associations listed above run Twitter accounts (see Appendix II). So many people are on Twitter that I won't list individual accounts here. The best place to start is with @EAL_naldic and @EAL_journal: see who is following them and whom they follow, then search using the hashtag #EAL to see who's talking about EAL online. The hashtag #multilingual is also good for EAL (and if you're not sure what hashtags and tweets are, try the beginner's guides at the end of this section).

There are a small number of EAL-focused blogs and these are also worth following. Online resources can come and go fairly quickly, but at the time of writing the following were stable and shared great content.

- *EAL Journal* (https://ealjournal.org). The *EAL Journal* blog is a great place to start. It offers the same mix of practice, activism and research as its print cousin. It also

includes contributors from the UK and around the world, sharing what they do in the classroom.
- *EAL in the Daylight* (https://ealdaylight.com). Jonathan Bifield, an EAL coordinator at a large secondary school, runs a blog with the aim of 'keeping EAL in the daylight'. The posts are reliably well informed and thoughtful, and would make a good starting point for discussions in your local group. The site also includes some materials, book reviews and links.
- *Across Cultures* (https://www.axcultures.com/teacher-guidance). This blog, from the team behind the award-winning Learning Village website, is rich in practical ideas and includes a lot of posts about using technology in the classroom.
- *Empowering ELLs* (https://www.empoweringells.com). Tan Huynh is a teacher, bilingual learner and trainer who has worked in the United States, China, Laos, Vietnam and Thailand. His blog contains a wealth of ideas, many with accessible infographics, and innovative 'bathroom briefs' to pin up in the loo so that everyone gets a little PD while they pee.

More blogs and resource sites are listed in Appendix II.

Task 12 Getting connected online

If you're an old hand at social media, skip this task.

☐ Make a Twitter profile (see the guide below if you need ideas). Add a photo and find 10 people to follow. If you're not sure, start with @EAL_naldic and @EAL_journal: they're good starting points because a lot of EAL people follow them. You can also search for the accounts posting using the hashtag #EAL and follow them.
☐ Send your first message! If you want to find more people to follow, you can say that you're new to social media and ask for recommendations. Use #EAL and tag some EAL people into the tweet so that it shows up on their timelines.
☐ Schedule time to check your account regularly until you get a feel for who's sharing what. Try to reply to people and engage in conversations: goodwill and generosity are usually returned in kind.

Beginner's guides to Twitter

You can find a host of guides for using Twitter online (including on Twitter). If you're just getting started, this one takes you through all the basics (including what tweets are and how to make a profile): https://ditchthattextbook.com/a-beginners-guide-to-twitter-for-educators. The Teacher Toolkit has good ideas on using social media generally: https://www.teachertoolkit.co.uk/2017/02/04/social-media-secrets.

For More Established EAL Specialists

Once you have the first term or two under your belt, you can start looking ahead to how you want your role and your school to develop. The following chapters are written to help you do that. They follow the same structure as those for new EAL specialists (Chapters 17–20), but go into more depth, reflecting an increasing level of complexity in the role. EAL specialists do not (or should not) work in isolation: the role extends across the curriculum and is a vital part of developing a whole-school approach to language. The next chapter accordingly looks at 'making friends and influencing people' – or getting to grips with how your role interacts with those of your colleagues. It covers different approaches to leadership in EAL, models of provision and making more fundamental and lasting change to the way in which multilingualism is perceived in school. Later chapters explore how we might shift from a monolingual to a multilingual mindset and what CPD looks like for experienced EAL specialists. This section also includes two case studies, although these are longer and written in a slightly different style. The first is a double-length chapter based on interviews with senior Ofsted inspectors. These help to show the breadth of the EAL specialist's role and how it is connected with the work of others across the school. The second is by Anne Margaret Smith, who brings her expertise in SEN and language development to the discussion.

21 Making Friends and Influencing People

For more experienced specialists, the challenge is to influence language-rich teaching across the school. This chapter looks at different approaches to doing so.

The first half of Part 3 looked at the priorities for the first term or so. They are largely focused on your own actions – getting to grips with the role, establishing effective assessments, welcoming students and building a network of likeminded colleagues. It also recognised that our education system currently takes monolingualism as the default state: real change for bilingual children means tackling these assumptions and the structures that marginalise their experiences and their voices. Change of that kind is hard for one person alone; it needs people working together, and that needs leadership. This chapter looks at what leadership might look like for an EAL specialist, a role that could combine advocacy, research and expert practice.

Beyond the First Year

Let's take a moment to look back at your personal EAL plan from Chapter 17. It contains a mixture of administrative tasks, goals for specific groups of learners, ways to promote a whole-school approach to language, your own professional development needs and your longer term aspirations. We called those aspirations the 'points on the horizon' that you are aiming for. The aim of Task 13, below, is to put these aspirations in context and to start turning them into action.

Personal and positional leadership

EAL teachers don't always have a very senior position in the school hierarchy. In fact, as our discussion of Ofsted will show, EAL is particularly easy to ignore. There is a ready-made excuse for low aspirations (they don't speak English!) and the effective absence of EAL from initial teacher education (ITE) means that few teachers have more than a working familiarity with the discipline. Angela Creese (2005: 4–5) talks of the different 'epistemological authority' of subject and EAL teachers. She argues that we often talk about EAL in ways that position specialists in a supporting role, and assume that they have no subject-specific or class teaching expertise of their own. This book has sought to challenge that assumption by setting out the body of evidence and theory that underpins EAL's special status as a cross-curricular, specialist discipline. Changing your role means tackling those discourses – those ways of thinking and speaking about EAL that become so deeply ingrained that we stop noticing them – and replacing them with a different outlook.

A good starting point is to distinguish between positional and personal leadership. Positional leadership comes from holding a position of authority – such as a head of department or senior leadership role – where you are focused on individuals and your responsibilities for the work of others. Personal leadership, sometimes called 'post-heroic' leadership, does not depend on your place in the hierarchy. It can best be described as a set of shared practices and relational skills; it is more focused on your responsibilities *to* others than *for* their work. Theories of personal leadership often emphasise that leading and following are two sides of the same coin: when we empower others to make a difference, we recognise that we are dependent on each other for our success.

Your success as an EAL specialist depends, in this sense, on how confident your colleagues across the school are to deliver language-rich and culturally appropriate teaching. Doing all the work for people does not achieve this. Leading by example and ensuring that others have the resources they need to succeed, as the case study authors amply demonstrate, does make a difference.

Task 13 Reviewing your personal EAL plan

☐ Revisit your personal EAL plan. What aspirations did you note for the whole-school approach to language?
☐ For each one, write down why it is important and what would count as success.
  ○ Who else needs to be involved as you achieve this aspiration?
☐ Then add the barriers you can see to getting there.
  ○ Who else is affected by (or contributes to) these barriers?
☐ Finally, note how each barrier can be overcome or avoided.
  ○ Who do you need to work with to overcome or avoid them?

You may find that a small group of colleagues is enough – a close-knit team that shares your aspirations. You might equally want to work with a broader network of people: a couple of interested teachers and teaching assistants in each subject or year, some parents, a local supplementary school. A lot will depend on who your colleagues are.

Building your team

Seán Bracken, Catharine Driver and Karima Kadi-Hanifi, in their 2017 book on teaching EAL in secondary schools, set out a series of 'pointers of good practice', adapted from Ofsted's (2013) research into literacy teaching. They recognise that 'there are no quick fixes' and that the 'vision and direction of the headteacher and senior leaders' is vital. They also recommend drawing on the expertise of others, such as the school librarian and English or MFL teachers – anyone who has an existing interest in language and literacy (Bracken *et al.*, 2017: 62–65). Working with this network of 'EAL-interested' people allows you to break down bigger aspirations into more manageable goals: before getting language embedded in every lesson, work with a small number of colleagues to build language into their lessons. With time you can develop a more distributed approach to EAL leadership, with knowledgeable colleagues spread throughout the school. Strategies like this demonstrate personal leadership. Your success depends on theirs, and your understanding of how language works in different subjects grows with their understanding of how language works beyond the boundaries of their discipline.

Models of Provision

The type of provision you are able to offer will depend on your team, your other commitments, your colleagues' level of knowledge in EAL and your learners' needs. Broadly speaking, there are four main approaches:

- Management only, supporting class teachers to work with EAL learners through whole-class strategies and differentiation.
- Team-teaching with a subject teacher: both model language and activities together before you support the focus group of learners.
- Supporting a specific learner or group of learners in class: subject teacher leads the lesson and the EAL specialist is in a supporting role.
- Working with EAL learners in withdrawal, with or without input from a subject teacher in planning.
(Adapted from Bellsham-Revell & Nancarrow/NALDIC, 2019)

Christine Davison (2001) introduces a number of other dimensions: the timetabling options (frequency, size of group), pupil groupings (same age, proficiency, background?) and the support model (balance of social and academic language, extent to which curriculum content is integrated). Task 14 incorporates these criteria into a map of your EAL provision.

Task 14 Mapping provision

☐ Think about all the different groups of learners in your school and map the provision they receive on the grid below. If you only have small numbers you could do this for each pupil.

Learners	Support model	Timetabling options	Pupil groupings	EAL specialist role	Subject/Class teacher role

☐ Write a few lines for each pupil/group, explaining to yourself why they are receiving this pattern of provision and what will need to change as their proficiency develops.

154 Part 3: The EAL Specialist

Figure 21.1 The content–language continuum

This gives us a more detailed framework in which to think about EAL provision. It takes us down to the level of individuals and small groups of pupils, which is essential if we are to get more people involved. 'EAL-interested' colleagues might not want a fully worked out rationale at first, but being able to talk them through the dimensions of good provision for the learners they teach will help them to see the complexity of the discipline and how the EAL knowledge base can support fine-grained differentiation in the classroom.

One way to open the conversation about EAL provision is to use a continuum from content-rich language teaching to language-rich content teaching (Figure 21.1). This has the benefit of putting EAL specialists and subject specialists in direct relation to each other, on an equal footing and showing clear common ground in the middle. It emphasises the need for reciprocity and the value each person's expertise has for the other's work. A good starting point is to sit down with an 'EAL-interested' colleague and try to pinpoint individual learners on this continuum. This can generate a lot of discussion: for example, a new-to-English learner will likely be on the far left, with a major focus on basic English so that they can get by in school. Even here, you can talk about the need to embed subject language and concepts. At the far right are advanced bilinguals and monolingual pupils: you can discuss the differences between them and could bring up the value for all of having an EAL specialist contributing to language-rich subject teaching.

EAL Specialists as Language Leaders

Leadership in EAL also means setting the tone for how the school approaches bilingual learners. An increasing number of teachers and researchers, mostly in the United States, are moving towards the term 'emergent bilingual' to describe EAL learners. This is partly because of the history and pupil demographics of the United States, where a large majority of bilingual learners are Spanish speakers whose language is widely used in the community, but it also reflects a similar shift in emphasis to the one that first led ESL teachers in the UK to adopt the term EAL in the 1980s (see Leung, 2016). The terminology matters because it shapes how we think about bilingual learners.

Whose norms?

The advocates for 'emergent bilingual' are deeply concerned with the significance of what we teach, of the norms we ask students to adopt and what they mean for the learners' voices and experiences. They argue that grammar should be much less significant in our teaching than vocabulary because grammatical accuracy – adherence to the morphosyntactic patterns of the standard variety – has long been a justification for marginalising bilingual learners and speakers of non-standard varieties (among many others, Deborah Cameron [2005] and Julia Snell [Snell & Andrews, 2017] have researched how this works in UK schools). There is strong support for this in the second language acquisition (SLA) research: meaning drives language learning, as we saw in Chapter 5, and so focusing prematurely on grammatical accuracy can retard the development of proficiency.

Proficiency is not an objective concept. We have seen how a narrow focus on the morphosyntactic norms of 'native speakers' marginalises many bilingual learners. The main premise of translanguaging, for example, is to recognise the 'deployment of a speaker's full linguistic repertoire without regard for watchful adherence to the socially and politically defined boundaries' of named languages, such as 'English' or 'Arabic' (Otheguy *et al.*, 2015: 281). Some years earlier, Bernstein (1970) argued that:

> If children are labelled *culturally deprived*, then it follows that the spontaneous realization of their culture, its images and symbolic representations, are of reduced value and significance. Teachers will have lower expectation of the children, which the children will undoubtedly fulfil. (Bernstein, 1970: 345)

What could 'culturally deprived' mean in the context of 21st century EAL? We might see it in the assumption of monolingualism that underwrites much of the young people's experience of school, from the starting point that the first priority of bilingual pupils is to learn English, through to the lack of bilingual teachers and leaders in schools and the widely shared apprehension about allowing other languages to be used in the classroom. These are structural issues in our education system.

Structural monolingualism

How can a language leader and EAL specialist change structural features of the education system? It is not actually as daunting as it sounds. This book has advocated a distributed model of leadership – personal leadership – in which your success depends on the success of others. It has suggested ways of building up a network of EAL-friendly colleagues and working with them to develop expertise in different subject areas. It has also, as one of the first things for a newly appointed EAL specialist to do, recommended working out both an EAL policy for the school and a more ambitious plan for yourself. Sharing this with your EAL-friendly colleagues, perhaps in small conversations over the year, will help you to develop them as language leaders too.

A major project in the United States, the City University of New York-New York State Initiative on Emergent Bilinguals (CUNY-NYSIEB) has developed substantial resources for doing this, using the lens of translanguaging.

> **Task 15** How to teach bilinguals (when you're not one)
>
> ☐ Find a monolingual colleague (ideally someone outside your immediate team) to buddy up with. Start by finding time to sit down and talk about what you each feel the language of the classroom should be. Are there any instances when pupils can (or should) use L1 as part of their learning?
> ☐ Watch the first two videos from CUNY-NYSIEB (https://www.youtube.com/channel/UC5PE-qUgT9LHiYq6yuVJ1fw/featured). If you're watching them together, take a moment to make notes on the following alone then discuss them:
>   - What emotions are associated with students using L1? What does it mean for your role as a teacher?
>   - What does it mean to be an advocate for EAL learners? Is it a desirable role? Who can be an advocate?
>   - What examples of multilingualism can we see in the videos? Are they quite superficial or do they challenge the structural monolingualism of the school?
>   - The video is very clearly set in the United States. What would apply (or could be adapted) to UK classrooms?

Ms Condon-Kim, the first teacher in the video (Task 15) talks about her fear of losing control if she allows first languages into her classroom. It is an entirely legitimate concern: if you have been educated in a system that primarily values native-like proficiency in the major European languages, a multilingual classroom can provoke a sense of loss. You are letting go of the familiar and embracing a new and uncertain future. Language leaders have to recognise these feelings – often found in ourselves, too – and create opportunities for colleagues to explore how multilingualism can enrich their pedagogy and better serve their learners. You will likely face resistance from colleagues who feel that the school's approach is already good, validated by inspectors and others, and you will need to be resilient. Our case study authors show how this can be done: each interprets their role differently but they are united by their commitment to bilingual learners (as, if you've read this far, are you). The tasks will give concrete examples to work with; the next chapter takes us further into the theory before we return to practice with our discussion of Ofsted's role.

Chapter Review

This chapter has discussed how a more established EAL specialist might develop their role. It began by establishing the notion of 'personal leadership', in which you lead by example and succeed by building up others – in contrast to 'positional leadership', where your authority stems from holding a senior position. You reviewed your personal EAL plan and updated it for the wider scope of your work, and looked at different models of provision that you can establish in the school. We introduced a continuum from 'content-rich language teaching' to 'language-rich content teaching', which has several benefits: it places language specialists and subject specialists on an equal footing and identifies plenty of common ground between them, and it gives a handy reference point for talking about individual pupils or groups of pupils. We extended the notion of an 'EAL specialist' into that of a 'language leader', a role that many EAL specialists already play, and considered how we might work with a network of 'EAL-friendly' colleagues to develop lasting change for bilingual learners. These starting points are taken further in the next chapter.

22 From Mono to Multi

Limitations in the national data can give a misleading picture of EAL pupils. This chapter explores the implications of moving to a more multilingual approach.

In Chapter 18 we discussed how to put good assessments in place and how to make sense of the resulting data. We saw that much of the policy around EAL is based on an assumption that bilingual pupils should achieve the same language proficiency as monolingual pupils. Now we return to that theme, but from a different angle. We look briefly at findings that show multilingual pupils outperforming their monolingual peers when both languages are fully supported, and we discuss recent arguments that second language acquisition (SLA) research should be more 'responsive to the pressing needs of people who learn to live – and in fact do live – with more than one language at various points in their lives' (Douglas Fir Group, 2016: 20). In doing so we ask a challenging question: What would happen to EAL if we moved from a monolingual curriculum to one that fully embraced pupils' multilingualism?

Monolingual and Multilingual: A Problematic Comparison

If we look at the average attainment figures for monolingual and EAL pupils, we see a clear pattern. EAL pupils do broadly as well as monolingual pupils in standardised assessments. In 2016, for example, they made quicker progress than monolingual children and were more likely to achieve the English Baccalaureate. A recent DfE update noted that 'pupils from the Chinese, Asian and Mixed ethnic groups scored higher than average for Attainment 8 [measures]', whereas 'White pupils and Black pupils scored lower than average' (DfE, 2019). Similarly, the Sutton Trust noted that White British boys who received free school meals were at higher risk, achieving the 'lowest grades at GCSE of any main ethnic group' (Sutton Trust, 2016: 1). EAL pupils are doing fine, it seems.

The problem is that average attainment figures for EAL are 'profoundly misleading' (Hutchinson, 2018: 11). The group is too diverse to be treated as a single unit, but this diversity is obscured by missing baseline data. Monolingual assessments systematically underestimate academic ability because they are mediated by the pupil's proficiency in English and by the enormous variation that makes cohort-level averages misleading. Recent research has addressed this complexity directly. There is some evidence to suggest that pupils' mobility is associated with lower outcomes in all demographic groups

(Strand *et al.*, 2015; this particularly affects EAL pupils who arrive mid-year), but the most robust and consistent predictor of attainment is proficiency in English (Strand & Hessel, 2018).

We do not collect robust proficiency data at a national level, but several local authorities do. The work of Feyisa Demie and his colleagues in Lambeth is particularly worth noting: it uses a scale that is very similar to the one introduced (and then abandoned) by the DfE, giving us a robust and extensive data set to investigate the impact of proficiency on attainment. One recent study (Demie, 2018), for example, examined the results of 2,957 pupils at KS2 and 1,953 GCSE students. The proportion of GCSE learners achieving five good passes (here A*-C grades, as the study was conducted shortly before the move to number grades) was strongly correlated with their proficiency in English. Learners at stages D (Competent) and E (Fully Fluent) out-performed the monolingual (English-only) average. A similar pattern can be seen in the extensive work done by Steve Strand and his colleagues at the University of Oxford, drawing on data from several local authorities. Figure 22.1 shows attainment at an earlier age, using data on the proportion of pupils achieving the expected standard in Maths at KS1.

In this example, few pupils at the earliest stages of learning English achieved the expected standard. This is perhaps to be expected: if you can't understand the question, it's hard to give the answer. It is interesting that a significant minority of pupils at an intermediate level of English (Stage C) did reach the benchmark, suggesting that

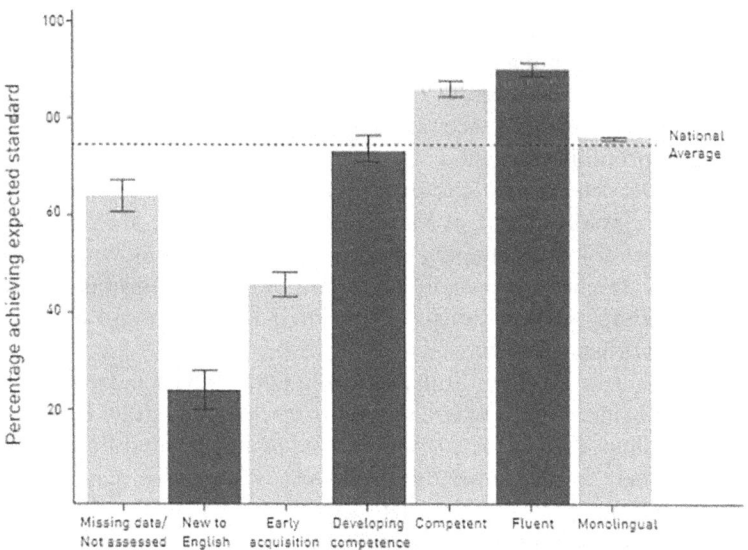

Figure 22.1 Percentage of pupils achieving expected standard in maths at KS1 for EAL pupils at different levels of proficiency in English and monolingual English speakers
Source: Strand and Hessel (2018).
Note: Error bars represent 95% confidence intervals around the mean. National average from DfE (2017).

students can succeed in the mainstream before their English is fully developed . However, the most striking finding is that highly proficient bilinguals (at Stages D and E) again outperformed monolingual children. This finding has been supported by similar studies at different ages and curriculum stages: although we are not able to pin down the causal factors, it appears that benchmarking bilingual pupils against a monolingual norm is inadequate. We need more 'intelligent benchmarks for EAL attainment to avoid complacency about outcomes for high-ability groups and to avoid the average masking the urgent needs of some sub-groups' (Hutchinson, 2018: 26).

A Challenge from SLA

What might a 'more intelligent benchmark' look like? A thought-provoking challenge comes from within the second language acquisition (SLA) literature, asking us to re-evaluate our assumptions about EAL provision and the role it plays in students' language development. There has been a significant shift in thinking in some quarters, recognising the importance of social life to language learning. One group of leading scholars has even argued that:

> A new SLA must be imagined, one that can investigate the learning and teaching of additional languages across private and public, material and digital social contexts in a multilingual world. (Douglas Fir Group, 2016: 20)

This has tremendous implications for EAL. A significant research agenda is beginning to investigate the multiple contexts in which additional languages are acquired – in schools, in faith groups, among friends, in the family and online. These may overlap: it seems likely that the classroom is only one of the places where young people learn their additional language, and other spaces are governed by very different norms and expectations. We often prohibit more fluid language practices in the classroom; the mixing of linguistic resources in creative and purposeful ways is often seen as a mark of low proficiency in the classroom and of high skill elsewhere. We are only beginning to understand how technology is shaping language learning among young people. Older learners, especially, might be physically present in our classrooms but are often simultaneously (and perhaps surreptitiously) using their languages and digital devices to communicate with others elsewhere.

This suggests that we might rethink the role of EAL provision, from being the main source of input to being a space where specialist teachers can draw together this wide range of learning, shape it to fit the curriculum and provide the explicit teaching on features that are unlikely to be acquired naturally elsewhere. This may sound like a tall order but there are some excellent precedents: Jean Conteh's work with bilingual storytelling and funds of knowledge (see Conteh, 2018) is a great place to start. She describes how her new-to-English primary pupils could produce rich and curriculum-relevant work by drawing on the culture and languages they brought to the school. Jim Cummins and Margaret Early's (2011) work on identity texts is similarly powerful; secondary schools might extend this with a programme like First Story (https://firststory.org.uk), which uses professional writers to help bilingual learners find their authorial voices. *The Economist*'s Burnet News Club (https://economistfoundation.org/burnetnewsclub), available for Primary and Secondary, challenges learners to discuss current events and could easily be adapted to develop first languages to advanced proficiency.

This would mean rethinking the EAL classroom, taking the well-established idea that EAL is a 'cross-curriculum discipline' (NALDIC, 1999) and transforming it for a world in which multilingualism and global connectedness are increasingly normal parts of life. Such a vision for EAL would be interdisciplinary and problem oriented: the book has so far argued that subject and class teachers should be involved in planning and co-teaching EAL lessons, but there is no reason why the EAL specialist should not orchestrate schemes of work that draw on multiple subjects, as well as parents and the community. Our commitment to the pupils' first languages means that we want to develop their full repertoire to a high level (the cognitive and academic language proficiency described in Chapter 11), and that will mean recognising the academic value of language learning in the home, supplementary school, faith and more.

What does this have to do with EAL data? In truth, very little – and that's the problem. The data we collect are often based on certain assumptions about language proficiency and attainment, about what languages are and what aspects we should measure. As we saw in Chapters 9 and 18, one common assumption is that high-proficiency bilinguals sound a lot like monolinguals. Once EAL pupils are proficient in English, the EAL teacher's job is generally considered done. Another is that some aspects of language proficiency can be separated from the communicative context and taught in isolation (such as phonics, some spelling and vocabulary, and much explicit grammar teaching). Still another is that language proficiency is universal – that one person's proficiency in English and Spanish can be equated directly with another's in Sylheti, Bengali and English. How do we capture that in our data, and how can we use those data to be accountable for our learners' progress?

To explore these questions, we will look closely at the inspection regime in England. It is different from those in other jurisdictions but the discussion should be easy to transfer. After all, it focuses not on understanding the demands of the current system but on the relationship between a broadly monolingual education system and a multilingual, often mobile student population. We will see that the 2020–2021 revisions to the English inspection system make these tensions particularly explicit, and that the role of the EAL specialist is more significant than ever. We will also see that even in an inspection – a high-pressure event with rigid statutory boundaries – this more nuanced way of thinking about EAL can be both practical and tremendously successful.

Chapter Review

The aim of this chapter was to pose a challenging question: What would EAL provision look like if we fully embraced the pupils' multilingualism? It began by looking at the challenges of comparing monolingual and multilingual pupils. The data collected by our education system are simply inadequate for the task, leading to 'profoundly misleading' averages that obscure the needs of some pupils and the abilities of others. We looked at a contrasting case, still using attainment data but this time at local authority level, to show that EAL pupils actually outperform monolinguals once they have reached a high level of proficiency. This raises important questions for the use of a monolingual standard. If success in learning English is defined as meeting the standard of their monolingual peers, how do we account for the fact that EAL pupils don't stop there?

This led to a thought-provoking argument that is emerging in the SLA literature, which has generally focused on the acquisition of one language at a time. An influential paper by a group of leading scholars (the 'Douglas Fir Group' took their name from the conference room in which they first met to discuss their ideas) argues that we should find ways to investigate how language learning stretches across multiple contexts, the material and digital worlds, and the learners' public and private lives. If we follow that train of thought, we find that the potential role for EAL specialists is near limitless.

Does this mean that we can redesign EAL from the ground up? Probably not: the institutional context of the specialist means there are real-world constraints on our work. But it is important to think more broadly before we address the next chapter, on Ofsted.

Case Study 6: Ofsted

Inspections exert enormous pressure on schools, so it is very important that inspectors are able to probe EAL provision insightfully and look for evidence of a language-rich curriculum across the school. This case study is based on wide-ranging interviews with senior inspectors: we discussed the new Education Inspection Framework (EIF), the principles underpinning Ofsted's approach, and the key questions that EAL specialists should be asking.

Ofsted has an uneasy relationship with EAL. We need inspectors who are well informed and able to challenge our schools to have the highest expectations for bilingual learners, but inspectors without the requisite insight lend legitimacy to provision that marginalises EAL pupils, even where the school's EAL specialist is a strenuous advocate for these young people. In general, the senior inspectors interviewed spoke highly of EAL and its importance to learning across the school. They argued that – where EAL is embedded in the curriculum – the inspection process should recognise its impact on language-rich teaching across the school. However, it is also clear from the discussions that where EAL is positioned more marginally, with less impact on subject classrooms, it can become invisible to inspectors even if there are high numbers of EAL pupils. This poses unique challenges for EAL specialists, who must now influence whole-school provision as well as being experts in their discipline.

This case study begins by looking at the big picture, then details the new inspection process and the implications for EAL specialists. It closes with advice on good questions to ask when the inspector calls.

The Big Picture: EAL Specialists, EAL Data and EAL Practice

Ofsted introduced the new Education Inspection Framework (EIF) for schools in September 2019. It marked a substantial shift in focus towards the curriculum, motivated in large part by concerns that outcomes-driven inspections were putting schools under pressure to narrow the breadth of learning. The new approach is designed to probe the school's curriculum thinking in more depth, asking how teachers and teaching teams work backwards from their disciplinary knowledge to structure teaching and learning. Ofsted is interested in how you are 'building your teaching on research, on principles, rather than quick fixes', say the senior inspectors:

> It's turning [the outcomes-based approach] on its head and saying, 'what is it you want your students to learn?' And when you plan that, how are you going to build on their starting points, and what is the destination going to look like in terms of what they know, understand and remember?

To support this, inspectors will no longer be able to look at schools' internal data. The inspection itself will instead be based around a series of 'deep dives into subjects' and professional conversations, asking teachers and school leaders to articulate their approach in a way that reflects their own principles and local context.

The implications for EAL are significant. The emphasis on evidence-led teaching, informed by clear principles and detailed understanding of local context, aligns very well with what many EAL teachers have been doing for years. Yet this emphasis on professional dialogue with inspectors carries risks. Inspectors are rarely EAL specialists (although there are some notable exceptions and Ofsted had, until recently, a well-regarded Lead Inspector for EAL) and may not be well equipped to engage in detailed discussion about the discipline. The reliance on professional dialogue means setting aside important data (such as pupils' PiE) that are fundamental to effective practice.

This is compounded by the lack of reference to EAL in the Framework: EAL pupils and their languages are often marginalised in an officially monolingual education system, and the principles that guide first language teaching are often inappropriate for those pupils who are learning the language of the school at the same time as they learn *through* that language. By removing the final references to EAL from the EIF and the relevant inspectors' handbooks, Ofsted risks further marginalising the specific needs of EAL learners and the specialist knowledge of their teachers.

Risks, however, are not certainties. The new approach widens responsibility for EAL to all teachers: being able to articulate how you build on learners' starting points involves recognising the linguistic, cultural and educational diversity of EAL learners. The challenge will be to maintain the visibility of EAL, both with colleagues and with inspectors, and to influence curriculum thinking across the school so that language is at the heart of all learning.

The Inspection Process

The EIF introduced a renewed focus on the curriculum and updated the four judgements (categories) against which schools are evaluated. Here, I will outline the thinking behind those changes before looking at the steps inspectors take in an actual inspection.

The Education Inspection Framework

The Framework is organised around four judgements, three of which are new:

- Quality of Education
- Behaviour and Attitudes
- Personal Development
- Leadership and Management

The first judgement, **Quality of Education,** is the most substantial and is also the most immediately relevant for EAL specialists. This is where the curriculum is assessed: Ofsted are looking for coherent understanding of how curriculum design connects to teaching and assessment, and how each stage of learning connects to what came before and after. Crucially, all pupils should receive the same broad and balanced curriculum. As Amanda Spielman, the Chief Inspector, said of SEND pupils:

> A child with severe or complex needs may well take longer to acquire and build that knowledge than other children but that doesn't mean we should assume it is irrelevant for them, or limit our efforts to help them achieve it. (Amanda Spielman, 26 January 2019)

The same is true of EAL pupils: different linguistic starting points do not mean lower aspirations. Inspectors should be looking especially for signs that EAL pupils are not being included in the full curriculum. Under the EIF, they should ask specifically about any pupils who are not in mainstream classes (for example, those who are withdrawn for extra English) and check that teachers can articulate their high aspirations for all EAL pupils.

Both **Behaviour and Attitudes and Personal Development** have some relevance for EAL, not least because they address culture, motivation, inclusion and character (the last of which has a more prominent place in the EIF). The guidance on outstanding provision specifically identifies a 'school environment in which commonalities are identified and celebrated, [and] difference is valued and nurtured' (Ofsted, 2019: 56) and where 'pupils have access to a wide, rich set of experiences' (Ofsted, 2019: 62). There is scope here for EAL pupils to make a substantive contribution to the school's overall evaluation.

Finally, the **Leadership and Management** judgement is where the school's high expectations for all learners will be reflected. This specifically includes 'ensuring that practices such as "off-rolling" do not take place' (Ofsted, 2019: 64), how leaders at all levels engage with parents and the community, and how high expectations of all pupils are embodied in day-to-day interactions. It is also significant because of the impact school leaders at all levels have on determining the curriculum and pedagogy, as well as on operational issues like staffing and the support available for continuing professional development (CPD). The school's EAL and language policies (see Chapter 17) are an important foundation for this, and it is important that school leaders can talk fluently (and with good evidence) about how they are putting those aspirations into practice. However, it is also important to note that inspectors are unlikely to look for evidence for this judgement in the EAL provision specifically. School leaders need to raise the work that they are doing with EAL pupils and make it visible in the inspection process.

The key messages from the EIF are around the curriculum. It should be broad and balanced, not narrowed so that pupils can receive extra interventions or language support outside the mainstream, and should clearly articulate how knowledge, skills and cultural capital are developed in a coherent and well-sequenced manner.

An inspection in six acts

The EIF assesses these criteria in six stages, corresponding to three broader themes. These are 'intent' (seeking to understand the thinking behind the curriculum), 'implementation' (how this thinking is translated into teaching and learning) and 'impact' (the effect this has on learners and learning). EAL could feature prominently in each theme, but at no stage are inspectors, school leaders or teaching staff required to report on the intent, implementation or impact of EAL practice specifically.

The six stages are outlined in Table CS6.1:

Table CS6.1 The six stages of an Ofsted inspection

Stage		Focus
1	Planning call with the head teacher	Intent
2	Meet senior and subject leaders in school	Intent > implementation
3	Lesson visits	Implementation
4	Meet with teachers ...	Implementation
5	... and pupils	Implementation > impact
6	Work scrutiny	Impact

Each of these has a distinct focus. The pre-inspection telephone call (which should last around 90 minutes on the day before the inspection) and the meetings with senior leaders focus on the big picture and strategic questions. The inspectors will be interested in the direction that the school is going in and the broad themes that the leadership team want to emphasise. This is the first point at which EAL can be raised, but it requires school leaders to make a strong and proactive case for looking at EAL provision more closely. Next are the 'deep dives' into subjects: longer conversations with people at all levels of the school, including pupils, to understand how the curriculum is implemented and what impact this has on learning. Inspectors will be particularly interested in the sequencing of the curriculum and the choices made about content, delivery, setting and programming.

The implementation theme is where the inspectors begin to triangulate their findings, for example by comparing notes from meeting a subject leader with lesson visits to subject classes in different year groups. The inspectors may again ask here about specific groups, but are unlikely to ask about EAL unless a specific issue emerges in the inspection. To get EAL into the conversation here, subject leaders would need to raise the topic with the inspectors and show how it informed their implementation of the curriculum.

The EIF has removed one-day inspections for most schools, to allow time for schools to comment and introduce more evidence on the second day. At the end of the first day, the inspectors will come up with a hypothesis and will share their thinking with the school leadership. The inspectors look to test that hypothesis on the second day, trying to establish what aspects of their hypothesis represent a systemic feature of the school. Here, they may drill down to look at specific areas or groups. The EAL coordinator may be involved, but it is more likely that EAL will be addressed through the SENCO or Literacy coordinator (even where the school has a separate EAL coordinator) unless the importance of the EAL coordinator's work to curriculum intent, implementation and impact has already been emphasised by others.

Inspecting Initial Teacher Education

The new Education Inspection Framework for ITE (Ofsted, 2020) was released as this book was going to press. It follows the same six stages as for school inspections, although for ITE the 'subject deep dives' are replaced with 'focused reviews', recognising that (especially in small providers) some subjects will need to be clustered with others (for example, language and humanities in Secondary or foundation subjects in Primary). EAL features in three areas: inspectors should ask about 'How trainees are taught to promote pupils' positive behaviour and attitudes, and how their practice in meeting the needs of

> pupils who speak English as an additional language (EAL) [...] is developed' (Ofsted, 2020: 16). It is also a point for discussion when inspectors meet trainees (Ofsted, 2020: 26). Importantly, EAL now features in the criteria for both outstanding and good provision – this is the direct result of EAL subject associations and practitioners making their voices heard through the consultation process, and shows that positive change is possible even in national-level policy.

Implications for EAL Specialists

The overwhelming implication of the EIF is that EAL specialists must now work across the school, building up the expertise of subject colleagues and school leaders, as much as working directly with pupils. This means that the *visibility* of EAL provision is an important characteristic, and this is where we begin our discussion of the implications.

Where can EAL be visible?

Under the EIF, more than before, EAL will be invisible to inspectors unless it is made visible by the concerted effort of teachers and school leaders. Invisibility is a huge risk: if EAL provision falls outside the main accountability structures, it will inevitably fall low on the list of priorities of most leaders in busy schools. We know from Parts 1 and 2 that EAL is most effective as a cross-curricular discipline that influences language-rich provision in all subject areas. The support of school leaders, subject leads and a large number of colleagues is therefore essential.

At the same time, the EIF does offer an opportunity to increase the visibility of both EAL and language across the curriculum. The new focus on the curriculum – that all pupils must receive their full entitlement, and that it should be ambitious in scope and depth – means that there is a strong reason for EAL specialists to be more deeply involved in curriculum subjects than before. It means that withdrawal teaching will need a more robust justification and will likely require the involvement of subject and class teachers in planning and preparation, just as EAL specialists will need to contribute to language-rich teaching across the curriculum. This is reinforced by the renewed emphasis on 'no preferred style' – that inspections should be an extended professional conversation in which schools can direct attention to aspects of curriculum provision that they feel are particularly effective.

All this changes the role of the EAL specialist, from someone who supports bilingual learners (often away from mainstream classrooms) to someone whose work can help secure an outstanding judgement in every inspection category. EAL is therefore a key characteristic of schoolwide provision.

Characteristics of good EAL provision

So what are the characteristics of good EAL provision, apart from its integration in curriculum provision? From an inspector's perspective, the distinctiveness of EAL practice may not be readily apparent. The renewed emphasis on the curriculum means that inspectors are looking at provision through the lens of subjects rather than groups of pupils (such as EAL learners generally). Good provision, so defined, is when pupils succeed in the curriculum.

This suggests the false equivalence, however, that the previous chapter explored. The practices that EAL specialists have advocated for years (such as close attention to the language of the curriculum, an emphasis on vocabulary learning, regularly recapping ideas and developing oral fluency to support literacy) work well for *all learners*. There is even some evidence emerging that all learners do better in multilingual classrooms, even those who are monolingual. However, provision that is good for the majority is often inadequate for pupils who are learning English and learning *through* English. It's not that good practice is good for everyone, but specifically that *good EAL practice* is good for everyone.

All good provision will demonstrate high aspirations for pupils, but expectations of EAL pupils should be higher still. Robust data show that bilingual and migrant learners make very rapid progress, especially in the early stages as their language proficiency develops. For example, we should expect Secondary-age EAL pupils to have Progress 8 scores of around 0.5. If high aspirations mean that we are content for EAL pupils to reach the national average, then we are significantly underestimating their potential. The inspectors described a culture of high expectations as central to Ofsted's vision for schools and to their mission as a 'force for improvement'. In good EAL provision, *all* teachers and leaders would be able to articulate how quickly their EAL learners should make progress, both in English and in their subjects, and have clear plans in place to support that. These will involve working closely with the school's EAL specialists, but also on their own account as they use the tools and techniques of EAL in their own teaching. This kind of differentiation is seen in conversation with teachers (Stage 4, see Table CS6.1) but becomes especially clear in the work scrutiny (Stage 6).

Supporting new arrivals

Some pupils bring experiences that are not easily reconciled with the expectations of our education system. Those who arrive mid-year, with limited English and interrupted schooling, for example, will require additional support. So will those who carry the burden of being separated from family, who have experienced trauma or who are navigating the asylum system. It can sometimes feel as if inspections are focused on the majority, and that the careful efforts to create a welcoming, supportive space for these learners are ignored in favour of those who fall more squarely in the mainstream. However, the broad principles that Ofsted proposes can be used to justify a rich and rigorous programme for pupils at any stage of their education.

Three principles allow us to align Ofsted with new arrivals. The first is the entitlement to the full, broad and balanced curriculum. This will be the main grounds on which inspectors can challenge the school's provision and the main lens through which non-specialist inspectors will seek to understand your work. The second is that different groups of EAL pupils will follow different trajectories. Here, there is likely to be an asymmetry between what you know and what the inspector knows: you can demonstrate how long pupils take to develop proficiency in English, how EAL pupils should make faster progress than their monolingual peers, and how academic and general English need to be balanced for new arrivals to make that progress. You can support your work with robust data and reference to an extensive literature. Although inspectors can no longer look at internal school data, subject teachers and school leaders can still talk about the patterns that emerge from the data and how they have influenced curriculum provision. Very little of this will reach the inspector automatically; they need to hear about it through conversations with subject and senior leaders.

The final principle is to use your assessments strategically. Good data on proficiency are an essential starting point, but you will also need to articulate what else informs your provision. Some key considerations are the pupil's experience of learning in other countries (and what can be transferred to the UK setting), any gaps in their curriculum knowledge (and, if they followed another country's curriculum, any areas in which they are more advanced than would be expected), and any knowledge about the pupil's current situation that might affect their learning (such as insecure accommodation, worries about family members, and so on). This responds to Ofsted's desire to see how teachers know and build on their pupils' starting points, but it goes beyond the basic data to incorporate your knowledge and understanding of your pupils.

Table CS6.2 Key principles for Ofsted inspections

Principle	Specialist knowledge	Link to Ofsted expectations
Curriculum entitlement	Part 2: EAL as a cross-curricular discipline; working with subject disciplines.	All pupils receive a full, broad and balanced curriculum.
Pupils' learning trajectories	Part 1: Components of language-rich teaching; trajectories for bilingual learners.	Ensuring inspectors have requisite information to evaluate your work.
Assessment and data	Part 3: Establishing effective assessments; making data work for you.	Knowing your pupils' starting point.

Withdrawing pupils

Where pupils are removed from the mainstream it can have a dramatic effect on a school's overall judgement. Reviewing large numbers of inspection reports reveals some interesting examples: inspectors explicitly cited the number of pupils being home-schooled as a contributing factor in one Requires Improvement judgement; in another, the use of a separate language centre for new arrivals was challenged by inspectors and the pupils were brought back into mainstream provision. Inspectors may also find evidence that EAL pupils are not accessing the full curriculum in the records of attendance, exclusions or poor behaviour, when they ask whether school leaders have identified any trends in those data.

The advice on withdrawing pupils for extra English is less clear-cut. Evidently, there will be real challenges in supporting some pupils in the mainstream, particularly those with very limited English proficiency and interrupted schooling. Many schools withdraw pupils from MFL lessons, for example. The inspectors cite a number of reasons for this: sometimes it is based on an assumption that learning English is enough of a challenge and that multilingual pupils 'can't cope with another language'; sometimes it is justified because they are already learning an additional language (English) and a further modern language is less important. Ofsted's position here is unequivocally that MFL is a statutory requirement. The National Director for Education, Sean Harford, recently wrote about the importance of MFL in a letter to the *Guardian*, and there are several examples of schools cutting modern languages as they sought to focus on core subjects and being rated Requires Improvement or Inadequate as a result.

This suggests that effective withdrawal, in Ofsted's terms, will have the following features: it will maximise opportunities for curriculum learning, involving pupils in subject learning even at the earliest stages of learning English; it will be time-limited, with clear goals and exit criteria, so that pupils spend the minimum necessary time outside the mainstream classroom; and it will involve class and subject teachers in planning and preparing (if not delivering) lessons. The new approach to inspection as a professional conversation means that these features also need to be clearly articulated so that all teachers can describe them and the impact they have on teaching.

> ### A combined EALCO and SENCO role?
>
> Many EAL specialists resist combining their role with that of the SENCO, fearing that the distinctiveness of EAL pedagogy will be lost and the distinctive needs of EAL learners obscured. The SENCO's role is better defined in policy, more widely recognised by inspectors and better supported by professional development opportunities. But many SENCOs already have responsibility for

> EAL, and SEN has visibility that can really benefit EAL provision. So should the roles be combined?
>
> The inspectors took no position on this, seeing it as a matter of internal school organisation. However, they did note the practical implications: SENCOs must be qualified teachers and achieve a recognised specialist qualification within three years of taking up the post, whereas EAL coordinators face no such requirements. This gives the SENCO a greater voice in the inspection process. However, SEN and EAL are both highly specialised roles, with distinctive knowledge and practices. Combining them could create an unmanageably complex role or lead to one being sidelined. Close collaboration seems the most obvious route to success.

Questions to Ask

Given that the EIF is based on an extended, professional conversation with teachers about the curriculum, we might ask what questions are likely to come up. There are few published accounts of inspections (and vanishingly few that focus on EAL, although see below for one teacher's experience), so I raised this question with the inspectors. Their approach would depend on the context, the number and needs of the EAL pupils and the experience of the teaching team.

For new EAL coordinators, the inspectors would often start by asking what training they had received and what expertise they bring to the role (recognising that many EAL coordinators are assigned the role with no guidance or support). The aim here would be to understand the EAL specialist's starting points as a context for evaluating the provision they lead. The inspectors were clear that Ofsted does not endorse specific professional development routes, but they noted that there were several well-known CPD providers and courses available (see Appendix II).

For more experienced EAL coordinators, the inspectors would be interested in how they are influencing the school as a whole, including senior leaders, subject leaders (around planning the curriculum) and the SENCO (if the roles are separate). They would hope to see evidence of an EAL team that has a clear strategy for supporting bilingual pupils which is well understood across the school, and not just responding to requests from subject colleagues (which one inspector described as 'firefighting'). At this stage, you might be asked how you see your role and how others see it, what level of seniority you have in the school and whether you are directly accountable to a senior leader. The inspectors might also ask about your approach to EAL, as well as the philosophy and rationale that underpin your work. They noted that qualifications in EAL were important, as evidence of sustained professional development, but were not in themselves sufficient to demonstrate outstanding practice.

Questions asked in a real inspection

There are few 'insider' accounts of inspections by EAL teachers. One of those few is from EAL specialist and blogger Jonathan Bifield, who shared the questions he was asked in a recent inspection. His secondary school is over 60% EAL and he reports that the inspector had both a 'reasonable grasp' of the A–E proficiency codes (see DfE, 2016, or https://schoolsweek.co.uk/eal-is-this-a-change-for-the-better) and recognised that learners at earlier stages need some degree of tailored support.

The inspectors asked:

- What interventions (if any) do you provide for EAL learners?
- What subjects do EAL learners miss out on?
- How do you monitor the progress of EAL learners?
- How do you assess their language proficiency?
- What strategies would you suggest for reading?
- How are you supported by senior leadership?
- How do you ensure that EAL learners are making progress?
- Tell me about the EAL department.
- What sorts of CPD do you give to teachers regarding EAL?
- Where can teachers find information on EAL learners at the school?

We can see evidence of three main concerns here. First, the inspectors asked about the curriculum: the specific interventions and the subjects that EAL learners were withdrawn from. The main concern here is to show that, whatever model of provision you choose, your learners receive a broad and balanced curriculum. Second, they asked about management and pedagogy: how you assess and monitor learners, and one question about reading strategies. Third, the inspectors wanted to know about Jonathan's role in the school: his department, the CPD he offers, his role in making sure that subject teachers know about their EAL learners and his relationship with senior leaders (https://ealdaylight.com/2019/12/02/what-might-ofsted-ask-you-about-your-schools-eal-provision).

The inspectors may also ask about the patterns emerging from the school's data, which could relate to specific groups such as EAL learners. Any withdrawal provision is likely to need a clear justification. Good proficiency assessment is important here: the data allow you to say clearly how EAL support is measurably successful. However, Ofsted does not support any one approach to assessment and it is up to the EAL specialist to articulate their methods of assessing progress. Good practice would be to supplement proficiency data with information on the pupils' other languages, their educational histories and any education-related community activities (such as Saturday schools or faith learning).

Addendum: The 'Fight for Fairness'

As this book was going to press, Ofsted announced that it would remove the post of National Lead for EAL, ESOL and Gypsy, Roma and Traveller pupils (the three areas were covered by a single lead inspector). It was done with no consultation and seemingly no thought for the impact it would have on the sector and on bilingual children. It is hard enough to keep bilingual children in the picture, but removing a key figure (whose work involved specialist support for inspectors as well as a strategic overview and liaising with professional bodies) deeply undermines our collective effort to raise attainment among minoritised pupils.

The move appears to be part of a wider response to the government's 'fight for fairness', announced by Minister for Equalities and Women Liz Truss (https://www.gov.uk/government/news/fight-for-fairness-speech-to-set-out-governments-new-approach-to-equality), in which a number of specialist posts were removed in favour of a generic focus on 'inequality'. The goal, announced the minister, is to combat a perceived 'soft bigotry of low expectations, where people from certain backgrounds are never expected or considered able enough to reach high standards'. It is hard to recognise this in the committed work of EAL specialists. Rather, as NALDIC argued in its response, we see instead 'the hard bigotry of no expectations, of pupils whose needs are clearly understood being failed because government departments and the inspectorate no longer think they are worthy of attention'.

It is a dismal end to a cautiously optimistic chapter, simply the latest withdrawal from the government's responsibilities to fully 20% of all pupils. It does, however, underscore the importance of a well-informed, committed professional community – working in the belief that evidence will be presented, that arguments will be won, and that policies will change.

Case Study 7: EAL and SEND

Anne Margaret Smith is a language teacher and specialist in specific learning differences. She has created resources to assess multilingual learners, holds a PhD in the field and now trains teachers to assess and support bilingual learners.

The ability to use other languages brings benefits to both individuals and society. However, in a monolingual environment it can present children with a range of barriers to their learning, particularly in the early stages of acquiring English. Not least, their 'EAL' identity masks some of the signs that teachers routinely look out for in identifying neurodiversity and SEBD (social, emotional and behavioural difficulties), and the indicative behaviours are often put down to cultural differences or frustration. This means that the tendency is to 'wait and see' how they develop, and precious time is lost just when early intervention would be most beneficial. The converse is also sometimes true, when teachers are too quick to attribute any lack of progress in their subject to 'special educational needs and disabilities' (SENDs) without taking into account the linguistic and cultural differences that the individual is experiencing. This can result in staff forming lower expectations of the student and inappropriate labels being applied that may even hinder the child's academic progress.

To avoid over- and under-identification of SENDs among our multilingual learners, we need to get to know them as well as possible, by building trusting relationships with the families and gathering very detailed background information that will help us to interpret the behaviours we see in school. Three common obstacles to achieving this are challenges around communication, linguistic and cultural differences, and assessment issues.

Communication With Families

In many, but not all, schools there may be members of staff who share a language with the child and who can assist with family liaison. It can seem frustrating if the lack of a shared language makes communication with learners or their families difficult, but communication becomes easier as we get to know people so it is always worth persevering in building relationships.

When there is no shared language, teachers might try using some simple communication support strategies, such as allowing extra time for processing information and formulating responses. Reformulation of questions should only be attempted after they have been repeated exactly as they were originally posed, in order to avoid confusing people with multiple questions. In some situations, communication may be hampered because learners or their families may not want to discuss the possibility of a difficulty, difference or disability. The topic may be distressing to them, or completely outside their experience, and therefore hard for them to understand. Differences in educational systems, or of expectations for individual children, may mean that the family/learner do not consider that there is any problem.

In most cases, it is better to avoid using diagnostic terminology (such as dyslexia or SEBD) which do not always translate neatly, and instead talk in functional and practical terms (e.g. 'I notice that you sometimes forget quite quickly what I have told you in the lesson. I would like to work with you on memory strategies so that you can remember more and learn faster.'). Most parents want the best for their children, and free interventions that do not entail additional work for them are rarely refused.

Since all behaviour is a form of communication, closely observing the interaction between the children and their families can also help us to understand the situation. Tensions within the household could explain some of the difficulties that the child is experiencing at school. Home visits may not always be possible, but they are an immensely valuable source of insight to help us get to know our learners and understand their responses to our teaching.

Linguistic and Cultural Differences

Our understanding of SENDs is largely formed by our experience and understanding of what typical development looks like, and in the UK that is based on a monolingual developmental pathway. It is important not to judge our multilingual learners by our monolingual norms. Our world view, and our brains, reflect the languages that were used to build them. Some languages are more similar to English than others, making it a little easier for speakers of those languages to develop their English proficiency. However, the writing system of English is notoriously difficult to master, so there are often large discrepancies between the oral and written language levels of multilingual learners.

The development of learners' first languages often influences their development of academic English. It is well worth exploring which languages the learners have been exposed to and feel able to use, to any extent and in any form. Children may be happy to reveal that they use many different languages (or language varieties) with different family members, neighbours and friends.

Finding out about the structural and phonological differences between these languages can help to explain behaviours that otherwise might be worrying. For example, if a child often leaves off the final consonants of words in either written or spoken form, teachers may wonder if there is a hearing loss or processing impairment preventing them from reproducing those words accurately. However, their 'errors' may be due to a lack of awareness rather than a cognitive or sensory difference, if their main language does not have many closed syllables.

Behavioural conventions (such as maintenance of eye contact or tolerance of silence) differ from culture to culture as well, which may lead to misperceptions. If there are concerns arising from behaviour, it is important to discuss them with colleagues and the child's family in a non-judgemental way, in order to establish what their cause may be and whether there are cultural norms that need to be understood.

Any information that can be gathered about the learners' linguistic repertoires, their home cultures and the families' perceptions of the education system is valuable in helping us to make sense of the behaviours and performances that we see in class, and potentially in identifying barriers to learning. Observation is the first step in gathering this information, and this can be made more systematic by the use of a simple recording system, such as a chart on which the teacher notes when certain behaviours or linguistic usage have been noticed. (I have produced a general behaviour chart, see link at end, and Farnsworth, 2016, offers a chart tracking pragmatic communication strategies.) Using a chart allows non-teaching staff to contribute their observations from different contexts, too. After a few weeks, patterns may begin to emerge, such that it becomes clear what the trigger for unusual behaviour might be.

Assessment Issues

Perhaps the biggest barrier to accurately identifying the needs of multilingual learners is that tests of language ability and cognitive function are usually standardised on a monolingual population, without taking into account the very different development patterns of multilingual children. EAL users will often score poorly on such tests, leading to false positive identifications, because learners either do not understand the tasks, or do not know how to answer in English, or draw on their broad linguistic knowledge to make sense of tasks and therefore give responses that do not fit the narrow marking scheme.

Instead of these potentially misleading assessment tools, teachers would be better advised to observe learners, as described above, and interpret the information gathered in light of the learners' family and educational backgrounds. Through liaising with other professionals with expertise in a range of SENDs, teachers can 'synthesize cultural, behavioural, academic and linguistic information' and determine the best course of action within their context (Carothers & Parfitt, 2017: 1).

Dynamic assessments (in which teachers offer learners coaching to complete tasks, and take into account how much and what kind of support was needed) also offer a much fairer form of assessment for multilingual learners. If possible, a first language assessment gives insights into how the learner is developing in their first or strongest language, which is also an important step in the overall evaluation of needs. If more formal assessment is required, tests should be used that do not rely on the learners' English language proficiency or cultural background knowledge (for example, my Cognitive Assessments for Multilingual Learners).

Overall, the best approach to identifying multilingual students whose barriers to learning are due to SENDs (rather than their diverse linguistic and educational experiences) is – of course – a whole-school approach, in collaboration with the families and carers. Locally, we need to build teams that include the SENCO, accessing the valuable input of (multilingual) teaching assistants, and working with external professionals whose expertise may be in occupational therapy, speech and language therapy, specific learning differences or SEBD. On a national level, by engaging with policy makers, providing them with reliable information from research and experience, and advising them how to take action, we can achieve the systemic change needed to ensure parity of opportunity for all our learners.

Note

Anne Margaret's multilingual assessment tools are available from her website: http://eltwell.com/dyslexia-assessment/spld-assessments-for-multilingual-people.

Commentary

Anne Margaret poses a challenging question: do our assumptions about multilingual children mean we hold back from assessing language disorders, missing an important opportunity to intervene and make a difference, or does overly quick diagnosis risk disadvantaging pupils? This may feel like a tightrope but Anne Margaret offers clear and evidence-based recommendations to find your balance.

First, as we found in Chapter 19, she recommends using observation to gather your initial insights into a pupil's language use. Talking to families and making a home visit (in Primary) or talking to pupils' subject teachers (in Secondary) are all good ways to supplement your direct observation. She recommends avoiding technical terms such as 'SEND' in the early days, because parents do not always share our assumptions about what these terms mean. Focusing on practical examples is helpful for both the teacher and the family.

She also recommends informing yourself about the pupil's first language. An excellent resource for this is Swan and Smith (2001), which gives clear summaries of how many languages differ from English. It is also a very useful way to begin stepping outside our monolingual mindset: rather than focusing on their difficulty in mastering English, we can understand that languages are structured differently, and that the greater the dissimilarity the more time it will take to incorporate them both into the learner's developing language system. In Part 1, we explored ways to enrich the input that learners receive and maximise their opportunities to use it in meaningful interaction. We also looked at the types of high-information feedback that helps learners process the difference between languages: these teaching techniques will help support language learning for all pupils.

Finally she recommends using accurate assessments. We know that bilingual learners are not going to demonstrate their full proficiency as soon as they are immersed in an English medium school: any assessments in the first six months will need revising after (see Chapter 18) and observation gives us much richer and more reliable data in the early days. When – and if – the time is right to use a formal language assessment, Anne Margaret recommends assessing the pupil's first languages as well as English. This is a good way to turn multi-competence thinking into practical teaching. It recognises that pupils use multiple languages for different purposes and with different people. Be cautious if the test reports low proficiency in L1: if it uses the cultural references and discourses expected of monolingual pupils, but translated into another language, it will give a less accurate result for pupils who might use L1 with their families but who are quickly becoming dominant in English at school and with their friends. There are language-development assessments available that do not rely on cultural knowledge or language proficiency (Anne Margaret has designed some herself).

The closing note is one of advocacy: making visible and amplifying the voices of young bilinguals, writing to policymakers and working with families as well as fellow professionals. We know the difference that a committed teacher can make to getting the right support, or preventing a child's normal development being medicalised because their bilingualism is not well understood. This is a specialist role, and one that requires ongoing professional learning.

23 CPD for EAL Specialists

This chapter outlines the opportunities for EAL specialists to continue their professional development and to support others to learn more about the discipline.

EAL specialists are in an unusual position, responsible for both their own professional development – in the absence of well-established routes to specialisation – and for the development of others, as they work across the curriculum to support and lead provision. This chapter looks at what CPD is available, what evidence underpins it and how you might craft an EAL CPD plan for yourself and your school.

Scope and Starting Points

The first step is to agree the scope of EAL professional development. It cannot be dependent on education policy: the teachers' standards for England, for example, say only that teachers must 'have a clear understanding of the needs of all pupils, including [...] those with English as an additional language' (DfE, 2011; Standard 5). The guidance in Scotland is more detailed and its counterpart in Wales does recognise bilingualism in the curriculum, but in all areas well-developed professional knowledge is needed to put policy into practice.

There are several good starting points. The *EAL Journal* has published two special issues on CPD (Issue 5, in Spring 2018, and Issue 10, in Autumn 2019). Two major reviews of the evidence on language and literacy interventions for EAL pupils have been published (Murphy & Unthiah, 2015, updated by Oxley & de Cat, 2019), with a similar review focusing on the United States (Larson et al., 2020). NALDIC conducted two national reviews of EAL training and development provision (NALDIC, 2009, 2014). There was also a major programme of workforce development in 2008–2009 that, although it was halted by the new government in 2010, produced a number of guidance documents and a review of the evidence (Andrews, 2009). Together they offer a small but robust body of evidence on which to plan CPD programmes.

This body of evidence needs to be adapted to local circumstances. The term 'EAL' covers such a diverse range of learners, needs and experiences that a single approach is unlikely to work for everyone. The professional landscape has also changed dramatically in the past decade, as the role of local authorities has decreased (in England) and come under increasing pressure (across the UK). EAL specialists report that they feel the professional community has fragmented, but at the same time social media has allowed teachers of all disciplines to connect with each other like never before, and teacher-led organisations like ResearchEd (https://researched.org.uk) are creating opportunities for teachers to engage directly with research. CPD for EAL is increasingly multifaceted.

Component Parts

What might an effective, school-wide EAL CPD plan address? Naomi Flynn (2018), writing in the *EAL Journal*, suggests that it should include a working knowledge of policy expectations, a strong understanding of the breadth of the discipline and specific knowledge of how to support the learners in your school. This three-part approach recognises the unique breadth of EAL but also gives it structure. There is an inherent risk that EAL CPD draws in a little of everything, trying to cover all bases, and is stretched thin as a result. By combining an overarching sense of what EAL *can* involve with detailed knowledge of the aspects that are relevant to your school, EAL specialists can begin mapping out an EAL CPD strategy for themselves and their colleagues.

Task 16 Mapping out an EAL strategy

☐ Make an initial map of EAL CPD needs in your school. Begin by sketching out the possible components of EAL knowledge for:
  ○ an EAL specialist;
  ○ an 'EAL-interested' colleague;
  ○ a colleague who hasn't given EAL a moment's thought (yet).
It may be helpful to go back through the book to identify key principles and findings.

☐ Then work out what you need to know for your school. You might consider the profile of your learners (mostly advanced bilinguals or new to English, for example?) and the expertise already in the school (the language-related strengths across the whole staff).

☐ Put these needs in a rough order of priority: What do you need to address first to build your own knowledge and to develop expertise across the school?

EAL specialists are often asked to deliver CPD for colleagues across the school, and so these plans will have two strands: one for yourself and one for others.

CPD Across the School

Several studies have found that CPD is especially beneficial when it builds capacity in the participants. This means that sharing research findings is not enough: people need a sense of their own ability to change things for the better, and this often means opportunities to apply and reflect on what they learn. Resist requests for isolated input sessions on broad topics: good CPD is sustained and closely tied to what participants do in their work. A balance of practice and theory is needed so that participants can link specific examples to the broader themes, and understand *why* a particular technique works (or doesn't) with a particular group of learners. It should also involve everyone, including school leaders and subject specialists. Several studies have shown that senior and middle leaders are vital to any programme of change. Including staff at all levels and from a range of disciplines is important to building support for and understanding EAL provision. Good CPD, then, shares a number of features: it is sustained, and closely linked to people's jobs so that they can apply the learning, but with enough theory to connect the work to broader themes and ideas. It should equip participants to change things and see the results of those changes, and it should include a range of staff at all levels of the school. In short: good CPD provision is about investing in colleagues and in yourself.

We Need to Talk about ITE

As we begin to think about CPD as part of a longer term development strategy, led by the EAL specialist but bringing in colleagues from across the school, we need to address people's different starting points. University-based initial teacher education (ITE) has been a historic point of weakness for EAL provision: a couple of hours is often all that trainee teachers will receive. Even this is sometimes combined with inclusion and diversity, obscuring the specialist knowledge and role of EAL staff. Trainee and newly qualified teachers have reported their dissatisfaction with this (see DfE, 2018), especially those who spend placements in linguistically diverse schools. School-based ITE can fare better, depending on the local expertise and pupil demographic, but there is little consistent input on EAL for new teachers. This means that a structured induction programme would be a very good investment.

CPD for EAL: A Practical Guide

Drawing on the findings above and in the book so far, a programme of continuous professional development for EAL would likely include the following elements:

Content

- How academic language differs from conversational language.
- Subject-specific vocabulary and how it is used in context (including general academic vocabulary).
- How the common texts and discursive patterns of a given subject are constructed and used.
- How experience of participating in subject talk and subject writing build subject knowledge as well as language knowledge.

Additional language learning

- The crucial importance of input, with many opportunities to use the language for meaningful interaction. Additionally, when explicit teaching is needed and when it constrains learning.
- How to use feedback effectively, both for students' written work and in everyday verbal interaction.
- The contribution that first languages make to additional language proficiency.
- The influence of age on the learning process, including the limits of that influence.
- The amount of time that EAL pupils will need to develop proficiency and what that means for curriculum and teaching.
- The constraints of a monolingual perspective and the need to engage the learner's whole linguistic repertoire in learning.

It is also important to use CPD opportunities to reinforce high aspirations for EAL learners. Research has shown that:

- We can expect 50% of additional progress of multilingual pupils over monolingual peers, as their proficiency grows rapidly in the early stages and unlocks their academic abilities.
- EAL pupils consistently outperform monolinguals at the highest levels of proficiency.
- Monolingual pupils often do better in multilingual classes (although the evidence for this point is still emerging).

We might also focus our CPD efforts on particular groups of pupils. Those who are new to English or have low proficiency are often a priority because their likelihood of succeeding at school is strongly influenced by their mastery of the language of instruction. However, this should not mean that more proficient learners have no support: there is a widely noted pattern of advanced bilingual learners struggling to reach the highest grades because they need explicit, focused instruction on the ways that texts work in their discipline. While the new-to-English learners often need close attention from the EAL specialist, advanced bilingual learners are best supported in the mainstream class and CPD should focus on equipping mainstream teachers to do so.

We might also focus on pupils belonging to language groups that have attainment below the national expected standard (at the time of writing, this included Pashto, Panjabi, Turkish, Portuguese, Czech and Slovak). We must do this critically. Are there other factors that lead these groups to attain below the expected standard and do these need to be addressed separately? If so, who do you need to partner with to ensure that the pupils and their families are fully supported? It is important to push back against any assumption that the EAL specialist will lead provision for any language group if the problems are not clearly linguistic, because where language and disadvantage are elided it separates the EAL specialist from the mainstream curriculum of the school. Complex challenges require interdisciplinary teams.

Task 17 Developing personalised CPD plans for your colleagues

- [ ] Work with two colleagues, at least one of whom is a subject or class teacher. Interview them on (at least) the following topics:
    - Their experience of teaching bilingual learners.
    - What they find difficult or wish would work better.
    - What seems to work well.
    - Any EAL or related CPD that they have done.
    - A specific challenge relating to EAL learners in their current classroom that they would like help with.
- [ ] Plan a personalised, realistic 12-month CPD plan for them. You should note topics covered and roughly when (e.g. 'straight after the Easter holiday, a peer observation focusing on ...').
- [ ] Share this with your colleagues and ask for their feedback. Does it look useful? Is there anything they would like to change? Is there anything they think is missing?
- [ ] Revise accordingly and store as part of your CPD bank.

Chapter Review

This chapter has examined the options for continuing professional development in EAL. It began by looking at the scope and starting points for CPD across the school. EAL is too diverse for a single approach to work, and so developing practitioners as language leaders keeps practice rooted in the needs of learners and their schools. We looked at the components of EAL CPD, recognising the need for an overarching view of the discipline and a detailed knowledge of the elements relevant to your work and your learners. We noted the absence of EAL in most initial teacher education (ITE) and set out a series of focal points for an integrated CPD programme. The chapter closed by considering how we might address particular groups of learners. The specifics of this will change with every school, but the overarching principles – that EAL should involve everyone, that it brings specialist knowledge but relies on the expertise of subject and class teachers too, that high aspirations for EAL pupils are both necessary and well justified by the evidence – can inform CPD in any setting.

24 For Everyone

This final chapter introduces the concept of 'funds of knowledge', reviews the key messages of the book and gives recommendations for further reading.

This book set out with a clear goal: to put before you, as simply as possible but with all essential detail, the evidence and principles you need to make informed decisions about your practice. In this chapter we review the evidence and principles for three audiences: parents, colleagues and EAL specialists. Before we do so, we will look at the knowledge that learners bring with them to the classroom and how that might influence our thinking about EAL.

Connecting Home and School: Funds of Knowledge

EAL learners do not arrive at school as blank slates. They come with their own experiences, expectations and ways of doing things, learned in the home and in the community. We can describe these 'historically accumulated and culturally developed bodies of knowledge and skills' (Moll *et al.*, 1992: 133) as 'funds of knowledge'. This approach grew from the work of a small group of researchers and teachers in the United States, working with predominantly working-class Mexican communities in Arizona. Cathy Amanti, a teacher and one of the research team, grew up in the area and describes her expectations at the outset:

> During my teacher training, I was led to believe that low-income and minority students were more likely to experience failure in school because their home experiences had not provided them with the prerequisite skills for school success in the same way as the home experiences of middle- and upper-class students. The result has been that traditionally low-income and minority students have been offered lessons reduced in complexity to compensate for these perceived deficits. (González *et al.*, 2005: 7)

Language plays a large part in these assumptions: if we replace 'low-income and minority students' with 'EAL learners', the argument holds true. Her experience of working in the school, however, was different:

> In my daily teaching practice I saw high levels of academic engagement and insight in my students who had typically been labelled 'at risk' because of their demographic characteristics. I saw they were as capable of academic success as students from any other background. Additionally, most were fluent in two languages! (González *et al.*, 2005: 7–8)

The funds of knowledge project found that learning in the community often revolved around children being respected as active participants alongside adults, interacting meaningfully and for sustained periods with others who were more expert than them. Their relationships were deeply trusting and secure; the activities were flexible and adaptive and involved a number of people across a number of settings. In the UK, a growing literature similarly describes how EAL children participate with adults in families, supplementary schools and faith settings.

Moll and colleagues argued that these participatory, trusting, sustained and nurturing activities 'contrasted [...] sharply with typical classroom practices', which they found typically involved an authoritative adult who plans and delivers programmes of study but does not participate alongside the young people. It is a striking argument, because many teachers would describe their classrooms as participatory, trusting, sustained and nurturing. The problem is that the deeply rooted assumptions of the education system are hard to get away from. EAL is premised on the development of the majority language, even though the research shows that supporting first languages contributes significantly to L2 proficiency. EAL learners need support until they can operate at a level equivalent to their monolingual peers, no matter if a better benchmark is whether they surpass the monolingual average ... and so on. The funds of knowledge approach encourages us to rethink what we know about EAL learners. Rather than asking if they are adequately prepared for the mainstream, for example, we might think about whether our education system is adequately prepared for 1.5 million bilingual children.

There are practical ways to address this locally. One approach is to make links to local supplementary schools and to make the connections between the different classrooms explicit. There are between 3,000 and 5,000 such schools in the UK (NRCSE, n.d.) and they generally teach a combination of heritage languages and cultures, usually in the evenings or at weekends. They are attended by both monolingual and multilingual children and often staffed by parents and members of the community, sometimes on the premises of mainstream schools and sometimes in community halls or private homes. These schools 'supplement' mainstream schools and they are spaces where young people are able to use their other languages for learning. Other approaches have been discussed throughout the book, such as using first languages for oracy, assessment and when creating bilingual resources.

Key Messages

To close the book we will briefly review the key messages for parents, colleagues and EAL specialists.

Parents

Parents get a lot of misinformation about raising bilingual children. They need reassurance that using their first language is the right thing to do, and that it will contribute to their child's development in English and in the curriculum. They also need help: Erica Field's case study on involving parents reminds us how much can be achieved with a little patience, a translator and a brew. Creating resources for parents and colleagues, as both Erica and Christine McCormack did, will take a lot of the pressure off others and only needs to be done once. Activities that involve families in learning, from bilingual homework activities to name trees (Chapter 19), are always welcome. Anne Margaret Smith also reminds us to moderate our specialist language if we think a child is having problems. Parents generally appreciate the work you do for their child and recognise when you go over and above.

The most important thing you can do for the parents of EAL pupils, though, is to get out there and meet them. Especially when you are new in post, spend some time at the school gates, ask to meet with supplementary schools and community groups, learn a few words of children's first languages and try them out, create activities that involve parents in subject learning – anything that breaks down the barriers between 'us' and 'them' and makes parents feel at home in the school.

Colleagues

First and foremost, we need to press the idea that language is every teacher's responsibility. The EAL specialist is there to support and to work directly with particular groups of learners, but in most schools the only practical way to ensure EAL learners can participate in the mainstream is for subject teachers to incorporate language into their teaching. The key is to work better, not more. If you're creating a worksheet and know how to incorporate rich subject language, it takes no extra time to do it that way. We need to ensure a culture of high aspirations, in which all teachers know that EAL learners make quicker progress than monolingual peers (because their developing English proficiency unlocks their knowledge and skills) and that they will, on average, achieve more highly than their monolingual peers once they reach a high level of proficiency.

Yourself

There is a lot to take on board for the EAL specialist. You are a source of expert guidance for colleagues as well as having your own teaching responsibilities. You are likely to be the leading advocate for multilingual children in your school, while trying to build up a network of supportive, 'EAL-interested' colleagues to share good practice with. You may also be the unofficial go-between for bilingual families and community organisations, all with the most rapidly changing group of pupils in the school. You probably won't be showered with gold for your efforts, but they are heroic nonetheless.

By this point you will have your own priorities and key messages, built up over the activities in Part 3. My only addition is to remember that there are very many advocates for EAL pupils out there. Many find it hard to meet others and would welcome a supportive professional network. If that includes you, look to the pages of the *EAL Journal*, to local groups and to social media. There are plenty of us who would love to work with you.

Where Can I Go Next?

So what next? The following recommendations are oriented towards the future. Some focus on the core tenets of the discipline, ideas and practices that you will add to through your own work. Others are resources to share with others when they ask for your reading recommendations. Several are from scholars and teachers who are challenging outdated assumptions and encouraging us to be ambitious for the field. I have tried to keep this list concise but would welcome you getting in touch with your own suggestions and questions.

On EAL

The best concise summary of EAL practice is still the NALDIC working paper on 'The distinctiveness of EAL' (NALDIC, 1999). It makes the case for EAL as a distinct specialism and outlines the main elements of the role. The termly *EAL Journal* (free to members of NALDIC) is also highly recommended because it is the only regular publication dedicated to EAL. By providing a space for shared professional dialogue, it plays an important role in sustaining the professional community. The EAL-bilingual online group and NALDIC's regional and special interest groups play a similar role (see Appendix II).

Several organisations make their material freely available. Among them, the EAL Academy and Hounslow Language Service stand out (the former especially for their regular analysis of EAL data). Contact details are given in Appendix II.

Recommendations for those new to EAL

Jean Conteh's (2015) *The EAL Teaching Book* is now in its 3rd edition and is an excellent primer on EAL. It is written with Primary teachers-in-training in mind but has much to recommend it to everyone. In two books, Canadian scholar Roma Chumak-Horbatsch (2012 and 2019) sets out simple and effective strategies for supporting first languages, which she calls *Linguistically Appropriate Practice*. The first book focuses on learners in the early years and is written for anyone who works with young bilinguals, including teachers, childcare workers, healthcare providers and speech therapists. The second book has a stronger classroom emphasis, but both are highly recommended. For Secondary learners, Esther Daborn, Sally Zacharias and Hazel Crichton's (2020) book on *Subject Literacy in Culturally Diverse Secondary Schools* is a valuable resource.

For day-to-day classroom activities, see three short and well-informed booklets: Alice Washbourne's (2011) *EAL Pocketbook*, *100 Ideas for Secondary Teachers: Supporting EAL Learners* by Chris Pim and Catherine Driver (2018) and the equivalent Primary volume by Chris Pim (2018). They are written by highly respected specialists and connect the body of evidence in this book to specific classroom activities.

Fresh ideas

Many challenges to the status quo concern assessment, especially in the United States where annual standardised tests of proficiency are required by law. Kate Mahoney's (2017) book, *The Assessment of Emergent Bilinguals: Supporting English Language Learners*, is an excellent resource. It sets out four principles for effective assessment: seeing assessment through a lens of promise rather than deficit; only using high-quality assessments; using a unified notion of validity; and recognising that translanguaging during assessments is important for English learners. For a critique of standardised assessments, see Menken (2009), Menken *et al.* (2014) and King and Bigelow (2018). These three papers focus primarily on the United States but raise issues of significance to EAL policy in the UK. Leung and Lewkowicz (2016) addresses language assessment in diverse populations and so is especially relevant to EAL.

Many of the most exciting projects are happening outside the education system. Amala (formerly Sky School, https://amalaeducation.org) works with young people who have missed out on formal education. It runs an innovative high school diploma with courses such as 'peace-building' and 'maths for change', which is run partly online and partly through local tuition (and often in very challenging locations). The Young Interpreters Scheme (run by Hampshire local authority but available across the UK, https://www.hants.gov.uk/educationandlearning/emtas/supportinglanguages/young-interpreters-guide) gives children and young people responsibility for newcomers to their community. Likewise, the New Scots strategy (https://www.gov.scot/policies/refugees-and-asylum-seekers/new-scots) puts an integrated approach to welcoming newcomers at the heart of government policy. The HundrED (https://hundred.org/en) showcases innovative education projects from around the globe. Their 'spotlight' theme for 2021 is 'Teachers for a Changing World'.

There is also huge creativity to draw on. The First Story project (https://firststory.org.uk) creates space for Secondary learners to put their experiences into their own words. It can be a powerful experience for those learners but can also make their voices heard across the school. Dual-language books are similarly important, especially where children and parents collaborate in their production: see the dual-language project at the University of East London (https://www.uel.ac.uk/research/dual-language-books) and the Multilingual Digital Storytelling project (https://goldsmithsmdst.com). MantraLingua, a UK-based company with a long history of supporting EAL learners, can turn children's own stories into published books and has a number of innovative tools to connect spoken and written language (https://uk.mantralingua.com). Annelies Kusters and Maartje De Meulder have produced a short guide to creating language portraits with children and young people who use spoken and signed languages (http://www.qualitative-research.net/index.php/fqs/article/view/3239/4452).

There is much still to do. Our understanding of mobile learners (a broad term to include both one-off and regular transnational movement, as well as the enduring connections to others inside and outside the local community) is sorely lacking. A slim volume by philosopher David Owen (*What Do We Owe to Refugees?*, 2020) is a thought-provoking starting point, as is Theresa Catalano's (2016) book of global migration stories and their implications for language teaching.

Finally, because this book seeks to put theory at the service of practice, there is the call to imagine a 'new SLA'. There is exciting and innovative work being done in the academic field and it will have far-reaching consequences, but only if teachers and researchers are genuinely in collaboration. The seminal paper by the Douglas Fir Group (2016) has sparked a number of others, including those (like Leung & Valdés, 2019) that apply such thinking to the multilingual classroom.

A note on academic journals

A well-informed specialist community needs access to the latest evidence, but much of the relevant literature is hidden behind paywalls. This leads to a difficult decision: whether to recommend only the most available sources, or to include those that most teachers will find it hard to access. I decided to focus on quality, using peer-reviewed studies even if they are not open access.

There are ways to access most papers. If you have a university affiliation (if you are training or taking a CPD course, for example) then the university should have access to all the sources recommended here. Many public libraries also have an arrangement with academic publishers that allows free access to many journals (this little-known tip was shared by a colleague who works for a major publisher). Many academics also upload 'pre-publication copies' to their personal websites or institutional repositories. They usually vary a little from the published version and so shouldn't be cited in your own academic writing, but are generally excellent quality. Searching online for the title of the article will often yield results, as can two sites where academics share their work: https://www.academia.edu and https://www.researchgate.net (you may need to set up an account but they are both free). All UK doctoral theses are published through the British Library's EthOS repository (https://ethos.bl.uk), which is an invaluable resource for exploring the academic field further.

The final way to get academic papers is to email the author. Almost all academics have profiles on their institutional websites and they are usually delighted to get enquiries from interested practitioners and to know that people are reading and using their work.

Appendix I: Checklist and Activities for the New EAL Specialist

Task 1 Getting to know your school
☐ Read through the questions above and make notes on your own school. Feel free to go beyond the questions and include your thoughts and impressions. ☐ Note one or two points that you would like to prioritise – then move on to Task 2.

Task 2 Establishing your role
☐ Make an appointment with your line manager to discuss your initial priorities. Give yourself enough time before the meeting to work through the rest of this chapter as it will give you plenty of solid points for discussion.

Task 3 Building your policy folder
☐ Use the list above to build your policy folder. Note any documents that are missing to discuss with your line manager. ☐ Make the folder accessible to other teachers (for example on a shared drive).

Task 4 Developing your own EAL plan
☐ Take a blank sheet of paper (or its digital equivalent) and set a timer for 20 minutes. ☐ Write down your aspirations for the role before the timer runs out. Try to keep writing non-stop to get as much on paper as possible. ☐ Develop this into your personal EAL plan (see below).

Goal	Why is it important to me?	How will I put it into practice?	How will I measure success?	How does it fit with my job description?	What theory & evidence support me?

Task 5a Identifying the focus of an assessment (i)

☐ Look at these two sample descriptors and note everything you can think of about the construct. Once you have your notes, move on to the next task.

A2	Can find specific information in practical, concrete, predictable texts (e.g. travel guidebooks, recipes), provided they are written in simple language. Can understand the main information in short and simple descriptions of goods in brochures and websites (e.g. portable digital devices, cameras, etc.). Can find specific, predictable information in simple everyday material such as advertisements, prospectuses, menus, reference lists and timetables. Can locate specific information in lists and isolate the information required (e.g. use the 'Yellow Pages' to find a service or tradesman). Can understand everyday signs and notices etc. in public places, such as streets, restaurants, railway stations, in workplaces, such as directions, instructions, hazard warnings.

Source: Common European Framework for Reference (CEFR) (Council of Europe, 2018: 62).

CONNECTION: *Common Core Reading Standards for Informational Texts, Integration of Knowledge & Ideas #7:* Integrate and evaluate multiple sources of information presented in different media or formats (e.g., visually, quantitatively) as well as in words in order to address a question or solve a problem.

EXAMPLE CONTEXT FOR LANGUAGE USE: Students review college or career marketing materials (e.g., print or online) according to personal preferences (e.g., affordability, location, time commitment, requirements, interest) to make informed decisions on post-secondary options.

COGNITIVE FUNCTION: Students at all levels of English language proficiency EVALUATE post-secondary options.						
	Level 1 Entering	Level 2 Emerging	Level 3 Developing	Level 4 Expanding	Level 5 Bridging	
READING	Sort information on post-secondary options from multiple sources with visual support with a partner	Identify important information (e.g., by highlighting) on post-secondary options from multiple sources with visual support with a partner	Categorize (e.g., best, maybe, unlikely) post-secondary options from multiple sources using illustrated graphic organizers	Make judgments about post-secondary options from multiple sources using illustrated graphic organizers (e.g., checklists of types of evidence)	Draw conclusions on post-secondary options from claims in multiple sources of information	Level 6 – Reaching

TOPIC-RELATED LANGUAGE: Students at all levels of English language proficiency interact with grade-level words and expressions, such as: priorities, vocation/trade, merit scholarship, cost of living, room and board, professional reference, résumé-building

Source: WIDA English Language Development Standards (WIDA, 2012: 40).

Task 5b Identifying the focus of an assessment (ii)

☐ Add to your notes:
  ○ *What types of language does each descriptor mention?*
  ○ *What types of text, situation or interaction are described?*
  ○ *What learner characteristics are implied by each descriptor?*
  ○ *What links do they each make to the curriculum and to academic language?*
☐ Finally, decide which is most appropriate for your learners and note why.

Task 6 Understanding the purpose of an assessment framework
☐ Go to The Bell Foundation's website and download a copy of the assessment framework (https://www.bell-foundation.org.uk/eal-programme/teaching-resources/eal-assessment-framework). You need to register an account but it is free. ☐ Watch the introductory video (five minutes) and read the introduction (two slides). ☐ Make a note on what information the assessment provides. Who might find it useful and why?

Task 7 A different perspective on language and community
☐ Visit the Multilingual Digital Storytelling website (https://goldsmithsmdst.com) and watch some of the student-made videos. Make notes on: 　○ What these videos tell us about the language and literacy skills that children bring into the classroom.[1] 　○ How we can help colleagues to understand the relevance of these multilingual literacy skills for curriculum learning. Note: [1] A detailed handbook for teachers accompanies the MDST project and is available from http://goldsmithsmdst.wordpress.com/handbook. See Chapter 8 of that publication for ideas on integrating multilingual literacies into the curriculum.

Task 8 From 'new arrival' to 'one of us'
☐ Gather your school's admissions procedures and welcome pack (if there is one). Ask around to find out what information is sent to staff – and whether it is actually used or gets lost in the email blizzard. ☐ On a fresh sheet of paper, draw a timeline from when you first get news of a new arrival, through the induction period, to when you might be confident that they are settling in. Add: 　○ Your key actions and where you need information or help from others. 　○ When others might need to act (for example, in their own classrooms) or need more information from you. 　○ What points the new pupil might find most disconcerting or need your help with. 　○ When you are going to check in with the pupil's buddies, teachers and family. ☐ Run this past a few colleagues. Does everyone know what's expected and is anything missing?

Task 9 Surveying the linguistic landscape

- ☐ Find some time to walk through the school slowly. Start in the reception area and work your way up to your classroom; then go around each department (in Secondary), the common areas and gathering places such as the hall, the dining hall and the playground. Take photos as you go, aiming to capture every instance of language that is visible.
- ☐ On a separate occasion, take a notebook and record what languages you hear. It's often worth pausing at places where students congregate and where they move from one space to another: coming out of lessons, into assembly, in the playground.
- ☐ Compare your notes and the images. Do you see the same languages that you heard? Were there times when you couldn't be sure what language was being used or where languages were mixed? The difference between the (teacher-controlled) visual environment and the (student-controlled) aural environment is a good indicator of how well the school reflects the languages of the pupils.
- ☐ Optionally, you might repeat this, but looking at/listening for cultural references rather than languages.

Task 10 Shadow a pupil

- ☐ Shadow a pupil for at least a lesson, a short break and a long break (so most of a morning). In Secondary, shadowing pupils in a range of lessons will give a richer insight into their experiences, allowing you to compare how teachers approach different subject areas and how the pupils respond.
- ☐ Note how others speak to the pupil. Is their name used accurately? Does their hand go up and is it noticed? Do teachers and others show patience if they need time to formulate their ideas? Do they have a supportive group of friends? How do they manage differences in language, experience and English proficiency?
- ☐ What specific techniques does the teacher use to ensure the pupil is included, supported and challenged? Do pupils do anything to the same end?
- ☐ What would you change for this pupil if you could? Share your insights with the colleagues concerned and ask if it matches their observations of the pupil. What next steps would they take as a result?

Task 11 Getting to know your subject association

☐ Find your subject association. Make a note of how much membership costs and what it offers you.

☐ Note three things you can do to build your network within this community. For example, is there a regional group in your area? If so, you could email the convenor to say hi and get details of the next meeting. Do they publish resources (like a blog or magazine)? If so, is there anyone you can buddy with to talk about what you read? Is there a conference that could go in your diary now? If so, add the details to your professional development plan (see Chapter 23).

Task 12 Getting connected online

If you're an old hand at social media, skip this task.

☐ Make a Twitter profile (see the guide below if you need ideas). Add a photo and find 10 people to follow. If you're not sure, start with @EAL_naldic and @EAL_journal: they're good starting points because a lot of EAL people follow them. You can also search for the accounts posting using the hashtag #EAL and follow them.

☐ Send your first message! If you want to find more people to follow, you can say that you're new to social media and ask for recommendations. Use #EAL and tag some EAL people into the tweet so that it shows up on their timelines.

☐ Schedule time to check your account regularly until you get a feel for who's sharing what. Try to reply to people and engage in conversations: goodwill and generosity are usually returned in kind.

Task 13 Reviewing your personal EAL plan

☐ Revisit your personal EAL plan. What aspirations did you note for the whole-school approach to language?

☐ For each one, write down why it is important and what would count as success.
  ○ Who else needs to be involved as you achieve this aspiration?

☐ Then add the barriers you can see to getting there.
  ○ Who else is affected by (or contributes to) these barriers?

☐ Finally, note how each barrier can be overcome or avoided.
  ○ Who do you need to work with to overcome or avoid them?

Task 14 Mapping provision

☐ Think about all the different groups of learners in your school and map the provision they receive on the grid below. If you only have small numbers you could do this for each pupil.

Learners	Support model	Timetabling options	Pupil groupings	EAL specialist role	Subject/Class teacher role

☐ Write a few lines for each pupil/group, explaining to yourself why they are receiving this pattern of provision and what will need to change as their proficiency develops.

Task 15 How to teach bilinguals (when you're not one)

☐ Find a monolingual colleague (ideally someone outside your immediate team) to buddy up with. Start by finding time to sit down and talk about what you each feel the language of the classroom should be. Are there any instances when pupils can (or should) use L1 as part of their learning?

☐ Watch the first two videos from CUNY-NYSIEB (https://www.youtube.com/channel/UC5PE-qUgT9LHiYq6yuVJ1fw/featured). If you're watching them together, take a moment to make notes on the following alone then discuss them:
  - What emotions are associated with students using L1? What does it mean for your role as a teacher?
  - What does it mean to be an advocate for EAL learners? Is it a desirable role? Who can be an advocate?
  - What examples of multilingualism can we see in the videos? Are they quite superficial or do they challenge the structural monolingualism of the school?
  - The video is very clearly set in the United States. What would apply (or could be adapted) to UK classrooms?

Task 16 Mapping out an EAL strategy

☐ Make an initial map of EAL CPD needs in your school. Begin by sketching out the possible components of EAL knowledge for:
  - an EAL specialist;
  - an 'EAL-interested' colleague;
  - a colleague who hasn't given EAL a moment's thought (yet).

It may be helpful to go back through the book to identify key principles and findings.

☐ Then work out what you need to know for your school. You might consider the profile of your learners (mostly advanced bilinguals or new to English, for example?) and the expertise already in the school (the language-related strengths across the whole staff).

☐ Put these needs in a rough order of priority: What do you need to address first to build your own knowledge and to develop expertise across the school?

Task 17 Developing personalised CPD plans for your colleagues

☐ Work with two colleagues, at least one of whom is a subject or class teacher. Interview them on (at least) the following topics:
  - Their experience of teaching bilingual learners.
  - What they find difficult or wish would work better.
  - What seems to work well.
  - Any EAL or related CPD that they have done.
  - A specific challenge relating to EAL learners in their current classroom that they would like help with.

☐ Plan a personalised, realistic 12-month CPD plan for them. You should note topics covered and roughly when (e.g. 'straight after the Easter holiday, a peer observation focusing on …').

☐ Share this with your colleagues and ask for their feedback. Does it look useful? Is there anything they would like to change? Is there anything they think is missing?

☐ Revise accordingly and store as part of your CPD bank.

Appendix II: Networks and Groups

Below is a list of useful networks, groups and organisations.

The advice in short is this: join NALDIC, follow everyone else on Twitter and make it to an MLIE conference if at all possible. From there you'll be in a good position to build your own network and reach out to others.

NALDIC, the subject association for EAL

Website:	http://naldic.org.uk
Email:	enquiries@naldic.org.uk
Social media:	@EAL_NALDIC, @EAL_Journal
Membership:	£30/40/100 (concession/individual/school). Discounts for groups of schools that join together.
Benefits:	*EAL Journal* (3 per year), conference, regional groups, resources for members on website.

SATEAL, the Scottish Association for Teachers of EAL

Website:	https://www.sateal.org.uk
Email:	Contact SATEAL through their website.
Social media:	@satealorg
Membership:	£ free
Benefits:	Conference.

ECIS-MLIE, the Multilingual Learning in International Education special interest group

Website:	https://www.ecis.org/mlie
Email:	mlie.ecis@gmail.com
Social media:	@ECISMLIE
Membership:	£ via ECIS
Benefits:	Conference.

EAL Research Network

Website: https://ealresearchnetwork.com
Email: Contact via website.
Social media: N/A
Membership: £ free
Benefits: Email list, events.

Many local authorities also maintain blogs and resource sites. Here are two to start with:

EAL Highland   https://www.ealhighland.org.uk
The EAL service in the Scottish Highlands post a lot of links and resources to their blog.

Hampshire EMTAS   https://emtas.hias.hants.gov.uk/blog
The Hampshire ethnic minority and traveller achievement service run a blog and regularly post resources. They also created the Young Interpreters programme and include a full description here.

Two further sites offer consistently good resources for free:

EAL Nexus   https://ealresources.bell-foundation.org.uk
Created by the British Council to complement its ESOL Nexus project for adult English learners, the EAL Nexus is now managed by The Bell Foundation. It is a rich repository of EAL resources, all created by teachers and organised by subject and age range.

Collaborative Learning   http://www.collaborativelearning.org
The Collaborative Learning Project, run by Stewart Scott, has been sharing talk-for-learning activities since 1983. Their website has a rich range of worksheets and ideas for different ages and curriculum subjects.

For a stronger research focus:

Bilingualism Matters   https://www.bilingualism-matters.ppls.ed.ac.uk
Based at the University of Edinburgh but with 26 branches around the world, the BM team share research on bilingualism and its importance for learning and society.

Centre for Literacy and Multilingualism   https://research.reading.ac.uk/celm
A research centre at the University of Reading, CeLM is an interdisciplinary hub for research into language, language acquisition and literacy. Their website hosts recent academic publications as well as a blog about their work.

Multilingualism: Empowering Individuals, Transforming Lives (MEITS) http://www.meits.org

The MEITS project investigated how the insights gained from stepping outside a single language, culture and mode of thought are vital to individuals and societies. The project was coming to an end at the time of going to press, but the site still contains valuable research findings and links to local networks.

Working with Consultants

If your school has the resources to bring in outside expertise, there are several very well regarded consultants who can mentor your team or work directly with your colleagues. The two largest are Hounslow Language Service and The EAL Academy, which grew from the Hounslow and Islington local authority EAL departments, respectively. Both have produced highly regarded resources: The EAL Academy run a kitemark for EAL and an online CPD course accredited through the University of Greenwich; Hounslow Language Service were partners in the nationwide EAL in the Mainstream Classroom Project. Both are very credible.

EAL Academy	Nationwide	https://www.theealacademy.co.uk
		contact@theealacademy.co.uk
Hounslow Language Service	Nationwide	https://www.ealhls.org.uk
		rehana.ahmed@ealhls.org.uk

Some smaller organisations are increasingly gaining recognition. These tend to focus on a particular geographical area and are often involved in local networks. Some are based in local authorities, some are private and some are social enterprises. All the organisations listed here are very reputable and have a track record of supporting schools.

Better Bilingual	South West	http://www.betterbilingual.co.uk
		info@betterbilingual.co.uk
Educator Solutions	East of England	https://www.educatorsolutions.org.uk
		enquiry@educatorsolutions.org.uk
Hampshire EMTAS	South	https://www.hants.gov.uk/education-andlearning/emtas
		emtas@hants.gov.uk
NASSEA	North	http://www.nassea.org.uk
		consultancy@nassea.org.uk
Leeds for Learning	North	http://www.leedsforlearning.co.uk
		leedsforlearning@leeds.gov.uk

CEC   International   https://www.crisfieldeducationalconsulting.com

                                             info@crisfieldeducationalconsulting.com

Courses and Qualifications

While it is fairly straightforward to get support from expert consultants, it is quite hard to find further qualifications in EAL. Many practitioners come to the field with an EFL qualification, such as the CELTA or Cert. TESOL. These contain a lot of useful ideas about language teaching, but they are not really suitable for EAL because they lack specialist knowledge about language in the curriculum. The DELTA qualification (https://www.cambridgeenglish.org/teaching-english/teaching-qualifications/delta) deserves an honourable mention, however. Where certificate-level courses tend to skip the theory in favour of developing practical skills, the DELTA engages more experienced teachers with evidence-informed approaches to language and learning.

These are good entry points to EAL, but what we really need are high-level specialist qualifications. There are not many available, but the ones below are well regarded. A good place to look is the *EAL Journal*, which for the past few years has run an annual CPD feature. This lists advanced programmes as well as short-course providers.

University of East London   **Primary PGCE with EAL**
https://www.uel.ac.uk/Postgraduate/Courses/PGCE-Primary-with-English-as-an-Additional-Language

UCL Institute of Education   **PGCE Languages with EAL Enhancement**
https://www.ucl.ac.uk/ioe/courses/teacher-training/languages-pgce

Oxford Brookes University   **Postgraduate Certificate in Teaching Multilingual Learners**
https://www.brookes.ac.uk/courses/postgraduate/teaching-multilingual-learners

University of Roehampton   **MA Educational Practice**
https://www.roehampton.ac.uk/postgraduate-courses/educational-practice

References

Alonso, J.G. and Rothman, J. (2017) Coming of age in L3 initial stages transfer models: Deriving developmental predictions and looking towards the future. *International Journal of Bilingualism* 21 (6), 683–697.
Andrews, R. (2009) *Review of Research in English as an Additional Language (EAL)*. London: Training and Development Agency for Schools.
Bak, T.H. and Mehmedbegovic, D. (2017) Healthy linguistic diet: The value of linguistic diversity and language learning across the lifespan. *Language, Society and Policy*. doi:10.17863/CAM.9854
Baker, C. and Wright, W.E. (2021) *Foundations of Bilingual Education and Bilingualism* (7th edn). Bristol: Multilingual Matters.
Beck, I., McKeown, M.G. and Kucan, L. (2013) *Bringing Words to Life* (2nd edn). New York: Guilford Press.
Bellsham-Revell, A. and Nancarrow, P./NALDIC (2019) *The EAL Coordinator: The First 100 Days*. Edinburgh: NALDIC.
Bernstein, B. (1970) Education cannot compensate for society. *New Society* 26 February, 344–347.
Blackledge, A. and Creese, A. (2010) *Multilingualism*. London: Continuum.
Bourdieu, P. and Passeron, J.-C. (1994) Introduction: Language and relationship to language in the teaching situation. In P. Bourdieu, J.-C. Passeron and M. De Saint Martin (eds) *Academic Discourse: Linguistic Misunderstanding and Professorial Power* (pp. 1–34). Stanford, CA: Stanford University Press.
Bourke, J. (2005) The grammar we teach. *Reflections on English Language Teaching* 4, 85–97.
Bourne, J. and McPake, J. (1991) *Partnership Teaching: Co-operative Teaching Strategies for English Language Support in Multilingual Classrooms*. London: Her Majesty's Stationery Office.
Bowyer, C. (2018) Making historians of sixth formers. *EAL Journal* 6, 34–36.
Bracken, S., Driver, C. and Kadi-Hanifi, K. (2017) *Teaching English as an Additional Language in Secondary Schools: Theory and Practice*. Abingdon: David Fulton.
Brisk, M.E. (2015) *Engaging Students in Academic Literacies: Genre-Based Pedagogy in K-5 Classrooms*. Abingdon: Routledge.
Brown, D. (2016) The type and foci of oral corrective feedback in the L2 classroom: A meta-analysis. *Language Teaching Research* 20, 436–458.
Bullock, A. (1975) *A Language for Life: Report of the Committee of Inquiry Appointed by the Secretary of State for Education and Science under the Chairmanship of Sir Alan Bullock F.B.A.* London: HMSO.
Cameron, D. (2005) *Verbal Hygiene: The Politics of Language*. London: Routledge.
Canagarajah, S. (1997) Safe houses in the contact zone: Coping strategies of African-American students in the academy. *College Composition and Communication* 48 (2), 173–196.
Carothers, D. and Parfitt, C.M. (2017) Disability or language difference: How do we decide? *American Journal of Qualitative Research* 1 (1), 1–12.
Carter, R. (ed.) (1990) *Knowledge About Language and the Curriculum*. London: Hodder & Stoughton.
Catalano, T. (2016) *Talking About Global Migration: Implications for Language Teaching*. Bristol: Multilingual Matters.
Chalmers, H. (2019) *The Role of the First Language in English Medium Instruction*. Oxford University Press Expert Series. See https://elt.oup.com/feature/global/expert/emi (accessed 1 June 2020).

Chomsky, N. (1965) *Aspects of the Theory of Syntax*. Cambridge, MA: MIT Press.
Chumak-Horbatsch, R. (2012) *Linguistically Appropriate Practice: A Guide for Working with Young Immigrant Children*. Toronto, ON: University of Toronto Press.
Chumak-Horbatsch, R. (2019) *Using Linguistically Appropriate Practice: A Guide for Teaching in Multilingual Classrooms*. Bristol: Multilingual Matters.
Cohteh, J. and Meier, G. (eds) (2014). *The Multilingual Turn in Languages Education: Opportunities and Challenges*. Bristol: Multilingual Matters.
Collier, V. and Thomas, W. (2017) Validating the power of bilingual schooling: Thirty-two years of large-scale, longitudinal research. *Annual Review of Applied Linguistics* 37, 203–217.
Commission for Racial Equality (1986) *Teaching English as a Second Language: Report of a Formal Investigation by the Commission for Racial Equality into the Teaching of English as a Second Language in Calderdale Local Education Authority*. London: Commission for Racial Equality.
Conger, D. (2009) Testing, time limits, and English learners: Does age of school entry affect how quickly students can learn English? *Social Science Research* 38 (2), 383–396.
Conteh, J. (2012) *Teaching Bilingual and EAL Learners in Primary Schools*. Exeter: Learning Matters.
Conteh, J. (2015) *The EAL Teaching Book*. Exeter: Learning Matters.
Conteh, J. (2018) Funds of knowledge. *EAL Journal* 5, 50–52.
Cook, V.J. (1991) The poverty-of-the-stimulus argument and multi-competence. *Second Language Research* 7, 103–117.
Cook, V.J. (2008) Multi-competence: Black hole or wormhole for SLA research? In Z.-H. Han (ed.) *Understanding Second Language Process* (pp. 16–26). Clevedon: Multilingual Matters.
Cook, V.J. (2016) Premises of multicompetence. In V.J. Cook and Li Wei (eds) *The Cambridge Handbook of Linguistic Multicompetence*. Cambridge: Cambridge University Press.
Cook, V.J. and Singleton, D. (2014) *Key Topics in Second Language Acquisition*. Bristol: Multilingual Matters.
Costley, T. (2014) English as an additional language, policy and the teaching and learning of English in England. *Language and Education* 28 (3), 276–292.
Council of Europe (2018) *Common European Framework of Reference for Languages: Learning, Teaching, Assessment (CEFR). Companion Volume with New Descriptors*. See https://www.coe.int/en/web/common-european-framework-reference-languages (accessed 21 July 2020).
Coxhead, A. (2000) A new academic word list. *TESOL Quarterly* 34, 213–238.
Coyle, D. and Meyer, O. (2021) *Beyond CLIL: Pluriliteracies Teaching for Deeper Learning*. Cambridge: Cambridge University Press.
Creese, A. (2005) *Teacher Collaboration and Talk in Multilingual Classrooms*. Clevedon: Multilingual Matters.
Crisfield, E. (2021) *Bilingual Families: A Practical Language Planning Guide*. Bristol: Multilingual Matters.
Cummins, J. (1979) Cognitive/academic language proficiency, linguistic interdependence, the optimum age question and some other matters. Working Paper on Bilingualism No. 19. Toronto, ON: Bilingual Education Project, The Ontario Institute for Studies in Education. See https://eric.ed.gov/?id=ED184334 (accessed 31 July 2020).
Cummins, J. (1981) Age on arrival and immigrant second language learning in Canada: A reassessment. *Applied Linguistics* 2 (2), 132–149.
Cummins, J. (1984) *Bilingualism and Special Education: Issues in Assessment and Pedagogy*. Clevedon: Multilingual Matters.
Cummins, J. (2000) *Language, Power and Pedagogy: Bilingual Children Caught in the Crossfire*. Clevedon: Multilingual Matters.
Cummins, J. (2001) *Negotiating Identities: Education for Empowerment in a Diverse Society* (2nd edn). Ontario, CA: California Association for Bilingual Education.
Cummins, J. (2005) A proposal for action: Strategies for recognizing heritage language competence as a learning resource within the mainstream classroom. *The Modern Language Journal* 80 (4), 585–592.

Cummins, J. and Early, M. (2011) *Identity Texts: The Collaborative Creation of Power in Multilingual Schools*. Stoke-on-Trent: Trentham Books.
Daborn, E., Zacharias, S. and Crichton, H. (2020) *Subject Literacy in Culturally Diverse Secondary Schools: Supporting EAL Learners*. London: Bloomsbury.
Datta, M. (2007) *Bilinguality and Literacy: Principles and Practice* (2nd edn). London: Continuum.
Davies, A. (2013) *Native Speakers and Native Users: Loss and Gain*. Cambridge: Cambridge University Press.
Davison, C. (2001) Current policies, programs and practices in school ESL. In C. Leung, C. Davison and B. Mohan (eds) *English as a Second Language in the Mainstream: Teaching, Learning and Identity* (pp. 30–50). London: Routledge.
DeKeyser, R. (1997) Beyond explicit rule learning: Automatizing second language morphosyntax. *Studies in Second Language Acquisition* 19, 195–221.
DeKeyser, R. (ed.) (2007) *Practice in a Second Language: Perspectives from Applied Linguistics and Cognitive Psychology*. Cambridge: Cambridge University Press.
DeKeyser, R. (2015) Skill acquisition theory. In B. VanPatten and J. Williams (eds) *Theories in Second Language Acquisition* (pp. 94–112). Abingdon/New York: Routledge.
Demie, F. (2018) English language proficiency and attainment of EAL (English as second language) pupils in England. *Journal of Multilingual & Multicultural Development* 39 (7), 641–653.
Derrick, J. (1977) *Language Needs of Minority Group Children: Learners of English as a Second Language*. Slough: NFER.
DES (Department for Education and Skills) (1971) *The Education of Immigrants: Education Survey 13*. London: HMSO.
DES (Department for Education and Skills) (1972) *The Continuing Needs of Immigrants: Education Survey 14*. London: HMSO.
Dewaele, J.M. (2018) Why the dichotomy 'L1 versus LX user' is better than 'native versus non-native speaker'. *Applied Linguistics* 39 (2), 236–240.
DfE (Department for Education) (2011) *Teachers' Standards*. See https://www.gov.uk/government/publications/teachers-standards (accessed 20 July 2020).
DfE (Department for Education) (2012) *Phonics Screening Check and National Curriculum Assessments at Key Stage 1 in England, 2011/2012*. See http://www.education.gov.uk/rsgateway/DB/SFR/s001086/sfr21-2012.pdf (accessed 21 July 2020).
DfE (Department for Education) (2016) *School Census 2016 to 2017 (Guide, Version 1.0)* (online). See https://www.gov.uk/government/statistics/phonics-screening-check-and-national-curriculum-assessments-at-key-stage-1-in-england-2012 (accessed 13 December 2016).
DfE (Department for Education) (2017) *Phonics Screening Check and Key Stage 1 Assessments in England*. London: Department for Education
DfE (Department for Education) (2018) *Newly Qualified Teachers (NQTs): Annual Survey 2017*. See https://assets.publishing.service.gov.uk/government/uploads/system/uploads/attachment_data/file/522546/2016_to_2017_School_Census_Guide_V1_0.pdf.
DfE (Department for Education) (2019) *GCSE Results ('Attainment 8'): Ethnicity Facts and Figures* (website). See https://www.ethnicity-facts-figures.service.gov.uk/education-skills-and-training/11-to-16-years-old/gcse-results-attainment-8-for-children-aged-14-to-16-key-stage-4/latest (accessed 1 July 2020).
DfE (Department for Education) (2020) *English Proficiency: Pupils with English as Additional Language*. See https://www.gov.uk/government/publications/english-proficiency-pupils-with-english-as-additional-language.
DfEE (Department for Education and Employment) (1997) *Excellence in Schools*. London: TSO.
Diamond, A. (2013) Executive functions. *Annual Review of Psychology* 64, 135–168.
Douglas Fir Group (2016) A transdisciplinary framework for SLA in a multilingual world. *The Modern Language Journal* 100 (Suppl.), 19–47.
Education Endowment Fund (2019) *Improving Literacy in Secondary Schools*. See https://educationendowmentfoundation.org.uk/tools/guidance-reports/improving-literacy-in-secondary-schools (accessed 1 August 2020).

Ellis, R. (1993) The structural syllabus and second language acquisition. *TESOL Quarterly* 27 (1), 91–113.

Ellis, R. (2015) *Understanding Second Language Acquisition* (2nd edn). Oxford: Oxford University Press.

Ellis, R., Loewen, S. and Erlam, R. (2006) Implicit and explicit corrective feedback and the acquisition of L2 grammar. *Studies in Second Language Acquisition* 28 (2), 339–368.

Ellis, R., Skehan, P., Li, S., Shintani, N. and Lambert, C. (2019) *Task-Based Language Teaching: Theory and Practice*. Cambridge: Cambridge University Press.

Farnsworth, M. (2016) Differentiating second language acquisition from specific learning disability: An observational tool assessing dual language learners' pragmatic competence. *Young Exceptional Children* 21, 92–110.

Festman, J., Poarch, G.J. and Dewaele, J.-M. (2017) *Raising Multilingual Children*. Bristol: Multilingual Matters.

Flege, J.E., Yeni-Komshian, G.H. and Liu, S. (1999) Age constraints on second-language acquisition. *Journal of Memory and Language* 41 (1), 78–104.

Flores, N., Kleyn, T. and Menken, K. (2015) Looking holistically in a climate of partiality: Identities of students labeled long-term English language learners. *Journal of Language, Identity & Education* 14 (2), 113–132.

Flynn, N. (2018) Continuing professional development for EAL: Mapping the field and filling in the gaps. *EAL Journal* 5, 58–62.

Forey, G. (2020) A whole school approach to SFL metalanguage and the explicit teaching of language for curriculum learning. *Journal of English for Academic Purposes* 44. doi:10.1016/j.jeap.2019.100822

García, O. (2008) *Bilingual Education in the 21st Century: A Global Perspective*. Oxford: Wiley.

García, O. and Li Wei (2014) *Translanguaging: Language, Bilingualism and Education*. Basingstoke: Palgrave Macmillan.

García, O., Johnson, S.I. and Seltzer, K. (2016) *The Translanguaging Classroom: Leveraging Student Bilingualism for Learning*. Philadelphia, PA: Caslon.

Gardner, S. and Donohue, J. (2020) Introduction to the special collection: Halliday's influence on EAP practice. *Journal of English for Academic Purposes* 44, 1–3.

Gebhard, M. (2019) *Teaching and Researching ELLs' Disciplinary Literacies*. New York and Abingdon: Routledge.

Genesee, F., Lindholm-Leary, K., Saunders, W.M. and Christian, D. (2006) *Educating English Language Learners: A Synthesis of Research Evidence*. Cambridge: Cambridge University Press.

Gibbons, P. (2002) *Scaffolding Language, Scaffolding Learning: Teaching Second Language Learners in the Mainstream Classroom*. Portsmouth, NH: Heinemann.

Gilbert, C., Husbands, C., Wigdortz, B. and Francis, B. (2013) *Unleashing Greatness: Getting the Best from an Academised System* (online). London: Academies Commission. https://www.thersa.org/reports/unleashing-greatness-getting-the-best-from-an-academised-system (accessed 25 January 2013).

González, N., Moll, L.C. and Amanti, C. (2005) *Funds of Knowledge: Theorizing Practices in Households, Communities, and Classrooms*. Mahwah, NJ: Lawrence Erlbaum.

Goo, J. and Mackey, A. (2013) The case against the case against recasts. *Studies in Second Language Acquisition* 35 (1), 127–165.

Grabe, W. (2008) *Reading in a Second Language: Moving from Theory to Practice*. Cambridge: Cambridge University Press.

Graf, M. (2011) *Including and Supporting Learners of English as an Additional Language*. London: Continuum.

Grosjean, F. (1989) Neurolinguists, beware! The bilingual is not two monolinguals in one person. *Brain and Language* 30 (1), 3–15.

Grosjean, F. (2021) *Life as a Bilingual*. Cambridge: Cambridge University Press.

Halliday, M.A.K. (1986/2007) *Language and Education* (ed. J. Webster). London: Continuum. See https://www.bloomsbury.com/uk/language-and-education-9781441131263

Halliday, M.A.K. (1990/2003) New ways of meaning: The challenge to applied linguistics. In M.A.K. Halliday and J. Webster (eds) *On Language and Linguistics* (pp. 139–175). London: Continuum.

Hammarberg, B. (2014) Problems in defining the concepts of L1, L2 and L3. In A. Otwinowska and G. De Angelis (eds) *Teaching and Learning in Multilingual Contexts* (pp. 3–18). Bristol: Multilingual Matters.

Hellman, A.B. (2008) The limits of eventual attainment in adult-onset second language acquisition. EdD thesis, Boston University.

Hopper, P. (1987). Emergent Grammar. *Proceedings of the Annual Meeting of the Berkeley Linguistics Society* 13, 139–157.

Hopper, P.J. (2001) Grammatical constructions and their discourse origins: Prototype or family resemblance? In M. Pütz, S. Niemeier and R. Dirven (eds) *Applied Cognitive Linguistics I: Theory and Language Acquisition* (pp. 109–129). Berlin: Mouton de Gruyter.

Hopper, P.J. (2012) Emergent grammar. In J. Gee and M. Handford (eds) *The Routledge Handbook of Discourse Analysis* (pp. 301–314). Abingdon: Routledge.

Hulstijn, J. (2005) Theoretical and empirical issues in the study of implicit and explicit second-language learning: Introduction. *Studies in Second Language Acquisition* 27 (2), 129–140.

Hutchinson, J. (2018) *Educational Outcomes of Children with English as an Additional Language*. London: Education Policy Institute.

Jaekel, N., Schurig, M., Florian, M. and Ritter, M. (2017) From early starters to late finishers? A longitudinal study of early foreign language learning in school. *Language Learning* 67, 631–664.

Jenkins, J. (2015) *Global Englishes: A Resource Book for Students* (3rd edn). Abingdon: Routledge.

Jenkins, J. and Leung, C. (2019) From mythical 'standard' to standard reality: The need for alternatives to standardized English language tests. *Language Teaching* 52 (1), 86–110.

Keck, C.M., Iberri-Shea, G., Tracy-Ventura, N. and Wa-Mbaleka, S. (2006) Investigating the empirical link between task-based interaction and acquisition: A meta-analysis. In J.M. Norris and L. Ortega (eds) *Synthesizing Research on Language Learning and Teaching* (pp. 91–132). Amsterdam: John Benjamins.

King, K. and Bigelow, M. (2018) The language policy of placement tests for newcomer English learners. *Educational Policy* 32 (7), 936–968.

Krashen, S.D. (1982) *Principles and Practice in Second Language Acquisition*. Oxford: Pergamon Press.

Krashen, S.D. (1985) *The Input Hypothesis: Issues and Implications*. New York: Longman.

Kroll, J.F. and Bialystok, E. (2013) Understanding the consequences of bilingualism for language processing and cognition. *Journal of Cognitive Psychology* 25 (5), 497–514.

Larsen-Freeman, D. (1997) Chaos/complexity science and second language acquisition. *Applied Linguistics* 18 (2), 141–165.

Larsen-Freeman, D. (2003) *Teaching Language: From Grammar to Grammaring*. Boston, MA: Heinle.

Larson, A.L., Cycyk, L.M., Carta, J.J., Scheffner Hammer, C., Baralt, M., Uchikoshi, Y., An, Z.G. and Wood, C. (2020) A systematic review of language-focused interventions for young children from culturally and linguistically diverse backgrounds. *Early Childhood Research Quarterly* 50 (1), 157–178.

Lemke, J. (1998) Multiplying meaning: Visual and verbal semiotics in scientific text. In J.R. Martin and R. Veel (eds) *Reading Science: Critical and Functional Perspectives on Discourses of Science* (pp. 87–113). London: Routledge.

Leow, R. (2007) Input in the L2 classroom: An attentional perspective on receptive practice. In R. DeKeyser (ed.) *Practice in a Second Language: Perspectives from Applied Linguistics and Cognitive Psychology* (pp. 21–50). Cambridge: Cambridge University Press.

Leung, C. (2001) *English as an Additional Language: Language and Literacy Development*. Royston: UKRA.

Leung, C. (2016) English as an additional language: A genealogy of language-in-education policies and reflections on research trajectories. *Language and Education* 30 (2), 158–174.

Leung, C. and Lewkowicz, J. (2016) Assessing second/additional language of diverse populations. In E. Shohamy, I.G. Or and S. May (eds) *Language Testing and Assessment*. Encyclopedia of Language and Education series (3rd edn). Cham: Springer.

Leung, C. and Valdés, G. (2019) Translanguaging and the transdisciplinary framework for language teaching and learning in a multilingual world. *The Modern Language Journal* 103, 348–370.

Leung, C., Harris, R. and Rampton, B. (1997) The idealised native speaker, reified ethnicities, and classroom realities. *TESOL Quarterly* 31 (3), 543–560.

Li Wei (2016) Epilogue: Multi-competence and the translanguaging instinct. In V.J. Cook and Li Wei (eds) *The Cambridge Handbook of Linguistic Multi-Competence* (pp. 533–543). Cambridge: Cambridge University Press.

Lightbown, P. (2014) Making the minutes count in L2 teaching. *Language Awareness* 23 (1–2), 3–23.

Lightbown, P. and Pienemann, M. (1993) Comments on Stephen D. Krashen's 'Teaching Issues: Formal Grammar Instruction'. Two Readers React. *TESOL Quarterly* 27 (4), 717–722.

Lightbown, P. and Spada, N. (2013) *How Languages are Learned* (4th edn). Oxford: Oxford University Press.

Local Government Act 1966 (c.42). London: HMSO.

Local Government (Amendment) Act 1993 (c.27). London: HMSO.

Loewen, S. and Sato, M. (2018) Interaction and instructed second language acquisition. *Language Teaching* 51 (3), 285–329.

Long, M.H. (1981) Input, interaction and second language acquisition. *Annals of the New York Academy of Sciences* 379, 259–278.

Long, M.H. (1983a) Native speaker/nonnative speaker conversation and the negotiation of comprehensible input. *Applied Linguistics* 4, 126–141.

Long, M.H. (1983b) Linguistic and conversational adjustments to nonnative speakers. *Studies in Second Language Acquisition* 5, 177–193.

Long, M.H. (1996) The role of the linguistic environment in second language acquisition. In W.C. Ritchie and T.K. Bhatia (eds) *Handbook of Second Language Acquisition* (pp. 413–468). San Diego, CA: Academic Press.

Lyster, R. and Ranta, L. (1997) Corrective feedback and learner uptake. *Studies in Second Language Acquisition* 19, 37–66.

Lyster, R., Saito, K. and Sato, M. (2013) Oral corrective feedback in second language classrooms. *Language Teaching* 46, 1–40.

Lytra, V. and Martin, P. (2010) *Sites of Multilingualism: Complementary Schools in Britain Today*. Stoke-on-Trent: Trentham Books.

Lytra, V., Volk, D. and Gregory, E. (2016) *Navigating Languages, Literacies and Identities: Religion in Young Lives*. Abingdon: Routledge.

Macken-Horarik, M. (2008) Getting 'meta': Reflexivity and literariness in a secondary English literature course. *English Teaching: Practice and Critique* 6 (4), 22–35.

Mackey, A. and Goo, J. (2007) Interaction research in SLA: A meta-analysis and research synthesis. In A. Mackey (ed.) *Conversational Interaction in Second Language Acquisition* (pp. 407–452). Oxford: Oxford University Press.

MacSwan, J. (2000) The threshold hypothesis, semilingualism, and other contributions to a deficit view of linguistic minorities. *Hispanic Journal of Behavioral Sciences* 22 (1), 3–45.

MacSwan, J. and Pray, L. (2005) Learning English bilingually: Age of onset of exposure and rate of acquisition among English language learners in a bilingual education program. *Bilingual Research Journal* 29 (3), 653–678.

Mahoney, K. (2017) *The Assessment of Emergent Bilinguals: Supporting English Language Learners*. Bristol: Multilingual Matters.

Martin, J.R. (1992) *English Text: System and Structure*. Philadelphia, PA/Amsterdam: John Benjamins.

Mauranen, A. (2012) *Exploring ELF – Academic English Shaped by Non-Native Speakers*. Cambridge: Cambridge University Press.

May, S. (ed.) (2014) *The Multilingual Turn: Implications for SLA, TESOL and Bilingual Education*. London: Routledge.

Mayberry, R. and Kluender, R. (2018) Rethinking the critical period for language: New insights into an old question from American Sign Language. *Bilingualism: Language and Cognition* 21 (5), 886–905.

McLaughlin, B. (1978) The monitor model: Some methodological considerations. *Language Learning* 28, 309–332.
Menken, K. (2009) No Child Left Behind and its effects on language policy. *Annual Review of Applied Linguistics* 29, 103–117.
Menken, K., Kleyn, T. and Chae, N. (2012) Spotlight on 'long-term English language learners': Characteristics and prior schooling experiences of an invisible population. *International Multilingual Research Journal* 6 (2), 121–142.
Menken, K., Hudson, T. and Leung, C. (2014) Symposium: Language assessment in standards-based education reform. *TESOL Quarterly* 48 (3), 586–614.
Ministry of Education (1963) *English for Immigrants*. London: HMSO.
Mitchell, R., Myles, F. and Marsden, E. (2019) *Second Language Learning Theories* (4th edn). Abingdon: Routledge.
Moll, L.C., Amanti, C., Neff, D. and González, N. (1992) Funds of knowledge for teaching: Using a qualitative approach to connect homes and classrooms. *Theory Into Practice* 31 (2), 132–141.
Montrul, S. (2008) *Incomplete Acquisition in Bilingualism: Re-examining the Age Factor*. Philadelphia, PA: John Benjamins.
Muñoz, C. and Singleton, D. (2011) A critical review of age-related research on L2 ultimate attainment. *Language Teaching* 44 (1), 1–35.
Murphy, V.A. and Franco, D. (2016) Phonics instruction and children with English as an additional language. *EAL Journal* 1, 38–42.
Murphy, V.A. and Unthiah, A. (2015) *A Systematic Review of Intervention Research Examining English Language and Literacy Development in Children with English as an Additional Language (EAL)*. Oxford: University of Oxford.
NALDIC (1999) The distinctiveness of English as an additional language: A cross-curriculum discipline. Working Paper No. 5. Luton: NALDIC.
NALDIC (2009) The national audit of English as an additional language training and development provision. See https://www.naldic.org.uk/Resources/NALDIC/Home/Documents/audit_englishasanatlanguage.pdf (accessed 21 July 2020).
NALDIC (2014) The national audit of English as an additional language training and development provision. See https://www.naldic.org.uk/Resources/NALDIC/Research%20and%20Information/Documents/NALDIC%20-%20EAL%20Audit%202014%20FINAL%20FINAL%20YF%20Oct%2014.pdf (accessed 21 July 2020).
Nation, I.S.P. and Hunston, S. (2013) *Learning Vocabulary in Another Language* (2nd edn). Cambridge: Cambridge University Press.
National Academies of Sciences, Engineering, and Medicine (2017) *Promoting the Educational Success of Children and Youth Learning English: Promising Futures*. Washington, DC: National Academies Press.
No Child Left Behind Act of 2001, P.L. 107–110 (2001).
NRCSE (National Resource Centre for Supplementary Education) (n.d.) *Supplementary Education* (web page). See https://www.supplementaryeducation.org.uk/supplementary-education-the-nrc (accessed 1 August 2020).
Ofsted (Office for Standards in Education) (2013) *Improving Literacy in Secondary Schools: A Shared Responsibility*. See https://www.gov.uk/government/publications/improving-literacy-in-secondary-schools-a-shared-responsibility (accessed 30 July 2020).
Ofsted (Office for Standards in Education) (2019) *School Inspection Handbook*. See https://assets.publishing.service.gov.uk/government/uploads/system/uploads/attachment_data/file/843108/School_inspection_handbook_-_section_5.pdf (accessed 11 July 2020).
Ofsted (Office for Standards in Education) (2020) *Initial Teacher Education (ITE) Inspection Framework and Handbook*. See https://www.gov.uk/government/publications/initial-teacher-education-ite-inspection-framework-and-handbook (accessed 30 July 2020).
Oliver, R. and Azkarai, A. (2017) Review of child second language acquisition (SLA): Examining theories and research. *Annual Review of Applied Linguistics* 37, 62–76.

O'Rourke, B. and Pujolar, J. (2013) From native speakers to 'new speakers' – problematizing nativeness in language revitalization contexts. *Histoire Épistémologie Langage* 35, 47–67.

Ortega, L. (2009) *Understanding Second Language Acquisition*. London: Hodder.

Otheguy, R., García, O. and Reid, W. (2015) Clarifying translanguaging and deconstructing named languages: A perspective from linguistics. *Applied Linguistics Review* 6 (3), 281–307.

Owen, D. (2020) *What Do We Owe to Refugees?* Cambridge: Polity Press.

Oxley, E. and de Cat, C. (2019) A systematic review of language and literacy interventions in children and adolescents with English as an additional language (EAL). *The Language Learning Journal*. doi:10.1080/09571736.2019.1597146

Paap, K.R., Johnson, H.A. and Sawi, O. (2015) Bilingual advantages in executive functioning either do not exist or are restricted to very specific and undetermined circumstances. *Cortex* 69, 265–278.

Panagiotopoulou, J.A. and Rosen, L. (2019) Recently arrived migrants as teachers in Greek complementary schools in Montreal: Views on multilingualism. In J.A. Panagiotopoulou, L. Rosen, C. Kirsch and A. Chatzidaki (eds) *'New' Migration of Families from Greece to Europe and Canada: A 'New' Challenge for Education?* Wiesbaden: Springer.

Paradis, J., Rusk, B., Duncan, T. and Govindarajan, K. (2017) Children's second language acquisition of English complex syntax: The role of age, input, and cognitive factors. *Annual Review of Applied Linguistics* 37, 148–167.

Parsons, S. and Branagan, A. (2014) *Word Aware: Teaching Vocabulary Across the Day, Across the Curriculum*. Abingdon: Routledge.

Peal, E. and Lambert, W.E. (1962) The relation of bilingualism to intelligence. *Psychological Monographs: General and Applied* 76 (27), 1–23.

Pfenninger, S.E. and Singleton, D. (2019) Starting age overshadowed: The primacy of differential environmental and family support effects on second language attainment in an instructional context. *Language Learning* 69, 207–234.

Philp, J., Borowczyk, M. and Mackey, A. (2017) Exploring the uniqueness of child second language acquisition (SLA): Learning, teaching, assessment, and practice. *Annual Review of Applied Linguistics* 37, 1–13.

Pim, C. (2018) *100 Ideas for Primary Teachers: Supporting EAL Learners*. London: Bloomsbury.

Pim, C. and Driver, C. (2018) *100 Ideas for Secondary Teachers: Supporting EAL Learners*. London: Bloomsbury.

Pinker, S. (1994) *The Language Instinct*. New York: William Morrow.

Polias, J. (2016) *Apprenticing Students into Science: Doing, Talking and Writing Scientifically*. Melbourne: Lexis Education.

Puig-Mayenco, E., González Alonso, J. and Rothman, J. (2020) A systematic review of transfer studies in third language acquisition. *Second Language Research* 36 (1), 31–64.

Race Relations Act 1976 (c.74). London: HMSO.

Rampton, A. (1981) *West Indian Children in our Schools: Interim Report of the Committee of Inquiry into the Education of Children from Ethnic Minority Groups*. London: HMSO.

Riches, C. and Genesee, F. (2006) Literacy: Crosslinguistic and crossmodal issues. In F. Genesee, K. Lindholm-Leary, W.M. Saunders and D. Christian (eds) *Educating English Language Learners: A Synthesis of Research Evidence* (pp. 14–63). Cambridge: Cambridge University Press.

Richmond, J. (1990) What do we mean by language knowledge? In R. Carter (ed.) *Knowledge About Language and the Curriculum* (pp. 23–44). London: Hodder & Stoughton.

Rose, D. and Martin, J.R. (2012) *Learning to Write, Reading to Learn: Genre, Knowledge, and Pedagogy in the Sydney School*. London: Equinox.

Rowsell, J. and Pahl, K. (2007) Sedimented identities in texts: Instances of practice. *Reading Research Quarterly* 42, 388–404.

Ruby, M., Gregory, E., Kenner, C. and Al-Azami, S. (2010) Grandmothers as orchestrators of early language and literacy lessons. In V. Lytra and P. Martin (eds) *Sites of Multilingualism: Complementary Schools in Britain Today* (pp. 57–68). Stoke-on-Trent: Trentham Books.

Sampson, G. (2017) *The Linguistics Delusion*. London: Equinox.
Saunders, W. and O'Brien, G. (2006) Oral language. In F. Genesee, K. Lindholm-Leary, W.M. Saunders and D. Christian (eds) *Educating English Language Learners: A Synthesis of Research Evidence* (pp. 14–63). Cambridge: Cambridge University Press.
Schmitt, N. and Schmitt, D. (2020) *Vocabulary in Language Teaching* (2nd edn). Cambridge: Cambridge University Press.
Seidlhofer, B. (2004) Research perspectives on teaching English as a lingua franca. *Annual Review of Applied Linguistics* 24, 209–239.
Seidlhofer, B. (2005) English as a lingua franca. *ELT Journal* 59 (4), 339–341.
Sharples, R., Hanks, J. and Conteh, J. (2019) Schooling, ethnicity and English as an additional language. In I. Abbott, P. Huddleston and D. Middlewood (eds) *Preparing to Teach in Secondary Schools* (pp. 275–287). Milton Keynes: Open University Press.
Sharwood Smith, M. (1993) Input enhancement in instructed SLA. *Studies in Second Language Acquisition* 15 (2), 165–179.
Snell, J. and Andrews, R. (2017) To what extent does a regional dialect and accent impact on the development of reading and writing skills? *Cambridge Journal of Education* 47 (3), 297–313.
Spielman, A. (2019) Amanda Spielman at the 'Wonder Years' curriculum conference. Speech, 26 January. See https://www.gov.uk/government/speeches/amanda-spielman-at-the-wonder-years-curriculum-conference (accessed 10 July 2020).
Strand, S. and Hessel, A. (2018) *English as an Additional Language, Proficiency in English and Pupils' Educational Achievement: An Analysis of Local Authority Data*. Cambridge: Bell Foundation.
Strand, S., Malmberg, L. and Hall, J. (2015) *English as an Additional Language (EAL) and Educational Achievement in England: An Analysis of the National Pupil Database*. Oxford: University of Oxford.
Sutton Trust (2016) Class differences: Ethnicity and disadvantage (research brief). See https://www.suttontrust.com/wp-content/uploads/2016/11/Class-differences-report_References-available-online.pdf (accessed 1 August 2020).
Swain, M. (1985) Communicative competence: Some roles of comprehensible input and comprehensible output in its development. In S.M. Gass and C.G. Madden (eds) *Input in Second Language Acquisition* (pp. 235–253). Rowley, MA: Newbury House.
Swain, M. (1995) Three functions of output in second language learning. In G. Cook and B. Seidlhofer (eds) *Principle and Practice in Applied Linguistics: Studies in Honour of H.G. Widdowson* (pp. 125–144). Oxford: Oxford University Press.
Swain, M. (2005) The output hypothesis: Theory and research. In E. Hinkel (ed.) *Handbook of Research in Second Language Teaching and Learning* (pp. 471–484). Mahwah, NJ: Lawrence Erlbaum.
Swan, M. and Smith, B. (2001) *Learner English: A Teacher's Guide to Interference and other Problems*. Cambridge: Cambridge University Press.
Swann, M. (1985) *Education for All: The Report of the Committee of Inquiry into the Education of Children from Ethnic Minority Groups*. London: HMSO.
Sweller, J. (1988) Cognitive load during problem solving: Effects on learning. *Cognitive Science* 12, 257–285.
Sweller, J. (2011) Cognitive load theory. In J.P. Mestre and B. Ross (eds) *Psychology of Learning and Motivation* (pp. 37–76). London: Elsevier.
Tomasello, M. (2012) The usage-based theory of language acquisition. In E.L. Bavin (ed.) *The Cambridge Handbook of Child Language* (pp. 69–88). Cambridge: Cambridge University Press.
Tyler, A. and Ortega, L. (2016) Usage-based approaches to language and language learning: An introduction to the special issue. *Language and Cognition* 8 (3), 335–345. doi:10.1017/langcog.2016.15
Umansky, I.M. and Reardon, S.F. (2014) Reclassification patterns among Latino English learner students in bilingual, dual immersion, and English immersion classrooms. *American Educational Research Journal* 51 (5), 879–912.
Unsworth, S. (2016) Early child L2 acquisition: Age or input effects? Neither, or both? *Journal of Child Language* 43 (3), 608–634.

VanPatten, B. (ed.) (2004) *Processing Instruction: Theory, Research, and Commentary*. Mahwah, NJ: Lawrence Erlbaum.

VanPatten, B. (2007) Input processing in adult SLA. In B. VanPatten and J. Williams (eds) *Theories in Second Language Acquisition: An Introduction* (2nd edn) (pp. 113–134). Mahwah, NJ: Lawrence Erlbaum.

Voice21: The National Oracy Education Charity (n.d.) Website. See https://voice21.org (accessed 31 July 2020).

Vygotsky, L.S. (1978) *Mind in Society: The Development of Higher Psychological Processes*. Cambridge, MA: Harvard University Press.

Walsh, S. (2015) *Classroom Interaction for Language Teachers*. Annapolis Junction, MD: TESOL Press.

Washbourne, A. (2011) *EAL Pocketbook*. Alresford: Teachers' Pocketbooks.

Weber, C. (2019) *The Changing Reading of the Hitler–Stalin Alliance*. Washington, DC: Wilson Centre. See https://www.wilsoncenter.org/blog-post/the-changing-reading-the-hitler-stalin-alliance (accessed 30 July 2020).

White, L. and Genesee, F. (1996) How native is near-native? The issue of ultimate attainment in adult second language acquisition. *Second Language Research* 12 (3), 233–265.

WIDA (2012) *The English Language Development Standards: Kindergarten–Grade 12*. See https://wida.wisc.edu/teach/standards (accessed 21 July 2020).

Wisniewski, B., Zierer, K. and Hattie, J. (2020) The power of feedback revisited: A meta-analysis of educational feedback research. *Frontiers in Psychology* 10, 3087.

Wood, D., Bruner, J. and Ross, G. (1976) The role of tutoring in problem solving. *Journal of Child Psychology and Psychiatry* 17 (2), 89–100.

Index

Note: References in *italics* are to figures, those in **bold** to tables; 'n' refers to chapter notes.

abbreviations and acronyms xv
academic journals 189
academic word list (AWL) 90, 91
acquisition-learning hypothesis 24, 26
Across Cultures (blog) 149
additional language learning 3, 15–16, 67, 182
affective filter hypothesis 25, 26, 27
age of acquisition 37–9, *38*
   and first significant contact 39–40
   key points 60
   and length of residence 39–41
   and ultimate attainment 39–41
   and vocabulary 37
   review 41–2
   resources 42–3
Alonso, J.G. 22
Amala 188
Amanti, C. 184
American Sign Language (ASL) 40–1
Andrews, R. 155, 179
Armitage, S. 93
assessment 134, 176–7
   basic features 134–6
   choosing the right test 137–8
   constructs 134–6
   formative assessment 136
   frameworks 136–7
   rating scales 134–6
   summative assessment 136
   review 138
   resources 188
attainment 158–9, *159*
attention 30–1, 32
audience 98
automatic knowledge 44, 45
AWL *see* academic word list
Azkarai, A. 28

Bak, T.H. 56
Beck, I. *et al.* 90
Bell Foundation 92, 109, 136, 137
Bellsham-Revell, A. 128–9, 153
Bernstein, B. 155
Bialystok, E. 56
BICS (basic interpersonal communication skills) 76–8, **77**
Bifield, J. 149, 172
Bigelow, M. 188
bilingualism 8, 21
   and the brain 55–6
   defined 18
   development of bilinguals 41
   emergent bilinguals 58, 154–5
   sequential bilingualism 18, 56
   simultaneous bilingualism 18
   see also reading in a new language
biliteracy 76
blogs 148–9
Bourdieu, B. 67
Bourke, J. 107
Bourne, J. 119
Bowyer, C. 99, 106, 107
Bracken, S. *et al.* 152
brain 55–6
Branagan, A. 112
Brisk, M.E. 102
Brown, D. 36, 48
Bullock Report (1975) 5, 51

Calderdale Report (1986) 6
CALP (cognitive academic language proficiency) 76–8, **77**
Cameron, D. 155
Carothers, D. 176
Carter, R. 74

case studies 4
 EAL and Maths 109–11
 EAL and SEND 174–7
 EAL in Wales 117–21
 EAL specialists 4, 131–3, 143–6
 language across the curriculum 4, 71–3
 Ofsted 162–73
 reading in a new language 87, 93–6, *94*
 teaching poetry 87, 93–6, *94*
 welcoming new arrivals 143–6
 working with families 131–3, 174–5
Catalano, T. 189
CEFR *see* Common European Framework fof Reference
Centre for Global Englishes, University of Southampton 117
Chalmers, H. 58
checklist and activities for new EAL specialist 190–6
Chomsky, N. 19
Chumack-Horbatsch, R. 187
clarification requests 47, 48
classroom power relations 6
cloze exercises 110
cognitive academic language proficiency *see* CALP
cognitive load theory 79
Cole, P. 117–20
collaborative learning 74, 85
Collier, V. 63, 65
collocations 89
Common European Framework of Reference (CEFR) 135, 136
common underlying proficiency (CUP) 53, 75–8, *76*
 BICS and CALP 76–8, *77*
 changing learner profiles 78
 key points 113–14
 review 78–9
 resources 79
complex clauses 106–7
constructs 134
Conteh, J. 11, 28, 142, 160, 187
context 32
continuing professional development *see* CPD for EAL: a practical guide; CPD for EAL specialists
Cook, V. 15, 54, 58
Cook, V.J. 43, 54

Costley, T. 12
Coxhead, A. 90, 91
Coyle, D. 93
CPD for EAL: a practical guide 181
 additional language learning 182
 content 181
 personalised CPD plans 183
CPD for EAL specialists 179
 component parts 180
 CPD across the school 180–1
 initial teacher education 181
 scope and starting points 179–80
 review 183
Creese, A. 151
Crisfield, E. 42–3
culture 99, 101, 175–6
Cummins, J. 53, 57, 62, 75, 76–7, 77, 79, 123, 160
CUNY-NYSIEB project 58, 155–6
CUP *see* common underlying proficiency

Daborn, E. *et al.* 109, 187
DARTs *see* directed activities related to texts
Datta, M. 76
Davies, A. 52, 58
Davison, C. 153
de Cat, C. 179
De Meulder, M. 188
declarative knowledge 44–5, 46
DeKeyser, R. 44
Demie, F. 159
Department for Education, England (DfE) 6, 7–8, 158, 159, 179
Derrick, J. 5
Dewaele, J.M. 52, 58
Diamond, A. 56
dictogloss 92
directed activities related to texts (DARTs) 88, 92
disciplinary language 103
 key points 115
 metalanguage and strategies 107–8, 109
 nominalisation and complex clauses 106–7
 register continuum 103–5, *104*
 teaching and learning cycle (TLC) 105–6
 review 108–9
 resources 109

Douglas Fir Group 28, 158, 160, 189
Driver, C. 187

EAL (English as an additional language) 1–2, 54
  as cross-curriculum discipline 161
  defined 7–8, 154
  GCSE results 159
  history of 5–7
  learners 9, *10*, 11–12, 24
  multi-competence 54, 58
  online data 12–13
  policy 7–8
  resources 187
EAL and SEND: case study 174
  assessment issues 176–7
  communication with families 174–5
  linguistic and cultural differences 175–6
  commentary 177–8
EAL-Bilingual Group 147
EAL in the Daylight (blog) 149
EAL Journal 92, 147, 179, 180
EAL Journal (blog) 148–9
EAL Research Network 147
EAL specialists 2–3, 6–7, 12, 123–5
  case studies 4, 131–3, 143–6
  checklist and activities for new specialist 190–6
  data and practice 163
  EAL audit 127–8
  effective assessments 134–8
  funds of knowledge 186
  getting connected 147–50
  key message for 186
  as language leaders 154–6
  and new arrivals 143–5
  newly appointed specialists 125, 127–31
  and Ofsted 167–71
  organisations 150
  policy folder 128–9
  role aspirations 129–31, **130**
  and SEND 174–5
  structural monolingualism 155–6
  welcoming students 139–46
  whose norms? 154–5
  working with families 131–3, 174–5
  review 131
EALCO/SENCO combined role 170–1
Early, M. 160
Economist, The: Burnet News Club 161

Education Endowment Fund 85, 93
EF (executive function) 56
EIF *see* Ofsted Education Inspection Framework
ELF (English as a lingua franca) 116
elicitation 47, 48
Ellis, R. *et al*. 43, 45, 46, 48
emergent bilinguals 58, 154–5
Empowering ELLs (blog) 149
England
  Department for Education (DfE) 6, 7–8, 158, 159, 179
  EAL data 12
  policy framework 1
English as a lingua franca (ELF) 116
English as an additional language *see* EAL
English-only policies 51, 53, 56–7
everyday language 76–7, 90, 98, 100, 105, 111–12
executive function (EF) 56
explicit correction 47, 48
explicit learning *see* implicit and explicit learning

families, working with 131–3, 174–5
Farnsworth, M. 176
feedback 31, 46, 49
  role in learning 47
  types of feedback 47–8
  resources 50
Festman, J. *et al*. 42–3
field 100
Field, E. 131, 186
first languages 50, 51
  bilingualism and the brain 55–6
  key points 61
  monolingual principle 51–3
  role in learning 53–5
  review 56–8
  resources 58
First Story 160, 188
Flege, J. *et al*. 37–8, *38*
Flores, N. *et al*. 64
Flynn, N. 180
Forey, G. 104–5, 106, 109
formative assessment 136
Fowkes, S. 90, 109–11
Freyer Model 92
Funds of Knowledge approach 12, 160, 184–5

García, O. et al. 54, 55, 58
GCSE results 159
Gebhard, M. 98, 100, 102
Genesee, F. et al. 39, 65, 86
genre 88, 98, 99, 101
Gibbons, P. 74, 81, 83, 93, 102
Global Englishes 117
González, N. et al. 12, 184
Goo, J. 36, 50
Grabe, W. 87
Graf, M. 5
grammar
    and age of acquisition 37–8, *38*
    explicit teaching 30–1
    language as a grammatical system 15–16
graphic organisers 88, 92
Greek supplementary schools 54
Grosjean, F. 8, 117

Halliday, M.A.K. 97, 104
Hamman, E. 116
Hammarberg, B. 22
Harford, S. 170
Hellman, A. 39
Hessel, A. 13, 63
history of EAL 5–7, 12
Hopper, P. 19
Hopper, P.J. 18
Hulstijn, J. H. 50
HundrED 188
Hunston, S. 92–3
Hutchinson, J. 13, 64, 160

identity texts 160
Impact 79
implicit and explicit learning
    feedback 46–8
    key points 60–1
    knowledge 44–5
    practice 45–6
    review 49
    resources 50
initial teacher education (ITE) 6, 151, 166–7, 181
input 26, 29–30
    and attention 30–1
    defined 29
    input processing (IP) 31–2, 36
    key points 60

processing instruction 32, 35
quality and quantity 30, 35
review 34–6
resources 36
Input Hypothesis 25, 34
institutional racism 6
interaction 29, 32–3, 36, 82–3
Interaction Hypothesis 33, 35
international context *see* national and international context
IP (input processing) 31–2, 36
IRE/IRF exchanges 82
ITE *see* initial teacher education

Jaekel, N. et al. 43
Jenkins, J. 117
Journal of English for Academic Purposes 102

Keck, C.M. et al. 36
key messages 185
    colleagues 186
    parents 185–6
    yourself 186
key principles 17–18, 59
key terms 18
King, K. 188
Kluender, R. 40
knowledge 44–5, 46, 49
Krashen, S. 24–5, 26–7, 28, 29–30, 31, 34
Kroll, J.F. 56
Kusters, A. 188

L1 (first language) 18, 53
L2 (second language) 18
Lambert, W.E. 55, 57
language acquisition 2, 18–20
    see also age of acquisition; learning or acquiring?
language across the curriculum 2, 3, 67–8
    case studies 4, 71–3
    five principles 73–4
    key points 113
    review 74
    resources 74
language as a grammatical system 15–16
language centres 5, 6
Language In the National Curriculum (LINC) project 68, 74
language processing 30, 31–2, 35

Larsen-Freeman, D. 46
leadership 151
　EAL specialists as language leaders 154–6
　and management 165
　models of provision 153–4, *154*
　personal and positional leadership 151–2, 155
　team-building 152–3
　review 156–7
learning environment 141–3
learning or acquiring? 23
　critiques and current thinking 25–7
　first languages to SLA 23–4
　key points 60
　Krashen's monitor model 24–5
　review 27–8
　resources 28
Lemke, J. 69
length of residence (LOR) 39–41
Leow, R. 35, 45
Leung, C. *et al*. 6, 12, 52, 87, 117, 188
Lewkowicz, J. 188
lexis *see* vocabulary
Li Wei 54, 143
Lightbown, P. 21, 26, 36
LINC project *see* Language In the National Curriculum
linguistic interdependence 75–6
literacy
　and multilingualism 86–7
　in secondary schools 93
　as social practice 68–9
　see also reading in a new language
Local Government (Amendment) Act (1993) 6
Loewen, S. 33
Long, M. 32–3
Lyster, R. *et al*. 47, 48, 50

McCormack, C. 111, 140, 143–4, 186
Macken-Horarik, M. 107
Mackey, A. 36, 50
McLaughlin, B. 26
McPake, J. 119
MacSwan, J. 79
Mahoney, K. 188
MantraLingua 188
Maths 68, 69, 76, 80, 90, 109–11
Mauranen, A. 52
May, S. 28
Mayberry, R. 40

MDST *see* Multilingual Digital Storytelling
Mead, M. 123
meaning and form 32, 33
Mehmedbegovic, D. 56
Meier, G. 28
Menken, K. *et al*. 188
Mercer, N. 83
metalanguage 107–8, 109
metalinguistic feedback 47, 48
metaphor 25, 93–5, 96
Meyer, O. 93
MFL *see* modern foreign languages
Mitchell, R. *et al*. 19, 21
MLIE (Multilingual Learning in International Education) 148
mobile learners 188–9
mode 100
modern foreign languages (MFL)
　Ofsted requirement 170
　pupil withdrawal from 170
　teachers 152
Moll, L.C. *et al*. 184, 185
monitor hypothesis 24, 26
monitor model 24–7
monolingual and multilingual 158–9
　challenge from SLA 160–1
　review 161–2
　see also Ofsted and EAL
monolingual principle 51–3
monolingualism 6
Montrul, S. 38
morphology 19
morphosyntax
　and age of acquisition 37–8, *38*
　defined 19
multi-competence 54, 58
Multilingual Digital Storytelling (MDST) 139–40, 188
Multilingual Learning in International Education (MLIE) 148
multilingual turn 28
multilingualism 5
　and literacy 86–7
Muñoz, C. 37, 39
Murphy, V. 92
Murphy, V.A. 179

NALDIC 9, *10*, 12, 147, 160, 173, 179, 187
Nancarrow, P. 128–9, 153

NASSEA 147
Nation, I.S.P. 92–3
National Academies 63
national and international context *10*
   current EAL policy 7–8
   EAL learners 9, *10*, 11–12, 24
   history of EAL 5–7, 12
   review 12
   resources 12–13
   see also practice-based approach to EAL
'native-like' proficiency 52
'native-speaker competence' 20–1
'native speakers' 6, 20, 52, 53, 58
natural order hypothesis 25, 26
negotiation 33
networks and groups 197–200
new arrivals 143–6
New Scots 188
nominalisation 99–100, 106–7
Northern Ireland: EAL data 12
noticing 34, 35

Ofsted and EAL 151, 152, 162, 163, 164
Ofsted Education Inspection Framework (EIF)
     163, 164–7
   Behaviour and Attitudes 164
   'Fight for Fairness' 173
   Initial Teacher Education 166–7
   inspection stages **165**, 165–6
   Leadership and Management 165
   Personal Development 164
   Quality of Education 164
   questions to ask 171–3
Ofsted EIF implications for EAL specialists 167
   characteristics of good EAL provision
     168, **169**
   combined EALCO/SENCO role? 170–1
   MFL requirement 170
   supporting new arrivals 168–9
   visibility of EAL provision 167
   withdrawing pupils 170
Oliver, R. 28
online community 148–9
online EAL data 12–13
oracy 73–4
   collaborative learning 74, 85
   defined 80–1
   key points 114
   multilingualism and literacy 86–7

   promoting oracy 83
   quality of interaction 82–3
   from talking to writing 81–2
   in the Welsh Curriculum 84
   review 83–4
   resources 84–5
Oracy Cambridge 84
oral language 89
organisations 147
   more established EAL specialists 150
   online community 148–9
   subject associations 147–8
   Twitter 148, 149
O'Rourke, B. 52, 58
Ortega, L. 22
Otheguy, R. *et al.* 54, 155
output 29, 33–4
Output Hypothesis 34, 35
Owen, D. 188–9
Oxley, E. 179

Paap, K.R. *et al.* 56
Pahl, K. 52, 76
Panagiotopoulou, J. 54
Paradis, J. *et al.* 40
parents
   key message for 185–6
   working with families 131–3, 174–5
   workshops 132–3
Parfitt, C.M. 176
Parsons, S. 112
Passeron, J.-C. 67
passive form 32
Peal, E. 55, 57
peer interaction 9, 26, 33
Pfenninger, S.E. 40, 43
Philp, J. *et al.* 28
phonics 88–9, 92
phonological awareness 88, 89
phonology and age of acquisition 37–8, *38*
PiE *see* proficiency in English
Pienemann, M. 26
Pim, C. 187
Pinker, S. 21–2
poetry 87, 93–6, *94*
Polias, J. 109
poverty of the stimulus 19
practical tools 92
practice 45–6

practice-based approach to EAL 8–11, *10*, 59, 61
  key points 59–61, 113–15
  proficiency development 62–4, 65
  review 65, 116–17
  resources 65, 117
preteaching 30, 31, 90, 91, 110, 111
procedural knowledge 44, 45
processability theory 26
processing, defined 31–2
processing instruction 32, 35
proficiency development 62, 113, 115–16
  critique 63–4
  policy context 116
  time in years 62–3
  time to proficiency, critique 65
proficiency in English (PiE) 7, 63, 64, 155
prompts 48
pronunciation and age of acquisition 37–9, *38*
Puig-Mayenco, E. *et al.* 22
Pujolar, J. 52, 58

quality and quantity of language 25, 30, 35

Race Relations Act (1976) 6
racial discrimination 6
Rampton Report (1981) 6
Ranta, L. 47, 48, 50
rating scales 134–6
reading in a new language 86
  case study (teaching poetry) 87, 93–6, *94*
  genres 88
  key points 114
  oracy, multilingualism and literacy 86–7
  phonics 88–9, 92
  reading as a skill 87–8
  strategies for developing confidence 91–2
  vocabulary 89–91
  review 92
  resources 92–3
recasts 47, 48
reformulations 48
register 100
register continuum 103–5, *104*
reinforcement 48
repetition 47, 48
ResearchEd 180
resources and recommendations 187
  academic journals 189
  age of acquisition 42–3

  assessment 188
  common underlying proficiency (CUP) 79
  disciplinary language 109
  EAL practice 187
  feedback 50
  first languages 58
  fresh ideas 188
  implicit and explicit learning 50
  input 36
  language across the curriculum 74
  learning or acquiring? 28
  national and international context 12–13
  oracy 84–5
  practice-based approach to EAL 65, 117
  reading in a new language 92–3
  theory of language 21–2
  for those new to EAL 187
  vocabulary 92
  writing 102
Riches, C. 86
Richmond, J. 68
Rosen, L. 54
Rothman, J. 22
Rowsell, J. 52, 76

Sampson, G. 22
Sato, M. 33
scaffolding 53, 73, 74, 93–6
Schmitt, D. 93
Schmitt, N. 93
scientific writing 97, 105, 109
Scotland 1, 179
  EAL data 12
  New Scots 188
  SATEAL 147
Scott, S. 85
SEBD (social, emotional and behavioural
    difficulties) 174
second language acquisition (SLA) 23–4, 28
  challenge from 160–1
  research 158
secondary schools 152–3
  good practice 152
  literacy in 93
  science teaching 109
  subject lessons 31, 73, 143
Seidlhofer, B. 116, 117
semantic knowledge 89
SENCO/EALCO combined role 170–1

SEND and EAL 174–7
sentence stems 110, 111
sequential bilingualism 18, 56
SFL *see* systemic functional linguistics
Sharwood Smith, M. 36
simultaneous bilingualism 18
Singleton, C. 37, 39
Singleton, D. 40, 43
situation 99–100, 101
Skill Acquisition Theory 44
SLA *see* second language acquisition
Smith, A.M. 150, 174–7
Smith, A.S. 186
Smith, B. 177
Snell, J. 155
social capital 52
social context 33
social, emotional and behavioural difficulties (SEBD) 174
social media 148–9
Spada, N. 21
Spielman, A. 164
Strand, S. 13, 63
structural monolingualism 155–6
subject associations 147–8
subject disciplines 31, 73, 143
summative assessment 136
Sutton Trust 158
Swain, M. 33–4
Swan, M. 177
Swann Report (1985) 6
Sweller, J. 79
syntax 19
systemic functional linguistics (SFL) 97–8, 99–100, 101

talk *see* oracy
Tan Huynh 149
target language 20–1
teacher-student interaction 33
Teacher Toolkit 149
teachers: key message for 186
teaching and learning cycle (TLC) 105–6
team-building 152–3
tenor 100, 105
terminology 18
theory of language 18
  key points 59–60
  nature of language 18–20

target language 20–1
review 21
resources 21–2
Thomas, W. 63, 65
TLC (teaching and learning cycle) 105–6
Tomasello, M. 19
translanguaging 54–5, 58, 155
Truss, L. 173
Twitter 148, 149
Tyler, A. 22

UK Proficiency in English (PiE) 63, 64
United States
  long-term English learners (LTELs) 64
  National Academies of Sciences, Engineering, and Medicine 65
  No Child Left Behind Act (2001) 63
universal grammar (UG) 19–20
Unsworth, S. 43
Unthiah, A. 179
usage-based theories 19, 20

vanishing cloze exercises 110
VanPatten, B. 31, 32, 36
Vazquez, M. 76, 93–6, 106
vocabulary (lexis) 73, 89–91
  academic vocabulary 90, *91*
  and age of acquisition 37
  frequency 90
  substitution tables 89–90, *90*
  resources 92
Voice21 80, 84–5

Wales 179
  EAL 12, 117–21
  oracy 84
  subject associations 147–8
Walsh, S. 82
Washbourne, A. 187
Weber, C. 107
welcoming students 139
  case study: new arrivals 143–6
  initial fact-finding 139–40
  learning environment 141–3
  linguistic landscape survey 142
  robust admissions, assessment, induction 140–1
  review 143
White, L. 39

WIDA English Language Development
    Standards 135, 136
Wisniewski, B. *et al.* 47
withdrawal of pupils 170
Wood, D. *et al.* 74
Word Aware Programme 109, 110, 112
word order 32
word type 110
writing 97
    audience 98
    culture 99, 101
    genre 88, 98, 99, 101
    key points 115
    multimodal meaning 100
    situation 99–100, 101
    systemic functional linguistics (SFL) 97–8,
        99–100, 101
    and talking 81–2
    review 101–2
    resources 102

Young Interpreters Scheme 188

For Product Safety Concerns and Information please contact our EU Authorised Representative:

Easy Access System Europe

Mustamäe tee 50

10621 Tallinn

Estonia

gpsr.requests@easproject.com